Exploring English with Online Corpora

An Introduction

Wendy Anderson and John Corbett

palgrave
macmillan

First published 2009 by
PALGRAVE MACMILLAN

Palgrave Macmillan in the UK is an imprint of Macmillan Publishers Limited,
registered in England, company number 785998, of Houndmills, Basingstoke,
Hampshire RG21 6XS.

Palgrave Macmillan in the US is a division of St Martin's Press LLC,
175 Fifth Avenue, New York, NY 10010.

Palgrave Macmillan is the global academic imprint of the above companies
and has companies and representatives throughout the world.

Palgrave® and Macmillan® are registered trademarks in the United States,
the United Kingdom, Europe and other countries.

ISBN-13: 978–0–230–55139–8 hardback
ISBN-10: 0–230–55139–4 hardback
ISBN-13: 978–0–230–55140–4 paperback
ISBN-10: 0–230–55140–8 paperback

This book is printed on paper suitable for recycling and made from fully
managed and sustained forest sources. Logging, pulping and manufacturing
processes are expected to conform to the environmental regulations of the
country of origin.

A catalogue record for this book is available from the British Library.

A catalog record for this book is available from the Library of Congress.

10   9   8   7   6   5   4   3   2   1
18   17   16   15   14   13   12   11   10   09

Printed and bound in Great Britain by the MPG Books Group Ltd.

For Christian J. Kay

Contents

List of Figures

List of Tables

Acknowledgements

We begin by thanking our colleagues in the Department of English Language at the University of Glasgow, and in particular Jean Anderson, Dave Beavan, Christian Kay, Jennifer Smith and Rachel Smith for their invaluable advice at various stages in the writing process. We are also grateful to James Butler and Marie-Thérèse McLaughlin for giving a student's perspective on the text.

Our editors at Palgrave Macmillan, Kate Haines and Kitty van Boxel, gave encouragement throughout, and the final text benefits from the constructive input of two anonymous reviewers. Needless to say, its shortcomings remain our responsibility.

We thank our colleagues on the Scottish Corpus of Texts & Speech and its successor project, the Corpus of Modern Scottish Writing, both of which have benefited from Resource Enhancement and Standard Research Grants awarded by the Arts and Humanities Research Council (www.ahrc.ac.uk).

We are grateful to the creators of the following corpora for permission to reproduce extracts and screenshots in this book:

BYU-BNC: The British National Corpus, TIME Corpus, Corpus of Contemporary American English, with thanks to Mark Davies.

Michigan Corpus of Academic Spoken English (MICASE), with thanks to Ute Römer.

English Language Interview Corpus as a Second-Language Application (ELISA), with thanks to Sabine Braun.

Speech Accent Archive, with thanks to Steven H. Weinberger.

Data cited in this book have been extracted from the British National Corpus Online service, managed by Oxford University Computing Services on behalf of the BNC Consortium. All rights in the texts cited are reserved.

We are also grateful to the copyright holders of the following texts for permission to reproduce extracts:

D. Biber for permission to use 'Representativeness in corpus design' in *Literary and Linguistic Computing* 8(4): 243–257 (1993).

M. MacMahon for permission to use *Basic Phonetics & Phonetics of Poetry*. Thirteenth edition. Department of English Language, University of Glasgow (2002).

Every effort has been made to trace all copyright holders, but if any have been inadvertently overlooked, the publisher will be pleased to make the necessary arrangements at the first opportunity. All website addresses are correct at the time of writing (January 2009).

Most of all, we acknowledge all the emotional and practical support given by our respective partners, Kenneth Austin and Augusta Alves. And we dedicate this book to Professor Christian Kay, in recognition of her outstanding contribution to the building of innovative digital text resources at the University of Glasgow, and her unfailing generosity towards her colleagues.

Introducing Online Corpora

This book has a number of intended readerships. It should appeal to

- students who are embarking on a formal course in English language, at upper school level or university;
- teachers who wish to know more about the technology available to support English language education in schools;
- learners and teachers of English as a foreign language, who wish to explore how language is used in a vast quantity of 'authentic' texts; and
- general readers who are simply curious about how the English language works and about new methods of exploring this topic.

All of its readers will be united by a common interest in the English language and a desire to explore its many written and spoken forms. However, the book assumes little or no previous formal experience of the study of the English language. A substantial part of the book, therefore, reviews some of the basic concepts that readers will encounter when they begin an exploration of how words work in English, how they form phrase patterns, sentences and ultimately entire texts and discourses. It also reviews some of the basic tools required to study the different accents of English. This introductory chapter sets out a number of concepts, some of which will be discussed in greater detail as the chapters unfold. The glossary at the end also provides an explanation for many of the concepts from linguistics and corpus linguistics which we draw on in the book. Readers, particularly those wishing to take corpus techniques further, may also find Baker, Hardie and McEnery's *Glossary of Corpus Linguistics* (2006) to be a useful reference work. Finally, readers will find a website to accompany the present book at www.palgrave.com/language.

Using a corpus

One of the most exciting developments in the exploration of English over the past 40 years has been the accumulation of vast electronic archives, or corpora, of written and spoken texts, texts stored on computers and manipulated easily and quickly by search programs. The availability of such corpora has changed the working practices of linguists, particularly those scholars interested in the meanings and patterns of words and phrases. Before the advent of electronic corpora, it was a long and arduous process to compile and search substantial bodies of data in order to confirm or challenge one's own intuition as a language user. Nowadays vast bodies of data are available at the touch of a keyboard and the click of a mouse. Early beneficiaries of large, electronically searchable, corpora of English were dictionary makers, who suddenly had hitherto inaccessible evidence for the meanings of words, and language learners, who also had access to materials constructed using corpus data that seemed to guarantee relevance and authenticity. Only in the last few years, however, have language corpora begun to be freely available online to the casual browser, language learner and relatively novice student.

A few years ago, Susan Hockey (2000, p. v) noted that 'The World Wide Web is good for looking at material but it does not provide many tools for analysing and manipulating that material.' Since then, happily, the resources available on the Web have improved to the extent that students of language and linguistics can make considerable inroads into linguistic study solely by using freely available corpora, provided that they know where to look, have an appreciation of a few basic notions, and know how to maximise the potential of language corpora, with all their idiosyncrasies and differences. So, as written and spoken corpora become available to an ever wider network of potential users, guidance is needed in the use of them to explore aspects of language. This book is designed to give that guidance.

The careful analysis of corpora can give insights into (i) how language is *really* used, rather than how people *think* it is used and (ii) how it is *commonly* and *typically* used. To see how true this is, you can try jotting down your immediate thoughts about the typical linguistic contexts of a word in real language and then compare your list with the sample of evidence from a corpus such as

---

TASK 1.1   Comparing intuitions and evidence

1. Without reference to a dictionary, write down a definition of the adjective *seedy* and some typical examples of the nouns that it describes.
2. On a computer, log on to the BNC interface at BYU: http://corpus.byu.edu/bnc/
3. In the 'Display' section, click on 'List'.
4. In the 'Search String' section, type *seedy* in the 'Word(s)' box.
5. The results will show you the number of occurrences of *seedy* in the 100 million words of the BNC.
6. Click on the word *seedy* in the 'Results' section in order to see some of the contexts of usage. Note down some of the nouns that are modified by *seedy*, for example *seedy affair*.
7. To compare your results with 360 million words of current American English, go to www.americancorpus.org and repeat Steps 3–6.

the British National Corpus (BNC) or the Brigham Young University (BYU) Corpus of Contemporary American English, both of which we'll introduce in more detail later in this chapter. For example, what sorts of nouns are modified by *seedy*? Now complete Task 1.1.

The results of these searches may confirm your expectations or surprise you. The term *seedy* derives from the notion 'gone to seed' and out of context it might suggest shabbiness or lack of care. Some of the results of the corpus search confirm such a definition. For example,

Harold Macmillan's seedy and stagnant Britain

However, the majority of examples in the BNC suggest something that is sexually unsavoury about the term *seedy*. For example,

seedy affair
seedy porn photos
seedy abortionist
a rake's progress of late nights, seedy bars and relentless beer bellies
the seedy world of prostitution
the film-maker's seedy little wife, pompously and unseductively nude
seedy northern beauty contest
a seedy image of people who use porn
gave up her seedy career and wrote an exposé of the porn business.

While by no means all the examples conform to this pattern of meaning (there is, for example, an innocent reference to British actor Will Hay's creation of the role of a *seedy, blustering and ineffectual teacher* and even a reference to *seedy grass-heads caught in my socks*), many do. These instances are enough to suggest that in contemporary English the 'sexually unsavoury' element of the meaning of *seedy* is strong enough to carry into contexts in which it is not necessarily explicitly mentioned; for example, *business friends who ran seemingly dowdy or seedy little second-hand enterprises in shops dark and dusty.* This element of meaning has not yet, however, found its way into the online Oxford English Dictionary.

At this very basic level, then, checking your intuitions against corpus data can help you confirm or challenge your preconceptions about words, what they mean and how they are used. We build up our intuitions, of course, from long experience of language read and heard in a linear fashion. We come across instances of words like *seedy* from time to time, perhaps once in a million words that we read or hear spoken. From each of these contexts we build up an evolving picture of what the word can mean in various contexts. By bringing a substantial number of these instances together in a small space – a corpus – we can become aware of patterns that remained below the surface of our consciousness. As John Sinclair, one of the pioneers of modern corpus linguistics, noted, 'The language looks rather different when you look at a lot of it at once' (Sinclair 1991, p. 100).

Choosing your corpus

There are some important issues that every corpus user should be aware of when choosing a corpus that will help you answer your own questions about language. We will return to some of them again in later pages. First of all, we need to consider what kind of collection of texts a corpus is, and what differentiates it from other online textual resources.

The nature of a corpus

A corpus may be described quite simply as a body of texts; in fact, this is the literal meaning of the word. Most corpus linguists, however, prefer to be rather more specific, and describe a corpus as a large principled collection of texts, that is, one which has been created for a purpose. This is now a widely accepted definition. Even more precisely, a modern corpus is a sample of naturally occurring language, in electronic form, which has been designed to represent a language, language variety, register or genre. The key word here is 'designed', and this is what distinguishes a corpus from its close relative, the text archive. While an archive may have no predetermined structure and is not intended to represent something larger, a corpus is motivated, created with a linguistic purpose in mind. The Web as a whole may be used as a resource for linguistic exploration, and with the arrival of online tools such as WebCorp, it has become much more straightforward to do so. Given its constantly changing size and nature, however, it is better treated as a massive archive rather than a corpus. Nevertheless, it is certainly possible to create a corpus from material on the Web, by selecting texts according to particular criteria.

It is important to bear in mind the principled nature of corpora when using online examples for research. Since corpora are usually compiled with a purpose, it is necessary to match your needs as a corpus user against the interests and goals of the corpus designers. Although many corpora do indeed contain vast quantities of data, it may not be the kind of data you are interested in. For example, the TIME corpus brings together 100 million words of text, easily putting into the shade the 4 million words of the Scottish Corpus of Texts & Speech (SCOTS) and the 1.8 million words of the Michigan Corpus of Academic Spoken English (MICASE). However, as its name suggests, the 100 million words of the TIME corpus consist entirely of texts taken from *TIME* magazine, and while this is a fascinating source of a particular type of journalistic data, it does not contain any spoken English, or other varieties of written English. On the other hand, the MICASE corpus contains exclusively spoken English, but only from the domain of academia – genres such as lectures, seminars and consultations with tutors. Alongside its written data, the SCOTS corpus contains 800,000 words of spoken data across a range of situations, from lectures to spontaneous child–parent interactions, but given its size it does not necessarily give you much linguistic data from each individual situation. Each corpus clearly has its uses, and as a user you need to think about which one is most appropriate for your own explorations. Fortunately, most online corpora explicitly set out their design criteria and contents, so that you can assess their suitability for your purpose before you begin, and then carry out a small, pilot investigation to see how searches work in practice.

This book contains a substantial number of tasks and activities that aim to use the most appropriate online resource or resources in each case. You should therefore find it easy to design your own follow-up studies and develop your own interests. It will normally be possible to attempt the same activity with a different corpus, or to use the same corpus but subtly modify the research question. This will give you a feel for the nature, design and strengths of the corpus you are using, and allow you to appreciate its (inevitable) weaknesses.

Representativeness

As hinted in the previous section, the issue of representativeness is a crucial one. It is possible to make valid generalisations about a language or language variety only if the corpus is a fair sample of that language or language variety. Just as no one would claim to be able to make valid conclusions about Singaporean English from analysing a corpus of Scottish English, so we cannot draw valid findings about the use of the word *like* in spoken language from a corpus which contains only written language, and vice versa. Similarly, we cannot assume that if a grammatical construction is common in a corpus made up of scientific articles then it is also commonly used in the language as a whole. Nonetheless, such a finding may form a good hypothesis on the basis of which further research can take place.

Also, it is important to bear in mind that a corpus can only provide positive evidence of a usage or construction. In other words, it cannot tell you what is *never* said or written. The philosopher Karl Popper neatly illustrated this point by observing that a naturalist who came upon any number of white swans would still not be in a position to make the claim that black swans do not exist (Popper 1959). However, it would only take a single black swan to come along to falsify the claim. The force of the argument lies in the seductive nature of corpus data, which might, for example, show thousands of examples of *had* in the active voice. An observer might be tempted therefore to claim that *had* only ever appears in the active voice. However, it only takes a single example of a passive construction – such as *a good time was had by all*, which is attested in the SCOTS corpus – to negate that claim.

A representative corpus should, however, be constructed so as to reduce the possibility of making false claims about the language based on partial or skewed data. A word of caution is also necessary here. Corpus linguists talk frequently of the representativeness of corpora, but rarely agree on whether it is even possible to attain perfect representativeness, let alone what would constitute the make-up of this ideal corpus. Occasionally, the issue is easy to address. If you want to investigate the use of greeting formulae in published correspondence in the UK in the eighteenth century, then the population of texts is finite and so, copyright matters notwithstanding, you could in principle select a fair and representative sample of the overall population, employing such criteria as decade of writing, gender and age of writer, and the level of formality of the letter.

Most of the time, however, the issue of representativeness is far from straight-forward, and it is particularly thorny if you want to make generalisations about a language as a whole. What are the 'right' proportions of written language and spoken language? How do we deal with the fact that some texts are very widely read or heard, over either a long or a short period of time (for example, the Bible, the Queen's speech or the Presidential address, the fiction of J.K. Rowling, front-page newspaper articles), while others are read or heard by few people, or small groups of people (for example, specialised scholarly monographs, horse-racing reports, sermons in a small village church). How can we make sure that the voices of people of all ages, genders, occupations, races, religions, types of upbringing and so on are fairly represented?

What about the sorts of language that are by nature private – personal diaries, intimate conversations, the words you mutter to yourself when working through the instructions to build a self-assembly bookcase? Can we justify not including them in a corpus? Most large corpora contain some ephemeral texts, spoken or written, that might seem odd out of context. On its own, for example, the following excerpt from the spoken section of the BNC might cause the casual user to question the principles of the designers:

> mm mm. Mm. Mm. Mm. Mm. Ma ah ah! Daddy! Daddy! Hello! Dee dee dee, dee dee dee dee, dee dee dee dee dee, dee dee dee! What is she meant to think about? Pauline? Ah yea yea yea yea yea yea! Ah, yea yea yea yea yea yea yea! Yea yea yea yea yea yea yea yea! Yea! Ooh ooh ooh ooh! Ooh ooh! Ooh! Ooh ooh! you didn't tell me it was on yet. Will you, shall I take her up tonight? If she'll let me. What? [BNC text KDG, conversation].

This spontaneous effusion in isolation might well tell us very little, but as part of a larger, representative corpus, it can function as a legitimate thread in the larger tapestry of language.

Representativeness can simply be thought of as the inclusion in a corpus of a large number of texts in a large number of registers and genres. However, there are also statistical measures of representativeness, which can guide the corpus designer – and these are discussed more fully in Chapter 2. Most general corpora will at least try to capture a snapshot of different types of speaking and writing, from casual conversation to carefully composed legal documents. Further discussion of the issue of representativeness can be found in most introductory books (see the further reading at the end of this chapter), or the articles by Biber (1993) and Clear (1992).

Size

The issue of size is a separate but related issue to representativeness. For applications in lexicography, it is important that corpora should be large, usually tens if not hundreds of millions of words in size. O'Keeffe, McCarthy and Carter

(2007, p. 4) observe that to obtain a sufficient range of prepositions that follow *bargain,* they needed to search a corpus of about 10 million words. Online corpora range from the 360 million words of the BYU Corpus of Contemporary American English (with more words being regularly added) to the 1.8 million words of MICASE. As O'Keeffe, McCarthy and Carter go on to state (ibid, p. 4),

> In terms of what constitutes a large or a small corpus, it depends on whether it is a spoken or a written corpus and what it is seeking to represent. For corpora of the spoken language, anything over a million words is considered to be large; for written corpora, anything below five million is quite small.

Nevertheless, a lot of interesting research can be done on the more frequent or 'core' words, constructions and features of a language with corpora of even a few tens of thousands of words. Size, along with design, is a feature of a corpus which should suit the purpose to which it is put. In the context of corpora for language learning, Chambers (2007, p. 9) notes that

> It is clear that, despite the corpus linguist's need for corpora to be as large as possible in support of the researcher's quest for the elusive quality of representativity, several of those who focus on classroom applications and who have experience of working with learners have become aware of the usefulness of the small corpus.

Several online corpora are very large indeed, but many others are relatively small and precisely focused. Rather than necessarily having a large corpus, it is more important to have a good understanding of the nature of the corpus being used, and therefore the level of faith which one can put in findings from it. A list of currently available free online corpora, with some details about their nature, is given in the Appendix.

Type of corpus

It should already be clear that the features of online corpora for linguistic study can be diverse in nature. While it is not necessary to provide a comprehensive survey of corpus types here, it is helpful to be aware of a few general distinctions.

One important distinction is between synchronic and diachronic corpora, that is, between corpora which contain texts from a particular time period (such as English from the 1990s) and seek, therefore, to provide a snapshot of language usage, and those which can be used to investigate language change over time, as would be the case for a corpus of personal correspondence between 1700 and 1900, for example, and is the case for the TIME corpus, which spans most of the twentieth century. Diachronic corpora can be used to investigate neologisms or new coinings, or changes in grammatical constructions over time. A specific type of diachronic corpus, known as a monitor corpus, is one to which new texts are continually added: the BYU Corpus of Contemporary American English is an example of a monitor corpus.

Some corpora have been specifically designed to study translation, and there is a distinction to be drawn here between parallel and comparable corpora. Although the terminology varies, a parallel corpus is generally taken to be one which contains the same texts in a number of language versions, while a comparable corpus contains texts which are functionally equivalent in two or more languages. So while a collection of translations of the same novel would, by this definition, constitute a parallel corpus, a collection of (original, not translated) newspaper articles in different languages about the same issue would be termed a comparable corpus. Actual translation corpora may have features of both types.

Annotation

Annotation refers to the process of adding information to a corpus, so that it becomes possible to search for features that lie below the surface of language. Consider the problem: it is easy to search a corpus for the sequence of characters *e-a-r-n*, but the computer will not know to retrieve instances of the inflected forms *earns, earned, earning* as well. If you want to retrieve these forms of the verb from an unannotated corpus, you would have to either type each form into the search facility in turn, or use wildcards if this facility is available (for example, *earn** to retrieve *earn* followed by any number of characters, including zero – but note that this would also find the unrelated *earnest*). Alternatively, you could use a corpus which was lemmatised, that is, annotated so that each form of the verb is attached to a headword or 'lemma', which is generally the form of the verb found in the dictionary. Similarly, if you are interested in the word *search* as a verb but not as a noun, then a corpus in which every word form in context is tagged with the right part of speech would allow you to specify that you want only the verb spelt *s-e-a-r-c-h* and not the noun with an identical form.

Lemmatisation and part-of-speech tagging are two of the most common types of annotation, but in theory any feature of language can be tagged. Imagine you wanted to find in a corpus all of the words which had to do with the concept of EATING. In that case a semantically tagged corpus would help: searching for EATING might retrieve *eat* itself, *devour, munch, gobble, feed, graze, dine, nibble* and so on. The possibilities for corpora annotated with semantic information are limitless: a first step in this direction is the possibility of searching the BNC, TIME corpus and BYU Corpus of Contemporary American English for synonyms as identified by a thesaurus.

Annotation is generally expensive and time-consuming, especially if it has to be done manually rather than automatically. Because of the work involved, tagging tends to be reserved for small corpora which are used to investigate specific research questions but are not made generally available. Larger corpora, like the three just mentioned, have been tagged automatically. However, with a bit of ingenuity, and trial and error, you can find out a lot about words, meanings and grammar even with an untagged corpus.

The tradition of corpus analysis of English

If we understand corpus linguistics to mean simply the empirical analysis of language, that is, the exploration of language using authentic texts as data, then it has a long history. Manual analysis of texts has been used for over a century for research into the areas of lexicography, dialectology, anthropology and grammar. To take just one example, Charles Fries' *Structure of English* (1952) is a description of English grammar that took as its data a quarter of a million words of recorded and transcribed telephone conversations. The advent of the computing age revolutionised the means, if not the methods, of corpus analysis. In the late 1950s, work began on huge mainframe computers, with data painstakingly entered by hand on punched cards. In the following years, advances in technology paved the way for such landmarks in corpus linguistics as

- the Brown corpus of 1 million words of written American English published in 1961, created at Brown University, Rhode Island, USA;
- its British English counterpart, the LOB Corpus (Lancaster–Oslo/Bergen Corpus); and
- the work on the Survey of English Usage at University College London in the 1960s, which led to major grammatical descriptions of English (for example, Quirk et al. 1985).

Since the 1980s, corpora have developed in two parallel ways: some have become larger, and others have remained fairly small but become focused on closely delimited types of language, such as child language, the language of learners and the many private corpora created to answer particular research questions. Legal constraints still mean that many corpora are available only to researchers (perhaps for an annual fee, sometimes with password system), but the impetus for this book is that more and more corpora can be accessed immediately and freely on the Internet. There is a long way to go, especially as regards corpora for languages other than English, specialised corpora of particular language varieties and multimedia corpora, but freely accessible online corpora promise to open up hitherto inaccessible riches of language data to the user at much earlier levels of language study. Of course, the user of online corpora is more or less at the mercy of the corpus compilers in terms of the textual content and design of the corpus and the analysis which can be carried out on the corpus through its integrated search tools. For the relative beginner, however, this can be a good thing, as having a limited number of possibilities can make getting to grips with corpus analysis rather less daunting.

It will no doubt have occurred to the reader that there are inevitable uncertainties that are bound to plague any book dealing with online corpora. In particular, there is the risk that particular corpora discussed here will cease to be available as corpus projects come to an end, technical support is no longer available or copyright licences expire. Other online corpora (such as the BYU Corpus of Contemporary American English, which went online literally days before the completion of the first draft of this book) promise to be regularly updated – which means that search results will change over time. Search tools might be enhanced, change their appearance or even disappear. Moreover, on the plus side, in the current climate, it is likely that new corpora will appear, existing corpora will be expanded and annotated, new portal sites will allow various corpora to be accessed together and online analysis tools will become more sophisticated. Such changes have occurred with regard to several corpora in the course of writing this book. Even so, the kinds of basic principles outlined in the book and the searches we recommend should be easily adaptable to new corpora and new corpus interfaces.

Five online corpora of English

Below we introduce five of the main freely available online corpora of English, which are frequently referred to in this book. Alongside each we suggest a straightforward task which will allow you to begin to find out more about the nature of these corpora and how they can be analysed. These corpora, along with several others, are also listed in the Appendix.

British National Corpus

The British National Corpus (BNC; www.natcorp.ox.ac.uk/) – because of its large size, level of annotation and availability – has become the gold standard among corpora of British English. It was completed in 1994, and contains

---

TASK 1.2   Using the British National Corpus

Using your intuition, jot down the words you expect to follow *high and _?*

1. Go to the BNC site at www.natcorp.ox.ac.uk/
2. Type 'high and' in the 'Look up' box under 'Search the corpus' and hit Return.
3. You will be given a random sample of 50 occurrences of the sequence from the thousand or so examples in the BNC.
4. Go through the examples, and pick out those where *high and* seems to you to be part of a fixed expression. How many expressions can you find? How many had you previously thought of? Did the corpus produce any surprises?
5. Look again at some of the examples which you have decided are not examples of fixed expressions. Can you explain in grammatical terms why you do not consider these to be fixed expressions?
6. Choose a small number of examples and try to identify what sort of text the example has come from. Click on the text ID code at the beginning of each example to see how accurate you were. Assuming that your guesses were at least partially correct, what does this indicate about the language of different sorts of text?

You will find more on performing word searches in online corpora in Chapter 3.

---

100 million words of British English texts from the late twentieth century. Ten per cent of the corpus is made up of transcribed spoken language of various genres, and ninety per cent is written material, again of a wide range of genres. Importantly, the corpus has been automatically part-of-speech-tagged. The BNC website contains further information and allows simple searches (of strings of characters, or words restricted by part of speech) to be carried out. The search results indicate the total number of hits, although the online system returns a random sample of only 50 examples in the context of the sentence in which they occur. From the search results, the user can click to find out details of the text in which an example occurs.

BYU-BNC: The British National Corpus

Another means of accessing the BNC online is through an interface created and maintained by Mark Davies at Brigham Young University (BYU; http://corpus.byu.edu/bnc/). This interface offers a number of additional features over the BNC's own online search system, in particular full results, the possibility of identifying collocates, comparing the use of a word across different registers (for example, spoken, fiction, news) and searching for synonyms. For reasons of copyright, it is not possible to see complete texts, and as with the BNC's own site, the surrounding text (the co-text) of a search word is limited. Given its ease of use, and additional features, BYU-BNC is the online version of the BNC that is used most in this book.

TASK 1.3   Using the **BYU-BNC**

From your own experience of language, do you think that passive constructions (for example, *he was followed by a big dog, the book was proofread twice*) are more common in spoken language or in written language?

1. Go to the BYU-BNC site at http://corpus.byu.edu/bnc/
2. Under 'Display' click 'Chart', and under 'Search String' type 'was *ed by' in the 'Word(s)' field. Click 'Search'.
3. Look at the resulting chart. In which of the five main registers (Spoken, Fiction, Newspaper, Academic, Miscellaneous) does the sequence have the largest raw frequency?
4. In which of the registers does the sequence have the largest normalised frequency, that is, the greatest frequency of occurrence per million words? Why is this answer different from the answer to Question 3?
5. Do the results confirm or challenge your expectations?
6. What words do you expect to occur most frequently in place of '*ed' in this search? Again, jot down your intuitions, and then check them against the corpus by selecting 'List' under 'Display' and rerunning the query.

You will find more on exploring grammar in Chapter 4, and more on interpreting quantitative data in Chapter 2.

BYU Corpus of Contemporary American English

Using the BNC as a model, Mark Davies has also designed an online corpus of American English currently totalling a massive 360 million words (and to be regularly updated; www.americancorpus.org). It uses similar search tools to the BNC and so offers a new and fascinating opportunity to compare British and American usages. For copyright reasons, it is again impossible to see complete texts, although short extracts around the search word are available for viewing.

TASK 1.4   Using the BYU Corpus of Contemporary American English

From your own experience of language, what adjectives do you expect to follow the adverb *real* in American English? Do you expect such expressions (for example, *real good, real important*) to occur more commonly in speech or in writing?

1. Go to the BYU Corpus of Contemporary American English site at www.americancorpus.org
2. Under 'Display' click 'Chart', and under 'Search String' type 'real' in the 'Word(s)' field. Click on 'POS List' and select 'adj.ALL' from the drop-down list, so that '[j*]' appears after 'real' in the 'Word(s)' field. Click 'Search'.
3. Look at the resulting chart. In which of the five registers (Spoken, Fiction, Magazine, Newspaper, Academic) is the construction most common?
4. Does there appear to be any change in frequency over time (for example, between the earliest texts in the corpus and the latest)?
5. Have a closer look at some occurrences, by clicking on a bar in the chart, to see a list of the most common instances of the search string. What adjectives occur most commonly with *real* in each register?
6. Compare your results with the British English data in the BYU-BNC. Does British English also make use of *real* as an adverb to qualify adjectives?

You will find more on exploring the connections between language and context in Chapter 7.

TIME Corpus

This third major online corpus site created by Mark Davies (http://corpus.byu.edu/time/) contains more than 100 million words of text from the US magazine *TIME* from 1923 to the present, and is accessible through the same interface as the BYU-BNC and the BYU Corpus of Contemporary American English. However, a novel feature of this corpus is the possibility of looking at frequencies of words as they appear decade by decade, allowing us to trace key cultural concepts, and the rise and dissemination of neologisms over almost a century of American journalism.

TASK 1.5   Using the TIME Corpus

Using your experience of language, jot down a list of adjectives which you think are likely to have changed dramatically in frequency or usage over time; that is, adjectives which you think have only become popular recently, or have fallen into disuse or have significantly changed in meaning. Here are a few to get you started: *funky, gay, pious, spooky, spunky.*

1. Go to the TIME Corpus site at http://corpus.byu.edu/time/
2. Under 'Display' select 'Chart', and then type one of your adjectives in the 'Word(s)' field. Click 'Search'.
3. Explore the adjective in terms of its frequency – a quantitative analysis. The tallest bar in the chart indicates the register in which the search term occurs with the highest normalised frequency, that is, the greatest frequency per million words (see Chapter 2 for further discussion of normalisation). Is there a clear tendency for your adjective to become more or less frequent, relatively speaking, over time?
4. Explore the adjective in terms of its meaning and common collocates – a form of qualitative analysis. Go back to the search box, and tick 'Show Sections'. In the 'Search String' section, click on 'Context' and use the 'POS List' below to identify nouns in the vicinity of the search word (try five words to each side).
5. Explore how collocation patterns with different nouns have changed over time. Do the collocates suggest a change in meaning in your adjective, or simply a change in use?
6. Go back and repeat Steps 2–5 for each of your adjectives.

You will find more on quantitative and qualitative analysis of corpora in Chapter 2.

Michigan Corpus of Academic Spoken English

The Michigan Corpus of Academic Spoken English (MICASE; http://quod.lib. umich.edu/m/micase/) contains close to 2 million words of audio recordings and transcripts of academic speech events collected at the University of Michigan, USA. MICASE is an example of a small but very focused corpus of spoken English in a restricted range of settings. The transcripts can be searched according to various criteria such as the academic role of speaker, type of speech event, academic discipline and so on. Complete transcripts can be viewed and also downloaded. Searching for a word displays a concordance view that can be sorted in various ways, and much more context can be shown than a few words on each side of the search item.

TASK 1.6   Using MICASE

Using your experience of language, and knowledge of academic situations, think about how you ask questions in the classroom, or in lectures, seminars and one-to-one sessions in a university context. How do you frame your question?

1. Go to the MICASE site at http://quod.lib.umich.edu/m/micase/
2. Click 'Search MICASE' and type the word 'question' in the search box. Leave the Speaker Attributes and Transcript Attributes at the default settings. When prompted, choose 'View all results'.
3. Scan the concordance lines to identify instances of *question* where the speaker (whether student or teacher) is using the word to signal that he or she is about to ask a question: for example, *I have a question, my question is, I guess my question for you is*. How many examples can you find?
4. Why do you think the speaker chooses to announce his or her question in this way, rather than just, say, asking the question bluntly? In other words, what purpose does the framing serve? You will probably find it useful in answering this question to read the wider context of some of the occurrences.
5. Spend some time looking more closely at a couple of transcripts. Go back to the Search page, and specify that you want speech events which are 'Highly interactive' in the 'Interactivity Rating' category. What other ways can you find of indicating that you are going to ask a question?

You will find more on exploring features of discourse through online corpora in Chapter 5.

Scottish Corpus of Texts & Speech

One of the main online corpora we shall be drawing on in this book is the Scottish Corpus of Texts & Speech (SCOTS; www.scottishcorpus.ac.uk). Compiled and maintained by a team at the University of Glasgow, SCOTS includes texts in Scottish English and varieties of contemporary Scots, plus a few texts in Scottish Gaelic. At 4 million words, SCOTS is small compared to the BNC and the BYU Corpus of Contemporary American English, but it offers advantages which in part compensate for its size, depending on the type of research to be undertaken. Four in particular are given below:

- SCOTS includes 800,000 words of spoken text, in audio and, in some cases, audio-visual format. These recordings are made available as audio-visual files (requiring Apple QuickTime™ to view them), with a synchronised orthographic transcription.
- Most of the texts in SCOTS are available as complete texts; they have been copyright-cleared, and while they cannot be republished without permission, they can be downloaded and analysed for educational and research purposes.

- Extensive sociolinguistic metadata is made available with every text and can be used to refine a search.
- The Advanced Search facility in SCOTS allows users to browse available documents, written or spoken, and download them in bulk to their own computer as plain text files. Other search software can then be used on this subcorpus.

In some respects, however, the user must still exercise caution in using the SCOTS resource. The corpus contains a wide range of genres (from spoken conversations and interviews to written prose fiction, poetry, correspondence, documents from the Scottish Parliament and so on), but the corpus is not balanced – that is, the quantities of texts in each genre do not represent the proportions of these which are produced in the respective language varieties. Nor is there a perfect geographical balance, although SCOTS does aim to cover as much as possible of Scotland and a map facility allows the user to see this coverage at a glance. In Teubert and Čermáková's terms (2007, p. 70), SCOTS is an 'opportunistic' corpus.

TASK 1.7   Using the SCOTS Corpus

Think about the characteristic Scottish features of pronunciation of which you are aware. Jot down some words which you think would help you to identify a speaker's accent as strongly Scottish.

1. Go to the SCOTS site at www.scottishcorpus.ac.uk. Click on the 'Advanced Search' option.
2. Build up a complex query in the following way. Under 'Select your criteria', click 'Spoken', choose 'Participant details' and 'Region of residence'. From the drop-down list, select 'Moray', and hit Return. Then under 'General', click 'Word search' and 'Word/phrase (concordance)'. Type 'fitt' in the search box, and hit Return.
3. Scroll down the page to the concordance of *fitt*, click on a few examples in turn to be taken to the document page, from which you can listen to the recording. What do you think *fitt* means?
4. Many speakers alternate between *fitt, what* and *whit* in the north-east of Scotland. Try the query again using these other forms. Can you find examples where it is actually difficult to say whether the speaker is saying *fitt* or *whit*?
5. Now repeat Steps 2–4 to listen to examples of *what/whit/fitt* by speakers living in other regions of Scotland.
6. Explore pronunciation variation in Scotland further by building up similar search queries based on the words you identified as likely to identify a speaker's accent as Scottish.

You will find more on exploring features of pronunciation through corpora in Chapter 6.

The DIY option: building your own corpus

In addition to the freely available online corpora detailed above and in the Appendix, you may find that your institution has a subscription to other corpora, which can be used for comparative purposes. It is also possible that you might want to build your own corpus. This might be the case if your interest lies in a very specific type of language, which is not included in any of the corpora described above, or if you want to create a new corpus to act as a point of comparison with an existing one. Additional online corpora can be accessed through the Sketch Engine program, available at www.sketchengine.co.uk, which can also help you to build your own corpus from web material. As the focus of this book is on using existing online corpora, we shall not dwell here on corpus building. Students seeking detailed advice on this should see McEnery, Xiao and Tono (2006), which contains an excellent unit on 'DIY corpora'.

Analysing online corpora

The previous section introduced five corpora that can be used as online resources for language study. This section previews the kind of questions that linguists ask, in their exploration of how language works. The corpora we focus on in this book all come with integrated analysis tools of various kinds, so that the corpora can be not only accessed but also interrogated online. The kinds of questions that different readers might ask of online corpora are diverse and wide-ranging. For example,

- How is the word *how* used by speakers in different parts of the world?
- How is reported speech signalled in conversation?
- How are different sounds typically pronounced by speakers in different parts of the English-speaking world?
- What prepositions commonly follow particular words, like *result* in English?

There are various ways to begin to answer these questions and others like them: indeed some are probably best answered using a variety of methods. It is difficult not to start by drawing on your own intuition, built up from years of experience as an expert user of English. Dictionaries and reference grammars may confirm or challenge your instincts. Widening the net beyond your personal expertise, you might devise a questionnaire to be completed by a wide range of native speakers and/or expert users of English as a second or other language.

A further perspective is offered by an appropriate language corpus. As we have seen, a language corpus is – ideally – a carefully designed collection of examples of language which were not originally written or spoken for that purpose. To that extent, at least, a corpus represents 'authentic' language use. In practice, some corpora owe their construction as much to accident as design, and others include language that is more or less spontaneous and more or less 'rehearsed'.

Even so, corpora are rich resources by which we can extend our knowledge of language from personal intuition to a large set of data that shows what people under different circumstances actually say and write.

For example, to answer the questions above, the interested reader could go to a computer with an Internet connection and search an online corpus such as SCOTS, which we mentioned above. Searches of the SCOTS corpus can quickly address some of these questions.

How is the word *how* used by speakers in different parts of the world?

By searching the SCOTS corpus, in ways that we shall shortly discuss, you will be able to find many different examples of the use of *how* by Scottish speakers. One sample conversation illustrates two possible uses of *how*:

(1) F643: //This used tae//
     M608: //uh huh//
     F643: be a post-office, *that's how we had a post-box.*
(2) M642: //Aye well that // covers your bare wire
     F643: //That's right.// But then ye see the rats were eatin the wires as well.//
     M642: //See, *that's how ye joined them.*

In the first example, *how* expresses a reason, and in other varieties this might well be expressed by *why* (as in *that's why we had a post-box*). In the second example, *how* expresses instrumentality, showing the way the wires were joined. In this case it cannot be paraphrased by *that's why ye joined them*. These two possible uses of *how* are typical of speech in Scotland; a search of other corpora would confirm whether these two uses are also found in other speech varieties.

How is reported speech signalled in conversation?

The means used to signal reported speech in conversation vary from generation to generation and from place to place. Searches of online corpora such as the SCOTS corpus, again, can show us some of the resources used to mark off reported speech in conversation:

     F1049: //But you know that way, when you're workin,// and then like somebody asks you something, so you go and get something and then before you've come back to them somebody else asks you //something, and *you're like* 'Wait a minute'. [laugh]//
     M1048: //Uh-huh, so you get nothing done.// 'Hang on I'm dealin with a customer just now', and then you just get a look. [laugh]
     F1049: Well I was dealin with this woman and *she had asked where the wine was* but I was on the way to give this vodka to another woman,
     M1048: Uh-huh.
     F1049: and then another *woman asked me where the cold meat was*, //and *I*//

M1048: //Uh-huh.//

F1049: *just went* 'It's down that, it's on aisle twenty-three or whatever it //was',//

M1048: //Yeah.//

F1049: and she went, like that. And *I was like* 'If you want to wait a wee second I'll take you to it, but I've got two customers just now'.

M1048: [laugh]

F1049: And *she went* 'Hm', like that. //And then this other customer//

M1048: //[laugh]//

F1049: 'I'll show you where it is', and *I was //like* 'She'll show you where it is', I don't//

M1048: //[laugh]//

F1049: care, [laugh]

In this conversation, the speakers either report the speech indirectly (for example, *she had asked where the wine was*) or report it directly, using the signals *like* and *went*. This kind of observation is useful to those who are interested in the way speakers dramatise their interactions with others in conversation; it is also useful to those who are learning and teaching conversational strategies.

How are different sounds typically pronounced by speakers in different parts of the English-speaking world?

Variation in accent is one of the most fascinating topics of language study. Many early corpora focused on written texts, and only in recent years have searchable archives of spoken English become readily available online. These allow you to hear speakers either interacting more or less spontaneously, or reading from a prepared text. Both types of corpus have their uses. The latter type of speech archive allows for easy comparison between different accents because the content of their speech is identical. The former type is more representative of the features associated with everyday speech. Chapter 6 focuses on ways of exploring different types of English pronunciation using online resources.

What prepositions commonly follow particular words, like *result* in English?

Some corpora contain information about grammatical parts of speech. The BYU Corpus of Contemporary American English, for example, currently allows the browser to search 360 million words of American English for sequences such as *result* + preposition. The most frequent preposition following *result* is *of*, mainly in sequences in which *result* functions as a noun, as in *chemicals that build up as a **result of** stress*. The second most frequent preposition to follow *result* is *in*, mainly in examples in which *result* functions as a verb, as in *it did* **result in** *division within the Cabinet*. Learners of English as a foreign language, for whom prepositional usage is a perpetual challenge, can compare a sample of the 7516 current instances of *result* + *in* in the Corpus of Contemporary

American English with the 60 instances of *result* + *on*; for example, *that may be the most important* **result on** *Sunday.* Here, *on* forms a phrasal unit with *Sunday* rather than with *result.* There are a few instances where *on* seems to follow *result* and indicate the nature of the result; for example, *I am extremely sorry that a poor choice of words on my part in any way would* **result on** *dishonour cast upon you.* The extreme rarity of these instances suggests that they might be slips of the tongue rather than genuine examples of possible variant uses.

The questions discussed above give just a taste of the way that corpora can be used to explore the use of English around the world. The corpora give evidence of variation in the use of vocabulary and grammar, and show patterns of usage that will interest the student and be useful to teachers and learners of English. We will pick up some of the topics touched on above and investigate them in greater detail in later chapters.

The organisation of this book

This introductory chapter has set out some of the essential information needed to begin corpus-based study of language, and sketched a brief history of the empirical exploration of English in the digital age. It has surveyed a number of freely available online corpora, focusing closely on the corpora which will feature most strongly in the case studies and tasks in the central chapters of this book, and discussing the kinds of language project to which each is most suited. The rest of the book is structured in the following way. Chapter 2 introduces you to some of the basic search techniques in corpus studies and discusses the strengths and limitations of qualitative and quantitative analysis. It also establishes the pattern of taking the reader through a number of case studies, each of which can be modified using different linguistic features and different corpora, to provide a means of approaching all sorts of research questions.

Chapter 3 begins our linguistic analysis proper, at the level of the word. This chapter introduces one of the most fundamental tools for corpus analysis, the concordance. Chapter 4 then turns to the grammar and syntax of English, exploring how online corpora can provide new insights in this area. Chapter 5 considers the strengths and weaknesses of corpora in the investigation of linguistic organisation above the level of the sentence, looking at the use of certain linguistic features to organise discourse. Next, Chapter 6 focuses on spoken language, examining how some online corpora and resources, through their multimedia nature, allow us objective insights into phonology, the study of pronunciation.

Chapter 7 brings together some of the issues discussed in Chapters 2–6 and further addresses issues of quantitative and qualitative linguistic analysis using corpus evidence. The case studies here examine the strengths and weaknesses of using whole texts versus extracts in corpus study, and show how linguistic data can be combined with metadata (that is, information about the social background to the speech event and participants) to provide a rich sociolinguistic analysis. Finally, Chapter 8 considers some developing trends in corpus-based language studies.

FURTHER READING

Adolphs, S. (2006). *Introducing Electronic Text Analysis: A Practical Guide for Language and Literary Studies*. Abingdon, UK: Routledge.

Biber, D., Conrad, S. and Reppen, R. (1998). *Corpus Linguistics: Investigating Language Structure and Use*. Cambridge: Cambridge University Press.

Kennedy, G. (1998). *An Introduction to Corpus Linguistics*. London: Longman.

McEnery, T. and Wilson, A. (2001). *Corpus Linguistics: An Introduction*. Edinburgh: Edinburgh University Press.

McEnery, T., Xiao, R. and Tono, Y. (2006). *Corpus-Based Language Studies: An Advanced Resource Book*. London: Routledge.

Sinclair, J. M. (1991). *Corpus, Concordance, Collocation*. Oxford: Oxford University Press.

Stubbs, M. (1996). *Text and Corpus Analysis*. Oxford: Blackwell.

Interpreting Corpus Data

2

This chapter offers an introduction to some basic techniques used to search and interpret corpus data. Its aims are as follows:

- Compare the relative advantages of quantitative versus qualitative analyses;
- Survey some key statistical concepts relevant to corpus linguistics;
- Introduce some simple statistical tools which will help in the interpretation of data from online corpora; and
- Discuss the strengths and weaknesses of statistical approaches to textual analysis.

Given its focus on statistical analysis, this chapter is necessarily technical in nature, and some readers might therefore find it more challenging than the other chapters in the book. If you find the content demanding, you might wish to read through the chapter quickly, and then return to it periodically, in order to study in more detail those sections that illuminate points made in later chapters.

Moreover, given the space available, this chapter cannot give a comprehensive introduction to statistical concepts or techniques. Several of these, such as the log-likelihood test, which we mention later, rely on a detailed knowledge of statistics that is not fully addressed here. For a comprehensive introduction to statistics in linguistic study, we refer readers to a textbook such as Baayen (2008), McEnery, Xiao and Tono (2006) or Oakes (1998). The discussion of quantitative analysis in this chapter is mainly limited to the use of statistical data that can readily be garnered from available online corpora. Some further statistical tests are briefly described towards the end of the chapter. At the outset, it is worth stating two general points that we wish readers to take away from this chapter. The first is that the digitised and searchable nature of corpora makes them particularly attractive to linguists who wish to count features of language automatically. The second is that those linguists need to be cautious about what and how they count – and what conclusions they are tempted to draw. This chapter will have succeeded, if it encourages readers to approach the quantitative data offered by corpus-informed language studies with due caution and a critical mentality.

Quantitative and qualitative analyses

The study of the English language has a foot in two camps – that of the linguistic sciences and that of the traditional humanities. This ambivalent position means that those who study English have shifting attitudes towards what comprises evidence for the claims that they make about the language. The more scientifically inclined among us search for empirical evidence that is explicit and open to objective analysis, while those who feel a greater affinity with humanities place a greater emphasis on individual insight and the kind of interpretation of texts that might be subjective and yet still be persuasive and illuminating. At first glance, corpus linguistics might seem to favour the former camp. By presenting a mass of text in digitised form, and constructing tools to search that mass of text, corpus linguistics brings to the table a set of data and tools that produce results that seem explicit and objective. And it is true that this surfeit of easily accessible, seemingly transparent evidence is one of the great virtues of corpus linguistics. However, as will be clear from this book, evidence always requires interpretation, and the interpretative, critical skills of the humanities researcher are still highly prized in the discussions about what corpus data actually *means*.

A common distinction, frequently discussed by corpus linguists, is that between quantitative and qualitative analyses of data (see, for example, McEnery and Wilson 2001, pp. 76–77). As noted above, corpus linguistics lends itself to quantitative analysis: that is, using corpora and search tools, we can count things, identify frequencies and distributions, and so we can propose, in principle, reliable and generalisable statements about how language works. We might look, for example, at the relative frequency of the use of *like* in samples of older and younger speakers of English and so conclude that there is a much greater likelihood of the word being used by younger speakers than older ones. So long as the corpus is well constructed and the search tools are reliable, it is difficult to argue against this fact.

However, the mere fact that younger people tend to use the word *like* more frequently than older people does not tell us much about *how* both groups are using the word, and it does not tell us *why* younger people are using it more frequently. Other, more sophisticated, statistical analyses might be used to address these questions. For example, is the use of *like* also related to some other social variable such as gender, ethnicity or even marital status? The issue of why certain groups of younger people have adopted *like* is even more difficult to address.

For this reason, many linguists supplement quantitative analysis with interpretative, qualitative analyses of corpus data. Corpora can as easily make data available for qualitative analysis as they can for quantitative. Qualitative analysts use corpora not as a source of frequencies but as a source of raw data, which can be quickly and easily assembled. A good corpus linguist should be able to handle both qualitative and quantitative analysis.

Representativeness

The question of what makes a corpus representative of a language as a whole was addressed in the introductory chapter to this book, but it is worth returning to it here, since it is a crucial, if thorny, problem. A key issue in any statistical analysis is whether a *sample*, or subset, of any *population*, or larger group, will accurately represent the *variables* or characteristic features associated with the population as a whole. To apply this to linguistics, if we are going to make claims that a linguistic feature (the variable) is or is not characteristic of the language as a whole (the population), then we need to be convinced that its incidence in the texts that make up our corpus (the sample) accords with its incidence in the language more broadly. In short, to make accurate claims about any variables, we need to ensure that our sample is representative of the population as a whole.

One obvious way of designing a corpus to be representative of language as a whole would seem to be to try to mirror the range and proportion of texts produced in everyday life. However, as Biber (1993, p. 247) points out, there are problems with this apparently simple approach to corpus design:

A corpus with this design might contain roughly 90% conversation and 3% letters and notes, with the remaining 7% divided among registers such as press reportage, popular magazines, academic prose, fiction, lectures, news broadcasts, and unpublished writing. (Very few people *ever* produce published written texts, or unpublished written and spoken texts for a large audience.) Such a corpus would permit summary descriptive statistics for the entire language represented by the corpus. These kinds of generalizations, however, are typically not of interest for linguistic research.

The problem, as Biber goes on to discuss, is that there are statistical and practical problems in basing the samples of a corpus on the proportion of text types found in 'everyday life' (and even since his article was published, email messages and mobile phone texts have probably come to outnumber 'letters and notes'). The practical problems lie in gaining ethical access to the more private kinds of speech and writing that people produce and in financing the transcription of a spoken-language corpus. To some extent, however, these issues can be resolved. The statistical problems lie in the fact that, while few people might actually produce published written texts, compared to conversation, these texts have a disproportionate influence in our daily lives – we read newspapers, books, journals and magazines, and we listen to scripted broadcasts, sermons and speeches. A truly representative corpus must, therefore, sample from the range of possible varieties of written and spoken language available. The 10 per cent of language that is *not* everyday conversation, therefore, becomes important in the construction of a corpus.

There are various statistical approaches to the construction of a representative corpus and to checking whether a given corpus is indeed representative of language at large. These approaches are based on the size of text samples and how the texts are distributed across different registers. Biber (e.g. 1988, 1990, 1993) has compared frequencies of linguistic items in different registers: conversations, public speeches, press reports, academic prose and general fiction. For example, in one study (Biber 1990), he extracted three sets of ten texts each from these registers and counted the mean frequency of six common linguistic features in each register: (1) first-person pronouns, (2) third-person pronouns,

(3) past tenses, (4) nouns, (5) prepositions and (6) passives. His results suggest that the mean frequency of these features is quite stable across the three ten-text samples, although he cautions against making similar assumptions about less common linguistic features such as relative clause markers or the use of particular kinds of subordinate clause such as conditionals. Since these linguistic features are rarer, larger sample sizes are required in order to give reliable information on how these features are used. Effectively, by comparing samples of text across corpora, Biber has produced estimates of sample sizes that will produce reliable results for a range of common and infrequent linguistic features.

Mean and standard deviation

The tables below (adapted from Biber 1993, p. 255) show figures for the mean and standard deviation relating to these linguistic features in three registers (namely, conversations, general fiction and academic prose), as calculated for a pilot corpus. It is worth taking some time to understand what these figures signify.

Most readers will understand the concept of the *mean*. To arrive at the mean number of nouns per text, in a collection of texts, you could follow these simple steps:

- Calculate the total number of nouns in each individual text
- Add the totals together to give an overall figure for the collection as a whole
- Divide that overall figure by the number of texts to arrive at the mean number of nouns per text.

The mean is what is commonly referred to as the *average*. However, as statisticians use different kinds of average to characterise data, we will use the term *mean* to refer to this simple calculation.

Of course, the actual number of nouns in any given text might vary considerably from the mean. For example, imagine that you have a collection of three texts of the same overall length. You calculate that the number of nouns in each individual text is 50, 170 and 360, giving a mean of 190. Notice that only the number of nouns in the second text (170) is relatively close to the mean of 190. It is therefore useful to have a measure of how far a variable is likely to *deviate* from the mean. Standard deviation is a figure that tells us how much variation we can expect to occur. To arrive at the standard deviation score, statisticians perform the following procedure:

- Look again at each of the individual values that were used to obtain the mean. In our three hypothetical texts, the mean was calculated by adding together the total number of nouns in each individual text (50, 170 and 360) to arrive at a mean of 190.
- Calculate how far above or below the mean each of these values is (that is, $50 - 190 = -140, 170 - 190 = -20, 360 - 190 = 170$). Square these differences to make them all positive. Then take an average of these squared

'deviations' ($140^2 + 20^2 + 170^2 = 48900$; 48900 divided by 3 = 16300). Finally, take the square-root of this average ($\sqrt{16300} \approx 128$). The standard deviation here is therefore 128.

A small standard deviation will tell us that on average the variation from the mean is quite low – although there might of course be a few exceptional examples that vary quite widely from the mean. A large standard deviation will indicate that the degree of variation is generally quite high. In our fictional example, the mean is 190 and the standard deviation is 128, telling us that we can expect a high degree of variation from the mean in our individual texts.

There are many times when it is useful to know the standard deviation as well as the mean. For example, if you were to go on holiday, you might like to know that the mean temperature at your holiday destination is 22°C. It would also be useful to know what the standard deviation from the mean was: if it was 2° you would know that the temperature did not vary much from the mean. You might be unlucky and get one or two exceptionally cold or hot days, but on the whole the temperatures would not vary too much. If the standard deviation were 8°, however, you would know that the temperature fluctuated quite a lot, and you would pack a wider assortment of clothes.

In the simple hypothetical example we have just given, based on the number of nouns in three texts, we made the assumption that all the texts are of the same length. Otherwise, of course, you would not be comparing like with like, and you might simply expect more nouns to occur in longer texts. When linguists like Biber compile corpora based on actual texts, they obviously do find that the length of texts varies. Therefore, in order to compare like with like, they perform a process known as *normalisation*. Normalisation is discussed in greater detail below. For the time being, it is sufficient to know that instead of using complete texts as the basis for his figures, Biber has adjusted his figures so that the mean values refer to the number of likely instances per 1000 words. That is, in Table 2.1, the figures of 137.4 nouns and 85.0 prepositions refer to their likely occurrence in 1000 words of conversation.

If we look now in more detail at the figures in Table 2.1, we can see that, for a range of conversational texts, Biber has the following frequencies:

Number of nouns: 137.4
Standard deviation: 15.6

These figures suggest that in the register of conversation, we should expect around 137.4 nouns to occur per 1000 words. If an individual conversational text displays variation to one standard deviation (that is, ± 15.6 occurrences from the mean), then that is very much to be expected. That text is not particularly 'deviant'. If individual conversations deviate greatly from this band of frequencies (say, by 6 or 7 times the standard deviation), then we can be relatively assured in our claim that they are unlike other conversational texts, at least in respect of the frequency of occurrence of nouns.

Table 2.1   Mean and standard deviation of linguistic features in normalised text samples from three registers

Linguistic feature	Conversation		General fiction		Academic prose	
	Mean	SD	Mean	SD	Mean	SD
Nouns	137.4	15.6	160.7	25.7	188.1	24.0
Prepositions	85.0	12.4	92.8	15.8	139.5	16.7
Present tense	128.4	22.2	53.4	18.8	63.7	23.1
Past tense	37.4	17.3	85.6	15.7	21.9	21.1
Passives	4.2	2.1	5.7	3.2	17.0	7.4
WH relative clauses	1.4	0.9	1.9	1.1	4.6	1.9
Conditional clauses	3.9	2.1	2.6	1.9	2.1	2.1

Source: Adapted from Biber (1993, p. 255)

If we accept Biber's sample as a balanced and fair one, from which reliable statistics can be adduced, what can we say about the relationship between the means and standard deviations for different linguistic features? The figures for nouns in conversation, general fiction and academic prose show a standard deviation from the mean of 15.6, 25.7 and 24.0, respectively. Given that the standard deviations for the two written registers (25.7 and 24.0) are higher than that for conversation (15.6), we might argue that the stylistic range of writing is greater than that of speech, accounting for the higher degree of variation found in the number of nouns found in the written registers.

The frequency of occurrence of nouns in text is a convenient measure for corpus linguists to consider, simply because most texts will contain a high frequency of nouns. Other linguistic features may be less suited to corpus analysis simply because they are less frequent. Notice, for example, the figures given for conditional clauses in Biber's study. The means and standard deviation for conditional clauses are obviously lower than those for nouns. Academic prose, for example, has a mean of 2.1 and a standard deviation of 2.1, indicating that it would be entirely reasonable to find a stretch of 1000 words containing no conditional clauses at all. If you wished to look in detail at a range of conditional clauses in a corpus, then, it is likely that you would need to look at passages of text considerably larger than 1000 words.

To gauge the reliability of Biber's figures, we can compare the figures he obtained from his pilot corpus with, for example, the figures available in a large, general corpus like the BNC. Task 2.1 sets out the steps involved in comparing the frequencies found in the BNC with the frequencies that Biber suggests are typical of representative corpora.

TASK 2.1   Part-of-speech frequencies

This activity considers the figures from Biber's pilot study in relation to the BNC online. Using the BNC-BYU interface, and a calculator, we can obtain frequency figures per million words for parts of speech across different genres.

1. Go to http://corpus.byu.edu/bnc/
2. In the 'Display' box, choose 'Chart'.
3. From the 'Parts of Speech' box, select *Noun ALL*, or, alternatively, enter [nn*] in the Word(s) box.
4. Click 'Search'.
5. Look at the results per 1,000,000 words for 'Spoken', 'Fiction' and 'Academic' and divide them by 1000 to compare with the range suggested by Biber's pilot study, which gives frequencies per 1000 words. Do the figures match up?
6. Try again with some other parts of speech, selecting these from the POS list, e.g. prepositions [pr*], present tense [v?z], past tense [v?ed], relative clauses [pnq].

The results for nouns in the BNC match up fairly closely with Biber's study in two out of three registers, conversation and general fiction. Biber's pilot study suggested 188.1 nouns per 1000 for academic prose, with a standard deviation of 24.0. The further the number of nouns in a text is from the mean, the more likely that text is to be atypical. Biber's mean frequencies and standard deviations (SD) for nouns are compared with the BNC figures in Table 2.2:

Table 2.2   Mean and standard deviation of nouns in three registers

	Spoken	*Fiction*	*Academic*
Mean score for nouns in Biber's pilot corpus	137.4	160.7	188.1
Standard deviation in Biber's pilot corpus	15.6	25.7	24.0
Mean score for nouns in the BNC	136.5	168.7	248.6

Source: Adapted from Biber (1993, p. 255) and incorporating figures from the BNC

The BNC mean figures for nouns correspond closely with Biber's pilot corpus in the registers of speech/conversation and fiction. The BNC scores fall well within one standard deviation. The BNC, however, has 248.6 nouns per 1000 words in its Academic section, which, at first sight, does not correspond so neatly with Biber's figures. The difference between Biber's mean score and the BNC mean score is 60.5, which is between 2 and 3 times the standard deviation of 24. This might suggest either a difference in sampling procedures by Biber and the BNC, or that one of the corpora over-represents or under-represents the typical number of nouns per 1000 words with regard to academic prose.

It will be clear from this activity that gauging representativeness on the basis of a sample of language – no matter how large – is always going to be problematical. The researcher first has to construct a corpus against which other corpora can be matched. The rewards for achieving a representative corpus are high, however, because once a corpus has been confirmed to be representative other questions can be reliably asked of it. Some obvious features of Biber's figures, based on his corpus, are the relatively high incidences of past tense verbs in general fiction and the high number of passive constructions in academic prose. Qualitative reasons for these quantitative results are not hard to find: general fiction is more commonly concerned with past tense narratives than are conversation or academic prose. Academic prose, on the other hand, favours agentless clauses, and so passive constructions are more frequently found in this register. In these two respects, the figures achieved by Biber's study confirm our impressions of the characteristics of these registers.

The statistical methods by which representativeness is gauged are, of course, more complex than those hinted at in this section. However, the basic methods should be evident from the discussion, and the activity above, and can be summarised as follows:

- Take a sample of texts from a range of registers, e.g. conversation, fiction, academic prose, etc.
- Select a range of linguistic markers to be counted, e.g. nouns, personal pronouns, prepositions, etc.
- Count the occurrences of the linguistic markers (the raw frequency).
- Calculate the mean number of occurrences per 1000 words (a normalised frequency; see further below).
- The standard deviation is then calculated using a statistical formula that calculates the mean variation from the mean (for further information on this formula, see Oakes 1998, pp. 6–8).
- Other texts are matched against the sample texts to find out if they (or the sample texts) are atypical.

While most people who are simply exploring English using online corpora will not need to calculate the representativeness of their samples on a statistical basis, it is still useful to be aware of the basis on which any corpus claims to be representative. It is also useful to consider how typical any text under detailed consideration is of other examples of its type.

Frequencies

Much information can be obtained by looking purely at frequencies of items in a corpus. The number of words occurring in a corpus is referred to as the _raw frequency._ While few online corpora allow you to search for the most and least frequent items, it is clear from the corpus linguistics literature that there are some basic differences between spoken and written language in relation to the frequency of particular items. For example, the twenty most frequent items in the CANCODE corpus of speech and a written sample of the Cambridge International Corpus (CIC) occur with the raw frequencies shown in Figure 2.1.

This table of frequencies confirms the expected high number of instances of the articles *the* and *a* in everyday speech and writing, as well as the common occurrence of the basic additive conjunction *and*. However, if we look closer at the items that occur most commonly in speech as opposed to writing, we

	CANCODE spoken corpus		CIC written corpus	
	Word	Frequency	Word	Frequency
1	the	169,335	the	284,174
2	I	150,989	to	132,335
3	and	141,206	and	125,526
4	you	137,522	of	122,903
5	it	106,249	a	114,381
6	to	105,854	in	84,940
7	A	103,524	was	59,454
8	yeah	91,481	it	51,642
9	that	84,930	I	50,871
10	of	78,207	he	50,007
11	in	62,796	that	46,195
12	was	50,417	she	41,607
13	it's	47,837	for	41,606
14	know	46,601	on	38,361
15	is	45,448	her	36,500
16	mm	44,103	you	35,773
17	er	43,476	is	34,871
18	but	41,534	with	33,829
19	so	40,071	his	32,535
20	they	38,861	had	31,420

Figure 2.1   Word frequency lists from CANCODE and Cambridge International Corpus, from O'Keeffe, McCarthy and Carter (2007, pp. 35–36)

begin to see a pattern. *I* and *you* occur much more frequently in speech than in writing —3 times as often in each case. Spoken language also has a high frequency of tokens like *yeah*, and markers of agreement or hesitation like *mm*, and *erm*, which obviously do not appear so frequently in writing. Even the marker of agreement, *yes*, does not appear in the fifty most frequent items in the CIC written corpus. The verb *know* appears frequently in the spoken corpus; further examination of the occurrences show that this is because it very often appears in the expression *I know*, which, like *yeah*, is a marker of agreement. So the frequencies suggest to us that speakers use these items for the purpose of 'projecting their self image, creating good relations with their interlocutors, understanding and using the basic grammatical and logical relations that underpin the less frequent vocabulary' (O'Keeffe, McCarthy and Carter 2007, p. 36).

Normalisation of frequencies

When looking at corpus data, we can distinguish between *raw* and *normalised* frequencies. For example, in O'Keeffe, McCarthy and Carter's samples from CANCODE and the CIC corpus, the search item *I* occurs 150,989 times in the spoken data and only 50,871 times in the written data. These raw frequencies are comparable because the two sets of data are of equal size, 5 million words each. Normalised frequencies are used when comparing two data sets of unequal size, say a sample of 5 million words versus a sample of 20 million words. Normalised frequencies usually tell us the number of occurrences that there are, or that we can expect, per thousand, or sometimes per million words (See Task 2.2).

Normalised frequencies can also be used with individual texts, although they are not completely reliable with very small amounts of text. For example, in the SCOTS corpus, *the*, which is the most frequent word in the CIC sample, occurs 7 times in a single 33-word poem by David Purves, 'Midnicht in Mey'. The same item occurs 15 times in the 264-word Minutes of a Scottish Parliament Committee Meeting on Justice, held on Wednesday 6 February 2002. It is difficult to compare the usage in these texts without looking at the normalised frequencies, which are 212.12 occurrences per 1000 words for the poem, and 56.82 occurrences per 1000 words for the Minutes, in each case making an assumption that the number of examples of this definite article would increase proportionately if the text were longer. The frequency of *the* in the parliamentary Minutes is much closer, indeed almost identical, to the normalised frequency for the CIC sample (which works out at 56.83 occurrences per 1000 words). By comparing normalised frequencies, then, we can say with some confidence that the frequency of *the* in the poem is some way greater than in the data from the CIC corpus. This observation might lead us to look at the seven instances in the poem and consider, qualitatively, how they contribute to its interpretation – how, perhaps, the concentration of noun phrases modified by *the* raises common ground between writer and reader and focuses our attention on a set of familiar images – frost, seasons, sun and stars – whose cyclical nature is being restated with poetic intensity.

TASK 2.2   Comparing written and spoken language

This activity compares the frequency of use of *I know* in a set of written and spoken documents in the SCOTS corpus.

1. Go to www.scottishcorpus.ac.uk.
2. Click on Advanced Search.
3. Click on General, then Word Search, and type 'I know' into the Word/Phrase (Concordance) box.
4. Click on General, then Document Details, Spoken, and click on Spoken.
5. Click on the general Spoken heading, then click on Audio Type and click on Conversation.
6. When the results have been displayed, scroll down the page and look at the normalised frequencies of the use of *I know* in the conversations listed. The normalised frequency gives the number of instances of *I know* per 1000 words. List the lowest and highest normalised frequencies, and note the documents in which they appear.
7. Click on Advanced Search to start another search. Repeat Steps 3–6 but selecting Written text and Prose: non-fiction.
8. Compare your results for the spoken and written documents. What kind of spoken documents have a low/high frequency of instances of *I know*? What kind of written documents have a low/high frequency of instances of the same phrase? Go back and look in detail at a concordance list of *I know* in the documents that show low and high frequencies of use. Does the use of this phrase really help to manage relations between speaker/writer and audience? If so, how?

It will be clear from the list above, compiled from the CANCODE and CIC data that by far the most common words to appear in English are the grammatical and discourse markers: those items that modify or say something about the status of much less frequent lexical items, that is, those verbs, adjectives, adverbs and nouns that carry much of the substantial meaning of any interaction. These lexical items have much lower frequencies in the language. However, an analysis of the frequency of lexical items can still be very revealing. In a discussion of the importance of frequency statistics in corpus linguistics, Paul Baker (2006, p. 48) suggests that frequency is useful because language is a set of conventional patterns that still manage to present individual users with a choice of possible expressions:

It is the tension between these two states – language as a set of rules vs. language as free choice – that makes the concept of frequency so important. If people speak or write in an unexpected way, or make one linguistic choice over another, more obvious, one, then that reveals something about their intentions, whether conscious or not.

As Baker indicates, the frequencies found are suggestive of ideological concerns. For example, the frequency of possible words referring to non-natives of Scotland in Scottish parliamentary discourse can be indicative of current attitudes and concerns.

TASK 2.3   Relative frequencies of lexical items

This activity compares the relative frequency of items referring to non-natives of Scotland in Scottish parliamentary discourse.

1. Go to www.scottishcorpus.ac.uk.
2. Click on Advanced Search.
3. Click on General, then Word Search, and type 'refugee*' into the Word/Phrase (Concordance) box.
4. Click on General, then Document Details, Spoken or Written, and click on Spoken.
5. Click on the general Written heading, then click on Text Setting and click on Government/politics.
6. When the results have been displayed, note the number of occurrences, the number of documents in which the words occur and the total number of words in those documents. Scroll down the page and list the names of the texts with the three highest normalised frequencies.
7. Repeat this search for *asylum seeker*, *immigrant*, *migrant*, *tourist*, *visitor*, *foreigner*, *overseas*, *indigenous*, *non-indigenous*.

An activity like Task 2.3 can be revealing about how a society and its institutions categorise groups of people. Do frequently occurring items indicate current ideological anxieties or concerns? How are non-natives of Scotland categorised, and how are those categories characterised? If you look at concordance results of the documents with a high normalised frequency, you can begin to see the words most likely to collocate with *refugee* as opposed to, say, *tourist*. Are other ways of categorising and characterising people possible?

Mutual Information

Identifying the frequency of individual words and phrases can be revealing, and further qualitative analysis, for example of concordance lines of documents containing a high normalised frequency of those words and phrases, can be suggestive of how these expressions are characterised. A glance at a concordance might hint that, for example, *refugee* is more likely than *tourist* to collocate with *problem*. However, further statistical measures, one of which is the Mutual Information (MI) measure, can offer more substantial evidence of how commonly individual words collocate with others. In corpus linguistics, MI scores give information about the probability of two words occurring close to each other in a text – say within a span of five words on either side. Some, though not all, online corpora give MI scores, as shown in Task 2.4 below.

TASK 2.4   Investigating Mutual Information Scores

This activity compares the MI scores of two words.

1. Go to http://corpus.byu.edu/bnc.
2. In the Display section, click on 'List', and then type 'refugee' into the 'Search String' box. Leave Context blank, and leave the span of words selected to five items on each side.
3. Click on 'Options' and then 'Sort by' and choose 'Relevance'.
4. Click 'Search'. This search gives you the most frequent collocates of *refugee* in the BNC as a whole. The search covers a span of five words to each side of the key word.
5. In Table 2.3, note the first five words and the respective figures in the adjacent columns.
6. Repeat Steps 2–5, substituting *tourist* for *refugee*.

Completing Task 2.4 will allow you to complete Table 2.3:

Table 2.3   Comparison of MI scores of collocates of **refugee** and **tourist**

	Collocates with refugee	*Total*	*All*	*%*	*MI*
1	Camps	103	1139	9.04	6.95
2					
3					
4	Kurdish	18	549	3.28	5.93
5					
	Collocates with tourist	*Total*	*All*	*%*	*MI*
1	Cowal	6	29	20.69	6.90
2					
3					
4	Attractions	71	885	8.02	5.96
5					

Table 2.3, when completed, shows a high MI score for *refugee* and *camps*, as well as a high MI score for *refugee* and a cluster of words around ethnic groups and nationalities, such as *Kurdish*. By contrast, *tourist* collocates more frequently with places, such as the *Cowal Peninsula* in Scotland and with positive terms such as *attractions*. In Table 2.3, the column headings along the top row spell out the following:

- a word with which the search item *refugee* co-occurs (within five positions to either side, as determined by this particular search), i.e. the collocate, *camps*

- the total number of occurrences of collocations such as *refugee + camps* (Total) in the entire corpus
- the number of occurrences of *camps* in the entire corpus, no matter what it occurs with (All)
- The percentage of all occurrences of the search item with the collocate. In this case, the number of times the search item occurs with the collocate (103) is divided by the total number of occurrences of the collocate (1139) and then multiplied by 100 to give 9.04.
- The Mutual Information score is given, a statistical measure of the 'semantic bond' between the search item and the collocate.

It is generally accepted that an MI score higher than 3 suggests a strong bond between the search item and its collocate (see, for example, Hunston 2002, p. 71). Here, therefore, the score of 6.95 shows a very strong bond indeed between *refugee* and *camps*. It will be clear, too, from Table 2.3 that the MI score is not a simple measure of frequency of co-occurrence. Looking at the collocates of *tourist*, it is clear from the table that *attractions* occurs much more frequently with *tourist* than *Cowal*. The total figures show that *Cowal* only occurs 29 times in the entire BNC; however, 6 of those 29 occurrences are within 5 words of *tourist*. The BNC therefore gives *tourist + Cowal* a very high MI score of 6.9. The careful interpreter of the figures must deduce not that *Cowal* is, as a general rule, very likely to occur with *tourist* but that in the BNC this low-frequency item occurs largely in the context of tourism texts. Indeed, it is only when the list of collocates reaches *attractions* that the total number of incidences of the collocate in the BNC is substantial.

Other measures of collocation

As ever, the interpretation of statistical information requires caution. Even so, by scrolling down the collocates of *refugee* and *tourist* it can become clear that each word is associated with a different set of collocates, with those relating to refugees being more negative in meaning than those to do with tourism. This observation can be further investigated by comparing the frequency of *refugee* and *tourist* with a particular collocate, like *problem*. Let us say you want to use the BNC to compare the frequency of occurrences of *refugee problem* versus *tourist problem*. Task 2.5 takes you through this analysis.

This activity will result in a set of figures that can be shown in a table, slightly adapted from that given by the BYU-BNC in Table 2.4.

This table shows that *refugee* occurs within the contextual range of five words before or after *problem* 33 times in the corpus while *tourist* appears in the same positions only once. This means that of all the occurrences of *refugee* and *tourist* before *problem*, the first search item modifies the collocate 97 per cent of the time, while the second search item modifies it only 3 per cent of the time.

The third and seventh columns show the relative percentages of the search items in the corpus as a whole: that is, of all the occurrences of either *refugee* or *tourist* in the BNC, 29.5 per cent are occurrences of *refugee*, and 70.5 per cent are occurrences of *tourist*. This simply shows that *tourist* occurs much more frequently than *refugee* in the BNC.

TASK 2.5   Comparing frequencies of collocations

This activity compares the frequency of two words with respect to a particular collocate that occurs immediately after the search item.

1. Go to http://corpus.byu.edu/bnc.
2. In the Display section, click on 'Compare words', and then type 'refugee' and 'tourist' into the 'Search String' boxes.
3. In the 'Context' box type 'problem', and leave the span of words selected to five items on each side.
4. Click 'Search'.
5. Note down the respective figures in the adjacent columns (compare Table 2.4).

Table 2.4   Comparison of frequencies of collocation of *refugee* and *tourist* with *problem*

Collocate	W1 Refugee	% Refugee/ tourist	Probability Refugee + Problem	Score	W2 Tourist	% Tourist/ refugee	Probability Tourist + problem	Score
Problem	33	29.5	0.97 (=97%)	3.30	1	70.5	0.03 (=3%)	0.04

The fourth and eighth columns show the percentages of occurrences of the two search items immediately before *problem*. That is, when you add together the occurrences of *refugee problem* and *tourist problem*, the former collocation occurs 97 per cent of the time, while the latter occurs only 3 per cent of the time. This result is despite the far greater frequency of *tourist* in the corpus.

The scores indicate the ratio of percentages of the search items overall against the search items plus the collocate, *problem*. And so the score for *refugee* (3.3) is arrived at by dividing the percentage of its occurrences with the collocate (97 per cent) by the percentage of occurrences in the corpus overall (29.5 per cent). Similarly, the score for *tourist* (0.04) is arrived at by dividing the percentage of its occurrences with the collocate (3 per cent) by the percentage of its occurrences in the corpus overall (70.5 per cent). Note that the scores are *not* calculations of MI; however the high score for *refugee* still shows its much greater likelihood than *tourist* to appear immediately before *problem* in 100 million words of British English text. While in principle both refugees and tourists could be considered problems or opportunities in any society, clearly, the discourse of British English tends towards the former option.

BYU-BNC: BRITISH NATIONAL CORPUS (100 MILLION WORDS, 1980s-1993)

Mark Davies / Brigham Young University

SEE CONTEXT: CLICK ON WORD (ALL SECTIONS) OR NUMBER (SPECIFIED SECTION)   [HELP...]

WORD 1 (W1): MALE (1.37)

WORD 2 (W2): FEMALE (0.73)

	WORD	W1	W2	W1/W2	SCORE		WORD	W2	W1	W2/W1	SCORE
1	CHAUVINISM	25	0	50.0	36.4	1	EAGLE	13	0	26.0	35.7
2	GAY	19	0	38.0	27.7	2	LAYS	24	1	24.0	33.0
3	SUPREMACY	18	0	36.0	26.2	3	TERMINAL	9	0	18.0	24.7
4	HEIR	30	1	30.0	21.8	4	DETECTIVE	8	0	16.0	22.0
5	TESTOSTERONE	14	0	28.0	20.4	5	EMANCIPATION	8	0	16.0	22.0
6	HETEROSEXUAL	13	0	26.0	18.9	6	PASSENGER	8	0	16.0	22.0
7	CHAUVINIST	23	1	23.0	16.7	7	REPRESENTATION	14	1	14.0	19.2
8	BREADWINNER	22	1	22.0	16.0	8	BLONDE	7	0	14.0	19.2
9	LOVER	11	0	22.0	16.0	9	CM.	7	0	14.0	19.2
10	SWINDON	11	0	22.0	16.0	10	EUNUCH	7	0	14.0	19.2
11	CHOIR	21	1	21.0	15.3	11	IMPERSONATOR	7	0	14.0	19.2
12	ABUSE	10	0	20.0	14.6	12	VAGRANT	7	0	14.0	19.2
13	MACHO	10	0	20.0	14.6	13	LEVEL	12	1	12.0	16.5
14	PIG	10	0	20.0	14.6	14	ANONYMOUS	6	0	12.0	16.5
15	QUALITY	10	0	20.0	14.6	15	ADVOCATE	6	0	12.0	16.5

More information...

KEYWORD IN CONTEXT (KWIC)

CLICK ON TITLE FOR MORE CONTEXT
SECTION: NO LIMITS

1	FP3	W_fict_prose	a portable cage and from it peered an eagle. An old eagle. A female eagle. A golden eagle! "It's Minch," whispered Creggan.
2	FP3	W_fict_prose	. The voice was faint and troubled, and sounded like that of an old female eagle. When they had carried him into his cage that afternoon and taken him
3	FP3	W_fict_prose	Cape Wrath. So you came from Cape Wrath ..." It was the old female eagle speaking from the darkness near him, repeating the name he had finally spoken
4	FP3	W_fict_prose	knew very well that this night was the one which would decide whether the old female eagle survived. For that evening, as work finished, the Zoo Curator himself
5	FP3	W_fict_prose	a portable cage and from it peered an eagle. An old eagle. A female eagle. A golden eagle! "It's Minch," whispered Creggan.
6	FP3	W_fict_prose	whose name was Helmut Wolski. He had a particular reason for regarding the old female golden eagle as special and, like Creggan, he was obsessed by it now
7	FP3	W_fict_prose	day to make him do so --; about the first time he had seen the female golden eagle in the Zoo. It had been the day he had gone to
8	FP3	W_fict_prose	round the Zoo by the Foreman, he came to the Cages just as a female golden eagle was being put in one of them. "That's our newest
9	FP3	W_fict_prose	drift away into memory and he found himself staring into the eyes of the old female golden eagle. And whatever it was she might have said, had she had
10	FP3	W_fict_prose	herself, he backed away across the path towards the benches. Then the old female golden eagle came out into the gloom to see what the fuss was. For
11	FP3	W_fict_prose	for fun. His only regret was that it was not his old friend the female golden eagle who had escaped. Mr Wolski knew what he was going to do
12	FP3	W_fict_prose	two years before, made a promise to stay on until his old friend the female golden eagle "went free", which to him really meant until she died
13	FP3	W_fict_prose	shadows far below, and the opening of great wings. It was a young female golden eagle, and she was going for the carrion he had left. He

Figure 2.2   Screenshot of BYU-BNC, showing significant collocates of *male* and *female*

This finding might seem like a statement of the obvious. However, a broader comparison of immediate collocations can result in more surprising findings. It is, for example, interesting to compare the immediate collocates of words like *male* and *female* (see Figure 2.2). Here the search items are more equally distributed in the BNC, with *male* accounting for 57.9 per cent of the occurrences and *female* the remaining 42.1 per cent. The highest scores for *male* suggest a tendency to favour discourses to do with attitudes and politics (*chauvinism, supremacy*) and also sexual orientation and performance (*gay, heterosexual, lover*). The collocates for *female* are more varied, perhaps, with suggestions of a concern with outward appearances (*blonde, representations, impersonator*), occupations and roles (*detective, passenger*), and political and sexual (dis)empowerment (*emancipation, eunuch*).

However, right at the top of the scores given for *female* is the collocate *eagle*. It has a high score – as high as the collocate *blonde* – and seems to form an association with *female* that is stronger than the collocation of *male* with *chauvinist*. The strength of this association seems counter-intuitive, and that in turn should lead us to examining the actual incidences of *eagle* with *female*, which we can do by clicking on *eagle* in the relevant column. Here, we find a concordance line from a work of fictional prose:

from it peered an **eagle**. An old **eagle**. A **female eagle**. A golden **eagle**!

In this line alone, the word *eagle* collocates 4 times within the span of five words to either side, and the description of the *old female eagle* recurs several times in the story. The inclusion of this piece of fictional prose in the BNC has clearly skewed the statistics so that they favour an apparent strength of collocation between *eagle* and *female*. It will of course be the case in any sample of texts that certain collocations appear to be stronger than we would expect them to be in the language as a whole. The larger the corpus, the easier it is to see beyond such idiosyncrasies of the sample.

As argued above, then, the quantitative analysis of statistical information from a corpus can be suggestive. Statistics can indeed indicate that a text or set of texts contains patterns of occurrence that conform to, or depart from, general norms; and they can suggest strengths or weaknesses of association between search items. But these are no more than suggestions. At times they will confirm our intuitions about how language works in general, as well as in particular texts. At other times, they will surprise us and make us think anew about how language works. However, statistical results are not in themselves an interpretation of a text or an explanation of why particular patterns occur. Qualitative analysis is often required to flesh out the interpretations we make of the unprocessed statistical data that online corpora invite us to investigate.

Key words

Key words are those expressions that have a significantly higher or lower frequency of occurrence in a text or set of texts than we would expect, given the frequency of occurrence of those expressions in a larger corpus used as a point of reference (Scott 1997). To an extent, they give us an indication of what a text is about. Texts can be characterised in relation to those expressions that have an unusually high – or low – frequency of occurrence in them. Compared to the statistical measures used above – normalised frequency analyses and MI scores – tests of 'keyness' are more sensitive to the size of a corpus and compensate for the fact that, for example, longer texts will contain fewer unique occurrences of particular words.

To achieve a measure of the keyness of an expression, the frequency of occurrence in the specific corpus (which might be one or more texts) is compared with the frequency of occurrence in a much larger reference corpus. The raw frequencies are then subjected to one of several possible statistical formulae to find out if the difference in frequencies is statistically significant – in other words, is the difference in frequencies a matter of pure chance, or is it likely to be motivated by some characteristic of the communicative event? One such statistical test is called the chi-square test and another common one is log-likelihood. It requires a detailed command of statistics to use either test in corpus analysis, and it is beyond the scope of this chapter to cover the complexities of these forms of analysis. We can only give a flavour here of how they might be used; readers who wish to know more are referred to more comprehensive statistical guides such as Oakes (1998).

Normally when log-likelihood is used to indicate key words in corpora (e.g. Baker 2006), the test reveals those words that characterise a set of texts by appearing more frequently (or indeed less frequently) than would be expected given the norms apparent in the language alone. No online corpus to date allows the user to calculate the key words in a corpus or subcorpus overall. However, Paul Rayson of Lancaster University has made a simple log-likelihood calculator available online, and it can be used to compute a measure of the keyness of given words used in two corpora. That is, the novice researcher who wishes tentatively to explore whether or not a set of given words are key can use Rayson's online log-likelihood (LL) calculator, which can be found at http://ucrel.lancs.ac.uk/llwizard.html. This at least allows the researcher to test his or her hypotheses about keyness, although more experienced analysts would wish to familiarise themselves with the statistical basis of the log-likelihood test. Rayson's website gives the full formula and references necessary for a fuller explanation.

For example, if you browse words such as *dialect, slang* and *language* in the spoken part of the SCOTS corpus, using the Standard Search page, you can see that it is used with different frequencies by different speakers, usually talking about different varieties of Scots. You might be interested to look at the measures of keyness to figure out whether the speakers use one term or another more frequently than would be expected from the norms as calculated from a much larger corpus. The results of this measure of keyness might conceivably indicate something about the speakers' language attitudes.

To find out the keyness of these three words, we need to look at the raw frequency of their occurrence in three documents of different sizes in the SCOTS corpus. We then compare each document in turn with a larger corpus of spoken language, which we use as a reference corpus. In principle, we could compare the frequency of occurrence with the spoken section of the SCOTS corpus as a whole, which currently stands at 800,000 words. However, we are going to choose instead the spoken section of the BNC, which stands at 10 million words. This activity gives us some practice in comparing results across online corpora. Using both SCOTS and the BNC, we are going to calculate a log-likelihood score for each search item, using Paul Rayson's interactive log-likelihood wizard. A step-by-step guide to this process is given in Task 2.6. As you complete the process, you might wish to complete Table 2.5. The current frequencies for the BNC spoken section are given, and the log-likelihood score for SCOTS Conversation 19 is already calculated for you so that you can check your progress in the activity.

Since this is a rather more complicated activity than the others in this book, we will take it in three steps, Tasks 2.6a, b and c. The figures you identify in Task 2.6(a) will give you the raw frequency of occurrence of the three given words in each of the documents chosen. These frequencies by themselves do not tell us very much; to know whether the words appear more or less frequently than we would expect, we need to compare these documents with a much larger reference corpus, such as the spoken section of the BNC. Now complete Task 2.6(b).

You now have all the figures you need to compare the occurrences of your search items in the SCOTS documents, with a much larger reference corpus, the BNC. The question is whether the difference in the frequency of occurrence in the documents and the reference corpus is a significant one. By applying the log-likelihood test, we can have a robust indicator of how significant any

Table 2.5   *Dialect, language* and *slang* in SCOTS and the BNC

Corpus/Text	Word	Size of text/corpus	Raw frequency	LL score	±
SCOTS	*dialect*	3743	5	45.06	+
conversation 19	*language*	3743	2	4.14	+
	slang	3743	1	6.51	+
SCOTS	*dialect*				
interview 12	*language*				
	slang				
SCOTS talk:	*dialect*				
Matthew Fitt	*language*				
	slang				
BNC spoken section	*dialect*	10,000,000	52		
	language	10,000,000			
	slang	10,000,000			

TASK 2.6(a)   Identifying word frequencies in a set of documents

1. Go to www.scottishcorpus.ac.uk.
2. Go to Standard Search and choose the Spoken part of the corpus by removing the tick on 'Written' in the 'Document' section.
3. Type 'dialect' in the 'Word/Phrase' box, and hit 'Search'.
4. Scroll down the results and choose three documents. To practise, select (i) Conversation 19: Two north-east teachers on Doric Language; (ii) Interview 12: Shetland woman talking about languages in Scotland; and (iii) Talk: Scots in Schools in the twenty-first century – Matthew Fitt.
5. Complete Table 2.5, showing the total number of words in each document, and the raw frequency of the search item, *dialect*, in each document.
6. Repeat Steps 3–5 for the search items, *language* and *slang*.

TASK 2.6(b)   Establishing frequencies in a reference corpus

1. Go to http://corpus.byu.edu/bnc.
2. Click on 'Chart' and 'Show Sections'.
3. Type 'dialect' into the 'Word(s)' box and click 'Search'.
4. Look at the results for the Spoken section of the corpus, and check the figures for the size of the corpus and the raw frequency of occurrence of *dialect* against those in Table 2.5.
5. Repeat Steps 3–4 for the search items *language* and *slang* and complete the table.

difference in frequency actually is. To do this, we compare the frequencies of occurrence of each search item in the three documents from the SCOTS corpus (Corpus 1) against the frequencies of the search items in the reference corpus, the BNC (Corpus 2).

TASK 2.6(c)   Calculating Log-Likelihood

1. Go to http://ucrel.lancs.ac.uk/llwizard.html.
2. Referring to your completed table, enter in the boxes under Corpus 1 the raw frequency of the search item *dialect* in SCOTS Conversation 19, and the total number of words in that document.
3. In the boxes under Corpus 2, enter the frequency of the search item *dialect* in the Spoken section of the BNC, and the total number of words in that section.
4. Click 'Calculate LL' and look at the results. In the table, note down the log-likelihood figure and whether the log-likelihood figure is + or −. In the log-likelihood wizard, + indicates over-use, while − indicates under-use. Scores of 3.8 or above are regarded as significant; that is, they are not likely to be the result of chance.
5. Repeat Steps 2–4 for the search items *language* and *slang*.

You now have a set of statistics that give an indication of how the frequency of occurrence of the three search items, *dialect, language* and *slang* in three spoken documents, compares to their expected frequency, based on 10 million words of the language. It is interesting to do this for these three documents – two featuring schoolteachers and a resident in strong Scots-speaking areas of Scotland and one featuring Matthew Fitt, an author, poet and translator into Scots – since 'Scots' is a contested term. Some people consider Scots a language, some a dialect and some consider it slang. In all three documents, the speakers are reflecting on language use in Scotland.

Looking, then, at the results that you should by now have plotted onto your table, you will see from the positive log-likelihood that in each of the three SCOTS documents there is a higher incidence than expected of occurrences of *dialect*, compared against the 10 million words of the spoken section of the BNC. In other words, all three of the SCOTS documents can be characterised in part by their focus on the concept of dialect. Moreover, the greatest log-likelihood score by far is that of the frequency of *dialect* in the conversation of the Shetland woman talking about languages in Scotland.

From the relative log-likelihood scores for *dialect, language* and *slang*, we notice that, in her discussion of her own speech, the woman from Shetland uses the term *dialect* much more frequently than *language*, and, indeed, the term *slang* neither appears in this document nor does it appear in the talk given by Matthew Fitt on language in schools: here, however, the term *language* appears with the greatest frequency, a much greater frequency than would normally be expected from the evidence of the BNC spoken corpus, with *dialect* still having a positive log-likelihood and *slang* again appearing less frequently than would be expected.

The very small negative log-likelihood figures for *slang* in the interview with the Shetland woman and the talk by Matthew Fitt suggest that the frequency of occurrence is not much less than would be expected. Given the size of the SCOTS documents, we would not necessarily expect a relatively low-frequency item like *slang* to feature anyway. However, given that these are spoken events that focus on language, *slang* appears surprisingly seldom.

This is not the case with the conversation between the two schoolteachers. As with the woman from Shetland, *dialect* occurs with the greatest frequency, much greater than normally would be expected. However, in the case of the teachers, *slang* appears more frequently than *language*, with both having a positive log-likelihood – that is, both search items appear more frequently than normal.

The 'keyness' indicators of the three search items, then, conform to what we might expect of a conversation, interview and talk about language in Scotland by a native of Shetland, two Scottish teachers and a Scots language enthusiast. For the Shetland woman, *dialect* is by far the most prominent key word, with *language* featuring in a distant second place and *slang* not featuring at all. For the two teachers, *dialect* is also the most frequent item, with *slang* in a distant second place, ahead of *language*. For the Scots language author and activist, *language* is significantly in first place, far ahead of *dialect* with *slang* not featuring. From the indicators of keyness, then, we would suggest that the woman from Shetland considers her speech and that of others in Scotland as dialect, while the Scots author and activist considers it a language. Neither seems to consider slang as a relevant theme in their interview or talk. The two teachers also focus on dialect, but slang also features as a significant topic area in their conversation: as educationalists, they are perhaps more likely to view dialect and slang as related, possibly problematic, issues in the classroom, where a written standard variety is normally promoted. They alone have *language* as the least key of the three search items.

To confirm or challenge these interpretations of the statistical results, one would have to go back and look in detail at the actual SCOTS documents. A qualitative analysis, for example, of Matthew Fitt's talk shows that he only uses *dialect* once in his talk, and that he distances himself from the term. He refers to *dialect* as the term used to describe Scots by the organisers of a minority language song competition that had excluded his entry:

And the response was was quite interesting. Erm apparently, [laugh] apparently Scots is a is a former dialect of a national language. Erm which that, I mean everyone's looking puzzled, and I'm extremely puzzled by that. [SCOTS document 1544].

It is clear from this excerpt that Fitt distances himself from the use of *dialect* to describe Scots; the keyness of *language* relative to *dialect* in his talk reflects this ideological stance.

A trawl through the key words in documents, or sets of documents, can give a general indication of what topics characterise these documents and how speakers and writers choose to articulate them. In an early article on key words, Scott (1997, p. 243) suggests that 'key word clumps and their members will play a part in critical text analysis within Sociolinguistics, Applied Linguistics, Political Science, etc.' He also suggests a role for key word analysis in English Language Teaching and literary criticism. A more sceptical view might be that key word analysis tells us little that is unexpected. Baker (2006, pp. 121–149) takes us in detail through an analysis of key words in a UK parliamentary debate on fox-hunting, showing that, for example, vocabulary associated with cruelty were positive key words in the contributions of the anti-hunt lobby, while vocabulary associated with civil liberties were positive key words in the contributions of pro-hunt supporters. While key word analysis shows in some detail how these lexical items are distributed amongst the factions, the general conclusion comes as no real surprise. Neither does it come as a surprise that a Scots-language activist might avoid the term *dialect* while a native of Shetland uses the term extremely frequently to characterise her own speech and that of others.

Even so, there are some virtues in analysing key words. As Baker (2006, p. 146) notes, key words are particularly interesting when one set of texts is to be compared with another, to explore ideological stance or linguistic style as shown in Task 2.7.

TASK 2.7   Exploring keyness using SCOTS and the BNC

Design your own investigation of documents from the SCOTS corpus in relation to the BNC, using the previous activity as a model. For example, you might look at the keyness of words like *nation, nationalist, nationalism, Scottish, English, British* in written documents from the 'Government/Politics' part of the SCOTS corpus, using the Written section of the BYU-BNC as your reference corpus. (To select SCOTS documents from the 'Government/Politics' section, go the Advanced Search page, click on 'Written' and then 'Text setting'.)

Other statistical tests

At the time of writing, the statistical data easily available from online corpora are largely limited to raw and normalised frequencies, and, in some cases, Mutual Information. With a little more effort, as we have seen above, we can explore the keyness of words and phrases. For other more sophisticated statistical investigations, the corpus linguist needs commercial corpus analysis software such as WordSmith Tools (Scott 1999) or Micro-OCP, or free online software such as TAPoR Tools or R, into which your own corpus texts can be fed (see Baayen 2008). Some corpora, such as the SCOTS corpus, allow their archives to be downloaded as text files, and these can then be used in conjunction with such corpus analysis software. Detailed guidance in the use of such software is beyond the scope of this book, since here we are mainly concerned with activities that you can perform directly with available online corpora. However, as online tools are developing quickly, we end this chapter with some general information about two more statistical techniques that may well shortly become available online.

Dispersion

Sometimes you might wish to find out more than the raw or normalised frequency of search items in a text or set of texts; you might also wish to find out more than the MI score between two search items. You might, for example wish to know *where* items 'cluster' in different parts of a document. WordSmith Tools (Scott 1999) is one corpus software package that allows users to derive frequency lists for groups of words and phrases that collocate. It then works out a 'dispersion plot' that tells you where those words and phrases occur within a text. Baker (2006, pp. 59–62) uses dispersion plots to track the appearance of frequent expressions in Club 18–30 holiday brochures. He finds, for example, that the phrases *don't miss out* and *work 2 live* appeared early in many brochures, and from this observation, he argued that the marketing strategy was to present the holidays quickly and forcefully to the young adult demographic as 'living' as opposed to 'working', and 'taking opportunities' rather than 'missing out'. Dispersion plots can indicate the flow of topics within a genre of texts.

Tests of statistical significance

As we have indicated in this chapter, raw frequencies by themselves often tell us little about how one text can be compared to another. We need to manipulate the raw frequencies to arrive at MI scores or log-likelihood values and to measure more robustly the relationship of one set of frequencies with another. Statistical tests allow us to determine more reliably whether the differences we see between sets of data are produced by regular patterns or a chance occurrence. The commonly used statistical term for data patterns that are unlikely to have occurred by chance is *statistically significant.*

The kinds of test used in corpus linguistics include log-likelihood, t-tests, ANOVA and chi-square tests (cf. Biber, Conrad and Reppen 1998, pp. 275–277). We have already used log-likelihood to calculate the 'keyness' of words, and, as noted above, Paul Rayson's log-likelihood wizard gives a brief summary of the equation used and some references for further exploration. When two groups of data are being compared, t-tests can be used to measure the difference between mean scores in the two data sets relative to the amount of variation that exists within each group. For example, you might measure the size of the difference between the mean frequency of occurrence of a grammatical construction such as *I've done* in two sets of texts, British and American, and then evaluate that difference against the variation within each data set. The resulting t value would take into account the size of the mean difference, the standard deviation and the size of the samples. Once we have a value for t, we can calculate a p value that tells us how likely it is that any difference arose by chance, rather than from an underlying difference in the usage of the two populations. A small p value indicates a low probability of the observed difference being the result of mere chance.

When more than two data sets are being compared – let us say British, American and Australian English – it is possible to use ANOVA (ANalysis Of VAriance) tests, again to calculate the differences between the respective data sets against the variation internal to each data set. In the ANOVA test, we obtain F values that indicate the size of the difference in the light of the variation. From the F values, we can again obtain a p value which indicates the statistical significance of the difference.

Finally, chi-square tests are often used to compare observed frequencies of a category with expected occurrences (see further, Oakes 1998, pp. 24–29). Chi-square tests are, therefore, alternatives to log-likelihood tests in the calculation of key words. Various online tutorials on the application of statistics in research, including the chi-square test, are available (see for example Anatol Stefanowitsch's page at www-user.uni-bremen.de/~anatol/qnt/qnt_dist.html; and the Georgetown University Department of Psychology pages at www1.georgetown.edu/departments/psychology/resources/researchmethods/statistics/8314.html).

Summary

This book does not delve much deeper into the methods of statistical analysis than it has done in this chapter. However, to exploit the strengths of corpora, on and offline, it is necessary to have at least a rudimentary sense of topics such as the following:

- how statistical techniques have contributed to our notions of the representativeness of the language in corpora
- whether or not the frequencies of occurrence of search items actually mean anything
- whether or not the comparisons we make of the relative frequencies of occurrence in two or more sets of data show statistically significant differences.

By introducing basic concepts such as raw and normalised frequencies, mutual information and keyness, we aim to have given you a general sense of the quantitative side of corpus linguistics. If nothing else, this chapter should alert you to the fact that statistics need to be used with caution. The explorer of linguistic corpora needs a variety of methods of analysis at his or her disposal – both quantitative and qualitative. Ideally these go hand in hand.

FURTHER READING

Baayen, H. (2008). *Analyzing Linguistic Data: A Practical Introduction to Statistics Using R.* Cambridge: Cambridge University Press.

Baker, P. (2006). *Using Corpora in Discourse Analysis.* London, New York: Continuum.

Biber, D., Conrad, S. and Reppen, R. (1998). *Corpus Linguistics: Investigating Language Structure and Use.* Cambridge: Cambridge University Press.

Hunston, S. (2002) *Corpora in Applied Linguistics.* Cambridge: Cambridge University Press.

McEnery, T., Xiao, R. and Tono, Y. (2006). *Corpus-Based Language Studies: An Advanced Resource Book.* London and New York: Routledge.

Oakes, M. P. (1998). *Statistics for Corpus Linguistics.* Edinburgh: Edinburgh University Press.

Exploring Lexis with Corpora

3

Corpora can be analysed for all sorts of linguistic purposes, as we will see throughout this book. However, the lexical route into a corpus is perhaps the most straightforward; the study of words and phrases is most accessible for students who have little or no previous experience of using a corpus. In this chapter, therefore, we look at how online corpora can illuminate the study of words in English and at the kinds of information that can be obtained from doing simple word searches and using basic tools such as concordancers. The topics covered are relevant to students of English language (both native speakers and learners of English as a foreign language), particularly those studying introductory courses on lexis and lexical semantics. This chapter will also be useful groundwork for students embarking upon the use of online corpora for the study of other aspects of language, as it explores some of the basic techniques for obtaining linguistic information from corpora. Some of the questions considered are as follows:

- From the perspective of corpus linguistics, how can we define a word?
- What information can we obtain from a corpus about words?
- How can we describe the typical environment of a word?
- How do common uses of a word relate to uncommon uses?
- What happens when words combine?
- How can we describe the linguistic patterns in which words are used?

There are two main reasons why words are an appropriate place to begin corpus research. First, the notion of a word is intuitively simple to grasp. Words are something in which people tend to be interested. This is why the BBC's peak viewing slots can include a programme like the recent series, *Balderdash & Piffle*, in which the presenter, with help from the public, seeks to trace early evidence of the use of words and expressions in English, or, in earlier years, *Call My Bluff*, a panel game in which contestants guessed the meanings of obscure words, like *immorigerous*, a seventeenth century term for *unyielding* or *rebellious*. This natural interest in words is also why some people become very worked up over what they perceive as misuses of certain terms in English – words such as *chronic, disinterested, flout, decimate* and so on – which are undergoing changes in meaning. We expect words to be fixed in meaning.

A second reason why lexis is a good place to begin is that searching for, and displaying occurrences of, words is something that computers can do very efficiently, without requiring much further intervention by the person or team who has built the underlying corpus. Some online corpora may not be suitable for the study of phonology or syntax, because the work involved in organising the data in a corpus to show phonological and syntactic information is time-consuming and expensive and is consequently not always carried out. In contrast, all corpora can be used to investigate the behaviour of words and phrases, although the types of analysis they facilitate may differ from resource to resource. It does not follow, however, that interpreting the evidence provided by corpora is always an easy task: creating dictionary definitions for words, for example, requires a great deal of skill on the part of lexicographers and demands huge corpora of hundreds of millions of words.

As you follow the activities suggested in this chapter, you might also find it useful to keep a piece of paper beside you in order to jot down other words you notice in the corpora which look as if they would repay further, independent investigation. One of the incidental pleasures of corpus study is in noticing intriguing patterns that are unrelated to the immediate object of your study, and it is an invaluable aid to memory to note these observations to follow up at a later time.

This chapter begins by briefly discussing the notion of a word as it relates to corpus linguistics and exploring how we can retrieve information about words from a corpus. However, words are of limited interest when extracted from their linguistic co-text and wider context, so we will move quickly on to look at various aspects of a word's linguistic environment, including the concepts of *collocation, colligation, multiword units* (such as idioms and metaphors) and the concept of *semantic prosody*. Although our focus here is on the words used in such patterns, and how they interact with their environment to create meaning, some of the analysis in this chapter will necessarily anticipate the investigations of later chapters, in particular Chapters 4, 5 and 7, on grammar, discourse and contextualisation of corpus data, respectively. It is important to understand that although we have chosen to divide language up into different 'levels' for the purposes of this book, these levels are for convenience only: meaning is not created at each level independently of the others but is rather created by choices made at multiple linguistic levels simultaneously.

What is a word in a corpus?

The question of what constitutes a word has long been discussed by linguists (see for example Crystal 1997, p. 91). In corpus linguistics, 'word' may be used to cover the concepts of both *word form* and *lemma*. The word form is the easier to define: word forms exist on the surface of language and are simply sequences of characters occurring between two spaces or between other characters such as punctuation marks, which word list software has been programmed to recognise as boundaries. *Is, are, was, were, being, been* are therefore all separate word forms. Lemmas (or, more formally, 'lemmata'), on the other hand, are forms which include all of the related inflected forms: in this case, the six word forms *is, are, was, were, being, been* are all included in the single lemma BE. This is considered to be the basic form of the word and is the form we would look up in a dictionary.

To see the distinction between word forms and lemmas in practice, go to the ELISA corpus (www.uni-tuebingen.de/elisa/html/elisa_index.html), and select 'Browse all words with Web Concordance'. This will take you to a page which lists all of the word forms in the corpus. Each clickable item on the list is a word form: note, however, that the related word forms have been grouped below the word form which is also the lemma, even where this disrupts the alphabetical list (see, for example, the lemma GO with word forms *goes, going, went, gone*). If you are looking in a corpus for all the variants of the lemma BE or GO, then it is clearly useful to have a lemmatised corpus that enables you to search for all the associated word forms. An unlemmatised corpus would not make the connection between, say, the word forms *be* and *is*, or *go* and *went*. Remember, however, that in English many word forms begin in the same way as their associated lemma (e.g. *walk, walks, walked*), so with careful use of truncation and wildcard characters (e.g. *walk**), you can make good progress even with an unlemmatised corpus. But watch out for the exceptions, like *be-was-were*, *goose-geese*, where you will have to search for each form separately.

A related issue is how corpus designers treat contracted words, which include an apostrophe, such as *I'd, didn't*. Sometimes a corpus word list facility will treat

---

TASK 3.1   Lemmatisation

1. Go to the ELISA homepage: www.uni-tuebingen.de/elisa/html/elisa_index.html
2. Click on 'Browse all words with Web Concordance'.
3. Expand the top frame, and click on the letter 'G'. Then scroll down the list until you reach the word form *grow*. Click on it and you will be taken to the concordance lines for *grow* as a word form, immediately followed by concordance lines for the other word forms related to the lemma GROW.
4. Look at the types of context in which each word form occurs. Can you make any generalisations about the typical uses of each in the interviews contained in this corpus?
5. Based on your findings, do you think it is useful in this case to consider the word forms together under their related lemma or separately?
6. Try this task again with other groups of word forms from the ELISA word list. Can you find instances where the word forms of a lemma typically occur (a) in similar patterns and (b) in different patterns?

See also Stubbs (2001, p. 27) for examples of patterning around word forms and lemmas.

an apostrophe as one of several characters that are used as word boundaries: this is the reason why under WOULD on the ELISA list you also find simple *d* (as in *I'd, they'd*) and under DO you find *doesn* and *didn* (as in *doesn't* and *didn't*). No single solution to issues like this will suit every research purpose, so it is simply a matter of finding out how the relevant word list has been configured when you are interpreting corpus data. In summary, two questions to consider when using any new corpus are as follows:

- Has the corpus been lemmatised?
- How are contractions such as *I'd* treated – as single word forms (*I'd*) or as separate word forms (*I* + *d*)?

Obtaining lexical information from a corpus

Two fundamental ways of obtaining information about the words in a corpus are through the word list and the concordance. A word list, as we saw with the ELISA corpus above, lists all of the lemmas or word forms in a corpus, along with their frequency of occurrence. Word lists can often be reordered according to either frequency or alphabetical order. If you are comparing the word lists from two different corpora, or from two parts of the same corpus (that is, sub-corpora), then it is usually appropriate to look at normalised frequencies rather than raw frequencies so that the potentially different sizes of the corpora do not disguise the underlying figures (see Chapter 2 for more on normalised frequency counts).

A concordance allows you to take the analysis a step further, by considering the context of a word as well as its frequency. In this way, it allows you to perform a basic qualitative analysis, as well as a quantitative analysis, that is, you can analyse aspects of the nature of the word, as well as simply how many times it occurs relative to other words. This is essential because words mean different things in different contexts. For example, without contextual information it would be impossible to tell whether the instances of a word form like *mine* which had been retrieved from a corpus were in fact the possessive pronoun (as in the example *No, that's mine, look* from the SCOTS corpus), the verb meaning 'to excavate for coal' or the noun meaning a type of bomb (among several other possibilities). Making the assumption that they were all examples of the noun would most likely lead you to false conclusions.

A concordance provides a means of viewing all of the occurrences of a specified word in a corpus, each in its immediate environment. The immediate environment is usually considered to comprise several words before and after the *node*, the search word itself. Let us begin by looking at a straightforward concordance of a relatively infrequent word. The screenshots below show the essential information, but if you are reading this book beside a computer with web access, you can try this for yourself online. You will then also have the options of seeing the titles of the texts containing the different occurrences, clicking to view the wider context or indeed the full text, and exploring the sociolinguistic information associated with each text.

If we look for the word *caravan* using SCOTS' Advanced Search, we obtain the concordance in Figure 3.1. The information returned by the search system also summarises this information, indicating that (at the time of writing):

- the word occurs 29 times in the whole corpus
- eleven of the texts in the corpus contain one or more examples of the word.

The full concordance also indicates the text in which each example occurs. Note that we are using the word 'text' here to include both written documents and transcribed spoken documents. The lines in the first concordance screenshot (Figure 3.1) have been sorted according to the node word (*caravan*); this is the default in SCOTS. This has the function of grouping the capitalised examples together at the bottom of the list. Sorting by the node word is particularly useful when you want to search using wildcards for all of the different inflected forms of a word.

Already we might make a couple of observations. Three of the capitalised examples are followed by the word *Park*, also capitalised, in the names of three different caravan parks: further investigation reveals that all three in fact come from the same text. There are a few capitalised names which in the context you are likely to interpret as place names, even if you are not familiar with

5 4 3 2 Left	Node	Right 2 3 4 5
and looked like paradise. Even the	caravan	sites and petrol stations were bright
worked there. And eh, he gied me a	caravan	tae live in. M608: uh-huh M642:
forward.// M642: so I slept in the	caravan	. //Monday night and Tuesday night.//
M642: prefab? That boy had his	caravan	inside the prefab. F643: Aye.
a good idea. He bought his big, long	caravan	eh?// Aye. He bought his big long
a prefab, and pit aw roond aboot his	caravan	//eh, for heat and everything, it
paper, an I went ower and he said, "My	caravan	's inside there." M608: [laugh]
dismantle it. Ye no wantin tae buy a	caravan	?" //Aye eh.// F643: //Two
a// M608: //[laugh]// M642:	caravan	? See the big ca- they big sheets o
small.// //Uh-huh, and she had a	caravan	// F814: //an everything.// F813:
to feed the //fish.// F835: //A	caravan	.// F833: //[laugh]// F834:
Edinburgh. M822: Mind we bade at a	caravan	site, [?]sooth at[/?] St Boswells
faur we were, cause Musselborough, the	caravan	site there, an we took the bus intae
holiday I remember was in Redcar in a	caravan	, er I think it rained //all week.//
a a mate of my dad's at work had a	caravan	and he used to to drive us through to
he used to to drive us through to the	caravan	site there. F718: Mmhm. F1077:
too far down there. I can see the	caravan	park, look. F1122: Me too. F1121:
that? Is that the girls' ca-	caravan	? M1110: No. F1109: I think it
it is. It's white. //It's a big	caravan	.// M1110: //It's big caravan,
a big caravan.// M1110: //It's big	caravan	, Mam!// F1109: And they go awa
Awa their holidays in the //	caravan	.// M1110: //Mam, Mam, Mam!//
the eastern boundary of Aird Donald	caravan	park. This enabled the work on the
of residents in the modern Innermessan	caravan	site in the summer season. And our
Messan Burn between the A77 and the	caravan	site will reveal short stretches of
they speak down there.' So he got a	caravan	, planted it outside their retirement
there? What do you see? F1122:	Caravan	. We could go, can we go back down
runs down the east side of Aird Donald	Caravan	Park. The owner, Bert Cassie, shows
and static caravans in Innermessan	Caravan	Park marks its progress through that
for the chalets in Cairnryan	Caravan	Park. Towards the end of the village,

Figure 3.1   SCOTS concordance of *caravan*, sorted by the node

them: Musselborough, Redcar, Innermessan and Cairnryan. There are also several codes (of the form *F814*, standing for a female speaker with the ID number 814), which are used in SCOTS to identify participants in transcribed conversations and interviews. So it is likely that many of these examples are from spoken rather than written language. All occurrences are of the modern sense of *caravan*, the towable house on wheels, rather than a group of merchants travelling through the North African desert, and all are instances of the noun form rather than the less common derived verb.

Click on 'Right' in the bar above the concordance lines and consider the same concordance, organised alphabetically according to the word immediately following the node. This is reproduced as Figure 3.2.

Now the association, or collocation, between *caravan* and *park* is more evident. It is used as a common noun or as part of a proper name (usually capitalised here). Ordering the concordance lines in this way also highlights the co-occurrence of *caravan* with *site(s)*. So we can conclude that about a third of the time in the SCOTS corpus *caravan* is used as a noun modifier and seems to have a particular preference for *park* and *site*. Of course, this may not come as a surprise to those familiar with caravan holidays, but here the corpus is providing evidence to support our intuition.

5 4 3 2 Left	Node	Right 2 3 4 5
holiday I remember was in Redcar in a	caravan	, er I think it rained //all week.//
a big caravan.// M1110: //It's big	caravan	, Mam!// F1109: And they go awa
they speak down there.' So he got a	caravan	, planted it outside their retirement
forward.// M642: so I slept in the	caravan	. //Monday night and Tuesday night.//
there? What do you see? F1122:	Caravan	. We could go, can we go back down
to feed the //fish.// F835: //A	caravan	.// F833: //[laugh]// F834:
it is. It's white. //It's a big	caravan	.// M1110: //It's big caravan,
Awa their holidays in the //	caravan	.// M1110: //Mam, Mam, Mam!//
small.// //Uh-huh, and she had a	caravan	// F814: //an everything.// F813:
a prefab, and pit aw roond aboot his	caravan	//eh, for heat and everything, it
a// M608: //[laugh]// M642:	caravan	? See the big ca- they big sheets o
that? Is that the girls' ca-	caravan	? M1110: No. F1109: I think it
dismantle it. Ye no wantin tae buy a	caravan	?" //Aye eh.// F643: //Two
a a mate of my dad's at work had a	caravan	and he used to to drive us through to
a good idea. He bought his big, long	caravan	eh?// Aye. He bought his big long
M642: prefab? That boy had his	caravan	inside the prefab. F643: Aye.
and static caravans in Innermessan	Caravan	Park marks its progress through that
too far down there. I can see the	caravan	park, look. F1122: Me too. F1121:
the eastern boundary of Aird Donald	caravan	park. This enabled the work on the
runs down the east side of Aird Donald	Caravan	Park. The owner, Bert Cassie, shows
for the chalets in Cairnryan	Caravan	Park. Towards the end of the village,
paper, an I went ower and he said, "My	caravan	's inside there." M608: [laugh]
faur we were, cause Musselborough, the	caravan	site there, an we took the bus intae
he used to to drive us through to the	caravan	site there. F718: Mmhm. F1077:
of residents in the modern Innermessan	caravan	site in the summer season. And our
Messan Burn between the A77 and the	caravan	site will reveal short stretches of
Edinburgh. M822: Mind we bade at a	caravan	site, [?]sooth at[/?] St Boswells
and looked like paradise. Even the	caravan	sites and petrol stations were bright
worked there. And eh, he gied me a	caravan	tae live in. M608: uh-huh M642:

Figure 3.2 **SCOTS concordance of *caravan*, sorted by the first word to the right of the node**

Finally, consider the same concordance lines sorted by the word immediately to the left of the node (Figure 3.3):

5 4 3 2 Left	Node	Right 2 3 4 5
paper, an I went ower and he said, "My	caravan	's inside there." M608: [laugh]
Awa their holidays in the //	caravan	.// M1110: //Mam, Mam, Mam!//
to feed the //fish.// F835: //A	caravan	.// F833: //[laugh]// F834:
worked there. And eh, he gied me a	caravan	tae live in. M608: uh-huh M642:
dismantle it. Ye no wantin tae buy a	caravan	?" //Aye eh.// F643: //Two
small.// //Uh-huh, and she had a	caravan	// F814: //an everything.// F813:
Edinburgh. M822: Mind we bade at a	caravan	site, [?]sooth at[/?] St Boswells
holiday I remember was in Redcar in a	caravan	, er I think it rained //all week.//
a a mate of my dad's at work had a	caravan	and he used to to drive us through to
they speak down there.' So he got a	caravan	, planted it outside their retirement
it is. It's white. //It's a big	caravan	.// M1110: //It's big caravan,
a big caravan.// M1110: //It's big	caravan	, Mam!// F1109: And they go awa
that? Is that the girls' ca-	caravan	? M1110: No. F1109: I think it
for the chalets in Cairnryan	Caravan	Park. Towards the end of the village,
the eastern boundary of Aird Donald	caravan	park. This enabled the work on the
runs down the east side of Aird Donald	Caravan	Park. The owner, Bert Cassie, shows
there? What do you see? F1122:	Caravan	. We could go, can we go back down
M642: prefab? That boy had his	caravan	inside the prefab. F643: Aye.
a prefab, and pit aw roond aboot his	caravan	//eh, for heat and everything, it
and static caravans in Innermessan	Caravan	Park marks its progress through that
of residents in the modern Innermessan	caravan	site in the summer season. And our
a good idea. He bought his big, long	caravan	eh?// Aye. He bought his big long
a// M608: //[laugh]// M642:	caravan	? See the big ca- they big sheets o
and looked like paradise. Even the	caravan	sites and petrol stations were bright
forward.// M642: so I slept in the	caravan	. //Monday night and Tuesday night.//
faur we were, cause Musselborough, the	caravan	site there, an we took the bus intae
he used to to drive us through to the	caravan	site there. F718: Mmhm. F1077:
too far down there. I can see the	caravan	park, look. F1122: Me too. F1121:
Messan Burn between the A77 and the	caravan	site will reveal short stretches of

Figure 3.3   SCOTS concordance of *caravan*, sorted by the first word to the left of the node

Now the proper names *Cairnryan, Aird Donald* and *Innermessan* come to the fore, along with the definite and indefinite articles. From this evidence, we can say that the noun *caravan* tends to appear in longer sequences ending in *park* or *site*, and is often preceded by an identifying place-name or proper noun, or an article that indicates whether the concept is being introduced into the conversation for the first time (as with the indefinite article in *Mind we bade at a caravan site*) or whether the concept is something the listener is expected already to know about (as with the definite article in *I can see the caravan park, look*). A possible association with the very common adjectives *big* and *long* might repay further investigation with a larger corpus.

Many concordancers also allow you to rearrange concordance lines to look for patterns of association between the node and words further from it (with SCOTS, up to five words to the left and to the right of the node). Using a larger corpus, or investigating a more frequent word, it is possible to make interesting and very subtle observations about the typical environments of words.

TASK 3.2   Reading concordance lines

1. Go to the BNC online at www.natcorp.ox.ac.uk.
2. Search for the word *chronic*. This will retrieve a random set of 50 examples from the 1688 examples in the entire corpus.
3. How many of these are instances of each of the following meanings: (1) Lasting a long time (the original meaning, related to time, from Latin *chronicus*); (2) Intense in a vaguer sense (similar to severe, dreadful, unpleasant)?
4. Are there occurrences where you cannot decide which meaning is intended? Why do you think this is? What would help you determine which sense is exemplified?
5. Run the same query again. Does the second random set of examples contain the same proportions of meanings as the first? Are there any examples of meanings you did not encounter with the first set of concordance lines?
6. Prescriptive style guides, such as early editions of Fowler's *Dictionary of Modern English Usage* (cf. Fowler 1926) condemn such extensions as the vaguer sense of *chronic* as 'illiterate'. Do you agree? Does the evidence from the corpus of the word give any grounds for this view?
7. Now try the same with the following words whose meaning is debated by purists: *decimate, dilemma, feasible, flout, mutual*. Alternatively, refer to an early edition of Fowler (the entry on 'Slipshod extension') or another prescriptive style guide for additional words.

For a thorough guide to using and interpreting concordance data, see Sinclair (2003).

Analysing lexical data

Both frequency lists and concordancers present data about language in a corpus, but this data is still to be interpreted and turned into valuable information. In this section, we consider the ways in which we can analyse lexical information through online corpora.

We begin by looking at words in their lexicogrammatical context, that is in a linguistic environment made up of other words and grammatical constructions. Key concepts here will be idiom, collocation and the more abstract notion of colligation. Secondly, we take a step towards abstraction to investigate the semantic context of words, considering the notions of semantic preference and semantic prosody, the latter a language feature which has only recently been recognised and which owes its current popularity to corpus analysis. Finally, we will look at words in their social context, focusing in particular on textual genre, time period and geography. The well-known British linguist, J.R. Firth (1957a, p. 14), wrote of collocation as 'actual words in habitual company'. The approaches we take here to lexical analysis all seek to illuminate the habitual company of words, whether this is their lexical company, grammatical company, features of the semantic environment or even the wider context of their use.

The lexicogrammatical environment of words

The term *collocation* refers to the tendency of words to occur in the close environment of particular other words. For example, Michael Halliday (1966, pp. 150–151) discusses the fact that the noun *tea* often co-occurs with the adjective *strong* but not with its near-synonym *powerful*; on the other hand, we might describe a car as *powerful*, but we would be unlikely to call it *strong*. The strength of collocation between words is a matter of degree. For instance, you can be fairly sure that if you see the word *kith* in a text then it will be followed by *and kin*, to form the fixed expression *kith and kin*; indeed out of 14 occurrences of *kith* in the British National Corpus, nine are followed directly by *and kin*, while four more are slight variants on the expression, still including the word *kin*. On the other hand, only nine of the 799 occurrences of *kin* are preceded by *kith and*, so the lexical environment of *kin* is less predictable, and *kin* has a weaker collocational relationship with *kith* than *kith* has with *kin*.

There are few words in English, however, whose immediate lexical environment can be predicted with such a level of certainty as *kith*, and where these do occur they tend to be part of idiomatic fixed expressions like this one where the meaning has become fossilised. Indeed, some automatic taggers, such as the one used to tag the XML edition of the BNC (the CLAWS part-of-speech tagger), treat some multiword units as single items: these include *a great deal, considering that, gee whizz*, and naturalised foreign expressions such as *a fortiori, aurora borealis, crème fraîche* and *spaghetti bolognese*. It is important to be aware of such tagging quirks when using a corpus: if you search for the single word *bolognese* in the XML edition of the BNC, you may find surprisingly few occurrences of *spaghetti* among the left collocates. Not appreciating the reason for this could lead to erroneous conclusions about the word's habitual patterning.

Collocation is an important concept in corpus linguistics. Our own knowledge and experience of language can suggest some of the combinations which go together (especially the set expressions like *spaghetti bolognese* and *kith and kin*). But collocation has been such a well-studied area in corpus linguistics, because it is one in which intuition often lets us down. Since it is essentially a statistical notion, collocation can only really come to light when we consider language in large quantities, as in an electronic corpus. Corpus analysis can reveal these and other patterns to us, even if we are not native speakers. This means that corpora are often the loci for surprising findings.

Set expressions and idioms

Here we look at some of the most predictable sequences of words and set expressions. Sometimes these are also idiomatic, that is, their overall meaning is not transparent from their component words, as in *pig in a poke, white elephant, the shoe is on the other foot*. The Oxford English Dictionary defines an idiom as: 'A form of expression, grammatical construction, phrase, etc., peculiar to a language; a peculiarity of phraseology approved by the usage of a language, and often having a signification other than its grammatical or logical one' (Oxford English Dictionary, *idiom*, sense 3a).

Using a large corpus of English, Rosamund Moon (1998) has shown that idioms are not always used in the form we might expect in texts. Instead, there are significant levels of variation within the form of the expression. This means, of course, that it can be difficult to find all of the examples which we would intuitively recognise as instances of a particular idiom. The SCOTS corpus for example contains the expression *a couple of turrets short of a castle*, which most native speakers of English would recognise in context as a creative, perhaps appropriately Scottish, form related to the more common expression *a few sandwiches short of a picnic*, used to describe someone who is lacking in intelligence. With the exception of the indefinite articles and *short of*, used prepositionally, the two expressions have no words in common.

TASK 3.3   Finding idioms

The BNC contains the following six instances of *gander* forming part of the expression *What is sauce for the goose is sauce for the gander.*

. . . what is sauce for the goose must be sauce for the **gander**. If this is the justification we seek for abandoning . . .

Sauce for the goose but not, apparently the **gander**! There is very little likelihood of confusion arising . . .

What's sauce for the goose is sauce for the **gander**. As for covering up the work . . .

. . . sauce for the goose was likely to be sauce for the **gander**. Because they saw the world as composed of groups . . .

. . . what's cash for the goose is cash for the **gander** . . .

What's sauce for the goose is sauce for the **gander**. And er if if it's appropriate . . .

Which of these do you think are standard uses of the expression? Which are creative uses? What are the implications of your findings for automatically retrieving examples of idioms and semi-fixed expressions from a corpus?

Now look for other idioms in the BNC. For example, *when in Rome . . .* , *don't count your chickens*, *dead as a . . .* , *. . . short of a . . .* (as in *a few sandwiches short of a picnic*). See Moon (1998) for many more examples. Do these behave in the manner you expect? What problems do you encounter in finding examples?

Sometimes the words in corpora are tagged for their part of speech (see also Chapter 4 on grammar). This means that information is added to the corpus to indicate the part of speech of each word, such as whether it is functioning as a noun, a verb or a preposition in the sentence. For example, in the BNC, 2433 instances of *pink* are tagged as adjectives (as in *The sergeant was stout and pink*); 193 are tagged as common nouns (*a bright pink which goes brilliantly with red*); and smaller numbers are tagged as proper nouns (*Mr Pink was given a script by his boss*) and even verbs (*try unleaded and if the engine doesn't 'pink' you're OK*). Although automatic taggers do not achieve perfect accuracy, this information is valuable for several reasons. First, a grammatically tagged corpus allows us to search either for words like *pink* specifically as a noun or as an adjective as we have seen. But it is also valuable because it allows the user to perform different types of search. A search system which allows you to indicate that you want a particular slot in the expression to be filled by an adjective, without having to specify which adjective that might be, will allow you to find creative forms of expressions.

If we search the BYU-BNC for examples of the noun *buff* when it is preceded by another noun (select 'noun.ALL' from the drop-down box and then type in 'buff') we find a number of more or less frequently repeated expressions such as *wine buff, film buff, computer buff, opera buff* and *cricket buff*; that is expressions describing people who are connoisseurs of particular activities. These fairly standard expressions are mixed in, however, with more creative one-off combinations such as *sausage buff, Wild West buff* and *folklore buff.*

TASK 3.4   Semi-fixed expressions

Analyse the contexts of occurrence of the adjective *proverbial* in a large general corpus such as the BNC. What semi-fixed expressions (idioms, proverbs etc.) can you identify in its co-text? What do you think is the function of the word *proverbial* in these instances?

Collocations

Words are found in the company of other words in a text or corpus for many reasons. It comes as no surprise that words are found together in language when the objects they denote are found together in the world: for example, if you were listening to a garage mechanic describe the work that needed to be done to your car, you would expect to find lexical items like *tyre, exhaust* and *brake fluid* within a short space of each other, so there is no surprise in finding that these words often occur close to each other in texts in a corpus. However, words collocate with each other in a text or corpus for less obvious reasons too. There is nothing in the denotation of the noun *balance* which leads it to be qualified by the adjective *delicate*, but this adjective is a frequent collocate (there are 53 occurrences of *delicate balance* in the BNC), compared with such near-synonyms as *flimsy* (which does not occur immediately before *balance* in the BNC), *fragile* (with 8 occurrences), *exquisite* (no occurrences), and *refined* (no occurrences). *Delicate balance*, as a chunk larger than a word, appears to be more readily accessible in our brains, through habitual use. We will return to this idea, in the form of the 'idiom principle' below.

It is relatively quick and easy to identify the usual collocates of a fairly frequent word like *balance* especially in larger corpora. However, smaller corpora may not provide enough evidence of infrequent words to build up a picture of their typical environment and will certainly not offer the quantity of information which a professional lexicographer needs to write dictionary entries. Indeed, even the largest corpora may provide only one or two examples of an infrequent word. Try searching for the word *discombobulate* and its inflected forms (by using an asterisk as a wildcard – *discombobul**) in the BNC. It turns out there are only three occurrences, which is scant evidence on which to base a description of the word's meaning and use. Now try Task 3.5, to build up a more thorough picture of the use of this word.

TASK 3.5   Infrequent words

Go to the TIME corpus at http://corpus.byu.edu/time/ and search for *discombobulate*, truncating to *discombobul** in order to find all forms of the word. Why do you think there are more examples of the word in this corpus than in the BNC?

Imagine you are a lexicographer. What information would you put in your dictionary definition of the word? These questions may give you some ideas.

1. Which inflected forms are most common?
2. Can you characterise the typical environment of the word?
3. What is the date of the earliest occurrences you can find?

Compare the information you find with the entry for *discombobulate* in a large dictionary such as the Oxford English Dictionary. Does the entry confirm your findings? Can you add anything to that entry?

With very large corpora or more frequently occurring words, the analysis of collocates can give us a picture of the typical environment of words and insights into unusual patterning. Try Task 3.6 to practise identifying collocational patterning.

As we saw above with the examples of *strong tea* and *powerful car*, collocational patterning can also allow you to distinguish between near-synonyms. The words *tangible* and *palpable* are generally considered to be synonymous; indeed etymologically both mean 'able to be touched'. However, corpus analysis shows that while out of context they mean the same, in practice they form part of distinct patternings.

Palpable is by far the less frequent term in the British National Corpus, occurring only twice for every nine occurrences of *tangible* (132 compared with 595). From the concordance of *palpable* we can see that it tends to describe something abstract, or rather something which is normally abstract but which is being described as taking on material form for emphasis: collocates include *reluctance, ambivalence, relief*. There are few repeated collocates, though it does

---

TASK 3.6   Building up a picture of typical collocations

1. Make a list of the words you would expect to find in the immediate environment of the adjective *rugged*. What things do you expect to be described in this way?
2. Now go to the Cobuild Concordance and Collocation Sampler, at www.collins.co.uk/corpus/CorpusSearch.aspx. Type the word 'rugged' into the Collocation Sampler and click to 'Show collocates'. (Select Mutual Information and T-score in turn as the measure of significance and compare the results – see Chapter 2 for an explanation of statistical measures.)
3. What are the most significant collocates of *rugged*?
4. Go back to the main page and type 'rugged' into the Concordance Sampler to see a selection of the surrounding lines.
5. In what ways can you group the collocates? Can you find a set of literal uses and a set of metaphorical uses?
6. You may have discovered that ruggedness appears to be a generally positive quality, especially when used of people's features. Can you find any counter-examples? What clues are there in the context that the word is being used in a negative way?

---

occur in the sequence *a palpable sense of* [+ something abstract, either positive or negative], and collocates with the noun *nonsense* (*To talk of . . . is palpable nonsense*). Notably, it also occurs in the medical text genre of the BNC, in the terms *palpable splenomegaly* and *palpable hepatomegaly*, referring to an enlargement of the spleen and liver, respectively.

Tangible on the other hand occurs not only much more frequently but also in different types of context. It has no particular connection with medical texts but instead very frequently precedes *assets* and *benefits* in the domain of finance. Like *palpable* it is used to describe abstract things which the speaker or writer would like to present as having a more concrete form than they do – evidence, results, proof. The BNC shows that it also collocates, although much less frequently, with things that can be touched, such as pieces of paper, sweat, fossil evidence.

Idioms and collocations both exemplify what the corpus linguist John Sinclair has called the 'idiom principle' of language: 'The principle of idiom is that a language user has available to him or her a large number of semi-preconstructed phrases that constitute single choices, even though they might appear to be analysable into segments' (Sinclair 1991, p. 110). This tendency may be contrasted with what he has called the 'open choice principle', according to which there is a free choice after every item in language of what will follow (ibid). Linguistic research on corpora over the last 30 years or so has built up much evidence in favour of the idiom principle, by demonstrating that while we may in theory have free choices in language, in actual usage we tend to rely heavily on frequent collocations and set expressions.

TASK 3.7   Distinguishing synonyms with collocation

The collocational patterning of a word can allow us to appreciate subtle differences in usage which may not be apparent through intuition alone. Go to the Cobuild Concordance and Collocation Sampler, and search for the words *stricken* and *ridden*. (Choose either Mutual Information or T-score as the measure of significance for both searches so that you are comparing like with like.)

What nouns collocate most frequently with *stricken* and *ridden* respectively? Begin by considering those nouns which collocate most frequently, and then consider whether individual words which collocate less frequently nevertheless exemplify similar meanings to the tendencies you are finding.

Bear in mind that *ridden* will also collocate with words related to horses and bikes! You can perform a word search to see the immediate context of words if the connection is not clear.

Now try the same task using pairs of similar adjectives: *childish-childlike, owlish-owl-like, godly-godlike, supporting-supportive*. (See Hamawand 2007 for more examples.)

Colligation

The notion of colligation is related to collocation. Colligation is usually defined as the tendency of a word to co-occur, not with another word or phrase, but with a grammatical category or construction. Thus, compared with collocation, colligational patterning lies at a more abstract level of language. In practice, however, the two concepts can be difficult to disentangle as a corpus may not give enough evidence to determine whether a word is co-occurring with a small set of words (surface forms) or an underlying grammatical feature which unites them. It can be helpful therefore to use a tagged corpus to investigate the colligational patterning surrounding words.

TASK 3.8   Colligation

Go to the BYU-BNC at http://corpus.byu.edu/bnc/. Search for the sequence of words *a matter of* followed by any noun (select the 'noun.ALL' tag from the box below the search box).

Here are the ten most frequent patterns:

1. A matter of fact
2. A matter of time
3. A matter of urgency
4. A matter of principle
5. A matter of weeks
6. A matter of seconds

⇨

TASK 3.8   (Continued)

7. A matter of law
8. A matter of minutes
9. A matter of policy
10. A matter of days

Can you divide this set into two categories? On what are you basing your division?

Now run the same search but with the sequence *in a matter of* followed by any noun. What do you notice? Does this confirm the categorisation you made above? Can you explain what *matter* means in each category of sequences?

Now investigate which sequences appear in different registers. For example, which are more typical of spoken language? Which are most typical of academic writing?

For more information on patterning of this sort, see Renouf and Sinclair (1991) and Siepmann (2005).

Colligation exemplifies the concept of lexicogrammar, that is, systems of wording encompassing lexis and grammar. In a well-known research paper (Hasan 1987, also reprinted in Cloran, Butt and Williams 1996), Ruqaiya Hasan discusses Michael Halliday's notion of 'lexis as most delicate grammar'. She suggests that lexical items can be seen as the result of very specific selections made in the system of choices that is grammar. In looking at colligation here, we have been approaching it from the lexical end of the lexicogrammatical continuum; in the next chapter, we approach it again but from the grammatical end.

The semantic environment of words

[handwritten annotation: meaning to the word]

The environment in which words tend to occur may also be characterised by semantic features, that is, the tendency of a word to occur with particular types of meaning. You will have seen this earlier in the chapter when we considered the collocational patterning of *stricken*: you probably found that the word collocated with words like *grief, panic, terror*. The overlap in meaning among these words may be sufficient for us to suggest that it is not the individual words but the concept of an unpleasant mental state which tends to co-occur with *stricken*. Other significant lexical items like *horror* and *guilt* seem to confirm this conclusion.

Semantic preference

Stricken may therefore be said to have a *semantic preference* for words which are examples of an unpleasant mental state. Using our knowledge of how the world works, and our knowledge of language, it is not difficult to find words which display semantic preferences. Knowing how the word *bottle* is used, it is not surprising that its most significant collocates tend to be the names of liquids which are typically contained in bottles: in the Cobuild Collocation Sampler we find *wine, champagne, water, whisky, beer* among the top ten most significant collocates (in this case using the T-score measure of significance).

TASK 3.9   Semantic preference

1. Look up the word *tome* (i.e. book) in the BYU-BNC at http://corpus. byu.edu/bnc. Set the search criteria to display the collocates, five words each side of the node.
2. Disregard the function words (articles, conjunctions, pronouns etc.) which collocate with *tome* and concentrate on the adjectives which occur at least 3 times. Note these down.
3. What generalisations can you make about the list of adjectives? Do they share an aspect of their meaning?
4. Can you find any other adjectives, occurring only once or twice, which support your findings?

Semantic prosody

The example above of *tome* actually may be said to exemplify another phenomenon of language, which has only recently received scholarly attention, having been facilitated by the study of large corpora. This is *semantic prosody* (sometimes also called *discourse prosody*, to stress the role of the phenomenon in the construction of discourse). Within linguistics, the word 'prosody' was originally used in the domain of phonology to describe features of pitch, rhythm and so on that extend over more than one sound segment. However, the word has a longer history in the domain of versification, in which it refers to the conventional rhythms that occur in the metrical line. Semantic prosody describes the fact that some words in language carry over some of the meanings they have in their typical, conventional contexts to new or less frequent contexts. That is, a word might begin to appropriate the meanings contained in longer, frequent collocations and thus take these meanings into newer linguistic contexts.

The verb *cause* in English is an excellent example of a word with a strong semantic prosody in English and for this reason has been much studied (see, for example, Stubbs 1996). Consider the following randomly selected concordance lines from the BNC (each tenth line in the results obtained from BYU-BNC). Look at the object of the verb *cause* in each case, that is what it is that is being caused. What tendencies can you identify?

1. problems that, unless addressed in a professional manner, can **cause** catastrophic consequences.
2. as a large change in atmospheric pressure may **cause** damage to some instruments.

3. because a wing can so easily go down and **cause** a bad swing as you slow down after landing.
4. And head lice can **cause** other, more serious infections if they are left untreated.
5. this will **cause** the panel to switch off, and thereby perhaps miss an actual score.
6. if a glass window shatters it may **cause** horrific and perhaps even lethal injuries.
7. processes involved when two dominant forms of ion are present can **cause** one ion form to screen the geomagnetic field effective on the other.
8. into a Bill dealing with embryos is a blatant attempt to **cause** confusion. There is no logic in the Pro-Life argument.
9. Pentagon, which estimated that any use of US troops would **cause** several hundred military and civilian deaths.
10. They are highly caustic and can **cause** terrible injuries to the throat and stomach if they are accidentally swallowed.

Cause has a strong tendency to occur with nouns in object position which point to a negative effect (similarly, you probably found that *tome* above occurred with adjectives with a shared meaning of *heavy*). However, *cause* does not occur simply with a set of semantically related words. Rather it appears to occur with a concept of negativity, which may take the form of disease, damage, confusion or something vaguer, as in line five, where we have the impression that the panel switching off is a bad thing, although there is not enough context to be absolutely sure. There is nothing in the dictionary meaning (the denotation) of the word *cause* to suggest that it will be found mainly with negative effects.

Now look at the following examples from the BNC, which all appear to be counter-examples; that is, positive outcomes appear to be *caused*. (Owing to their infrequency, this is not a random selection.) In each case, can you explain the apparently unusual use of *cause*? Greater co-text and a little context are given to help you.

1. A "point" is an idiosyncrasy or peculiarity about a work which may be held to determine priority of edition, impression or issue. A number of these are entirely legitimate and **cause** great excitement among devotees, who will be found anxiously scanning the title of Pickwick to see whether Sam Weller's name on the inn sign-board is spelt with a W or a V. [from a non-fiction book on book-collecting, 1986]
2. There are great expectations, pious hopes and myriad uncertainties which have coalesced to **cause** a frisson of excitement at the prospect of success, for success alone can be the only option that should be countenanced. [periodical concerning community care, no date given]
3. Such catalogues include accounts of relevant historical research, and may **cause** new original historical work to be done. Individual works may be studied more carefully for a catalogue entry than ever before. [from a book on art criticism, 1991]

The first example seems to confirm a point which Bill Louw has made about semantic prosody (e.g. Louw 2000, p. 50), which is that semantic prosodies relate to attitude and tone and may indicate irony on the part of the speaker/writer if used deliberately, or insincerity if used inadvertently. Irony works by violating expectations. So if a word has built up a consistent background pattern of negative contexts, an author can surprise or disarm a reader by introducing an apparently positive one. The new positive meaning is tainted by the expected negative patterning. The author of this non-fiction work may be gently mocking these devotees of book-collecting who are concerned with fairly inconsequential matters but derive a lot of frenzied excitement from them.

The object of *cause* in the second example also appears to be a positive outcome: a frisson of excitement. However, our view may change if we consider a little more of the co-text:

A concerned and confused practitioner sent in a cutting of the cataclysmic article and highlighted a paragraph which reads as follows: "There are great expectations, pious hopes and myriad uncertainties which have coalesced to **cause** a frisson of excitement at the prospect of success, for success alone can be the only option that should be countenanced." Surprisingly, after all that, the only bone of contention is the supposed "frisson of excitement" which the anonymous mole declares is impossible to find and seeks help, as certain members of the department "don't know where to look, or even what we are looking for". [periodical concerning community care, no date given]

The *frisson of excitement* here is caused by uncertainties among other things, and remains a *bone of contention*. Indeed, it is only hypothetical and may not even exist.

In the final case, the extent of the context is not sufficient to find a reason for this use of *cause* with an apparently positive object (*new original historical work*). Perhaps there is no particular reason: perhaps this is simply a rare, unironical use of *cause* in this way. Genuine counter-examples will certainly exist.

Now look at a list of the hundred most frequent nouns to follow *cause* by inserting the 'noun.ALL' tag after the word in the search box. Are any of these items positive? Click on those you are unsure about to see more co-text in each case.

TASK 3.10   Semantic prosody

Search for the following expressions or words in a corpus, investigate their typical environments and try to identify a semantic prosody: *a recipe for, laden with, break out, happen, set in*.

See also Louw (2000), Partington (1998) and Sinclair (1991) for these and further prosodies.

The wider social environment of words

A common charge against corpora is that they present linguistic data out of context (e.g. Widdowson 2000). This may seem paradoxical – surely the essential feature of a corpus is that you can access whole texts, or at least extended passages? Although there is usually no shortage of co-text, or linguistic context, it is fair to say that all corpora to some degree dissociate language from its wider context of production. While it is a simple matter to record individual facts about context, the number of contextual features which may affect language is potentially limitless, and in the corpus compilation process decisions will have been taken regarding which to highlight and which to suppress. Could it be significant that a conversation took place between two or three people rather than a larger number? Is it important to know whether a lecture was delivered extempore or read from a script? Would our interpretation of the language of a conversation change if we knew that all of the participants knew each other from school? Depending on the aim of the analysis, it is certainly possible. It is therefore especially important to take care to choose an appropriate corpus when you are interested in the connections between language and such contextual features as genre, time, the geographical origin of the speaker or writer, and so on. In the following section, we will look briefly at how words may vary in usage in texts of different genres, from different time periods and by language users from different speech communities. Chapter 7 looks more closely at how corpus texts can be combined with metadata for sociolinguistic analysis.

Genre and mode

With an appropriate corpus or set of corpora, we can investigate how words differ according to the type or genre of text in which they occur (prose fiction, personal correspondence, business reports and so on) or according to the mode of production, that is, whether a text is spoken or written.

The SCOTS corpus is useful for comparing usage across modes, as it contains around 800,000 words of transcribed speech, much of which is spontaneous conversation. Using the Advanced Search facility, search for the word *totally*, limiting your search to the written texts only. Here is a selection of ten of the 84 concordance lines which this search retrieves:

. . . used a Scots word, it produced a **totally** bewildered look around the place . . .

. . . a submission that contains four **totally** different opinions . . .

. . . and I went home early to bed, feeling **totally** exhausted . . .

. . . I felt that officers were being **totally** frank at the meetings.

. . . felt euphoric and had to fight off her **totally** irrational idea that the consultant's . . .

. . . the money is spent. However, it is not **totally** predictable . . .

. . . the sounds, grammar and vocabulary of **totally** strange languages.

. . . Unless I receive **totally** unambiguous advice that the trials . . .

... over the fact that the problem was **totally** unnecessary and resulted from ...
... for the union to say, 'You are **totally** wrong. It is necessary to go back ...

Look at the words which follow *totally*. What part of speech are they? How can you characterise the use and meaning of *totally* from these examples? Now look at the complete list of occurrences of the word in SCOTS' written texts. Does this support your findings, or do you have to revise your description?

Now carry out the same search, but limiting it to spoken texts only. Again, here is a selection of ten of the 147 concordance lines retrieved (bear in mind that the corpus contains 4 times as much written text as spoken text!):

... six academic papers in Scots, **totally**, totally answering the challenge that ...
... Yeah well, yeah, **totally**, totally.
... He was amazed. He was **totally** amazed [cough] that I had made such ...
... I'm speaking to you, I'm speaking **totally** different to // if I'm speakin to a ...
... [laugh] I just **totally** forgot, I was like ...
... Sure // sure in P.S.E. she was **totally** guilt-trippin me ...
... after that so everybody was like **totally** listening and nodding ...
... I thought you know, I was **totally** reminded of Rafi when we were ...
... So he's **totally** wasting his money.
... and I was like "this is just **totally** typical".

Again look at the parts of speech of the words following *totally*. How does this second set of examples differ from the first? Look at the complete list of occurrences in the spoken texts in SCOTS. Can you find additional examples of some of the patterns you have found or new patterns which need to be accounted for?

TASK 3.11   Genre-based usage

Using the MICASE corpus, at http://quod.lib.umich.edu/m/micase/, compare the use of the following words in the different available subgenres of academic spoken English. What grammatical constructions do they typically appear in, and what are their main collocates?

Faculty
Tenure
Semester

Compare the patterns of usage you have found in MICASE with those in a general corpus such as the BNC.

Time

Despite the fact that many people resist changes in meaning of words, as we saw at the start of this chapter, there is incontrovertible evidence all around us that language changes over time. A diachronic corpus, that is, one which has been designed to enable the comparison of texts from different time periods, can help us investigate changes in meaning and usage.

TASK 3.12   Diachronic change in usage

1. Using the TIME corpus at http://corpus.byu.edu/time/, search for the word *wireless*, viewing the results as a chart.
2. In which decades was the word most frequently used in *TIME* magazine? Can you account for this?
3. Look at the collocates of *wireless*, noting which occur in which decade. Do your findings correspond with your expectations? Which were the most common collocates in the 1920s? How can you characterise the lexical environment of *wireless* in US English in the 2000s?
4. Now look more closely at the concordance lines across the century. Can you summarise how *wireless* has changed in usage and meaning over a period of 80 years?

Geography

Another important dimension of variation in English is geography. Online corpora, including the web itself, can be very useful resources for finding out about lexical items which are typical of different varieties or dialects. But this can take a bit of effort. Unless geographical information has been specifically included

---

TASK 3.13   Geographical variation

1. The WebCorp site (www.webcorp.org.uk) returns concordance lines from a specified search engine such as Google or Altavista and lists these with the document URL. Search for the word *outwith* using WebCorp (selecting the search engine of your choice).
2. Now look at the URLs containing instances of the word which are retrieved: what generalisations can you make? What features of the URLs gave you clues?
3. Look at the immediate co-text of each instance: do these have anything in common?
4. What can you deduce about the meaning of the word from the examples of its use?
5. Now go to the SCOTS corpus (www.scottishcorpus.ac.uk) and investigate the word *outwith* in more detail. What textual genres does it tend to occur in?

in a corpus (as it has in the SCOTS corpus and the IViE Corpus, for example), or you are aware that this was one of the parameters for compilation, it can be difficult to obtain such information from a corpus. This is particularly true of the many corpora which have been compiled solely from online materials, which have the benefit of being readily available and large but tend to lack explicit contextual information. This makes quantitative analysis almost impossible for the general user. However, some clues may be gathered, which suggest hypotheses to guide further study using more focused corpora. Try Task 3.13 to see the sorts of clue which might help you.

Summary

This chapter has provided an overview of some of the possibilities which almost all online corpora offer, and an insight into how corpora can furnish data for lexical study, as well as tools for beginning to interpret that data. We have seen that a lot of work can be done with an untagged corpus but also that some forms of annotation, such as lemmatisation, may help lexical enquiry. We gradually expanded the scope of the investigation, from counting occurrences of words, to subtler analyses of the typical lexical environments of words and lexical items and, finally, to their wider social context.

The studies carried out had in common an attempt to identify patterns in often complex data sets: patterns in the immediate environment of words, and meaningful correlations between typical usage and contextual features. This pattern-hunting will continue to be a main concern in the remainder of this book, not least in Chapter 4 as we turn to the study of the grammar of English.

FURTHER READING

Biber, D., Conrad, S. and Reppen, R. (1998). *Corpus Linguistics: Investigating Language Structure and Use.* Cambridge: Cambridge University Press.

Partington, A. (1998). *Patterns and Meanings.* Amsterdam and Philadelphia: John Benjamins.

Sinclair, J. (1991). *Corpus, Concordance, Collocation.* Oxford: Oxford University Press.

Sinclair, J. (2003). *Reading Concordances: An Introduction.* London: Longman.

Stubbs, M. (2001). *Words and Phrases: Corpus Studies of Lexical Semantics.* Oxford: Blackwell.

Exploring Grammar with Corpora

4

In this chapter, we consider what grammar is and how online corpora can be used to explore the traditional areas of concern for grammarians, as well as some of the more novel issues raised by corpus linguists. The chapter focuses on the following:

- Attitudes to grammar revealed by corpus study
- Grammatical categories, such as words, phrases, clauses and sentences
- The exploration of grammar using corpus data
- The grammar of speech and writing
- The conventional grammatical patterns into which words fall

As Chapter 3 indicated, it is difficult to sustain the traditional boundaries between the study of lexis (words and lexical items), grammar (the organisation of words into sentences) and discourse (the organisation of speech and writing above the level of the sentence). Corpus studies have confirmed that these three levels of language are mutually influential and intertwined. The present chapter should therefore be read in combination with the chapters on lexis and discourse; there are many overlapping and complementary concerns in each.

Attitudes to grammar

The recent publication of an innovative, corpus-informed reference grammar of spoken and written English (Carter and McCarthy 2006) provoked the kind of response from one newspaper columnist, Dot Wordsworth, that is typical of the reaction of certain lay commentators on academic linguistic study (Wordsworth 2006). Under the headline 'Grammar is a question of manners', Wordsworth attacked the conventional stance taken by academics that grammars should be based on a dispassionate description of what people do, rather than an evaluative prescription of what they *should* do. Wordsworth argues:

> The two professors have been let loose with their search engines in a sample of "800 million words of real spoken and written English". This Sargasso Sea of

real live language is rather grandly called a "corpus", and the attitude implicit in fishing about in it for samples is: "Everything that is is right."

She then proceeds to rail against much that she disapproves of in current speech. It is easy to characterise the outpourings of commentators like Dot Wordsworth as being founded on prejudice and confusion: she seems to consider the discourse marker *you know* as a dialectal feature, and she admits that her distaste for expressions such as *I was, like, Wow!, You're* so *going to regret this* and *Whatever* are founded on their fashionable, and probably temporary, adoption by the young.

However, Wordsworth is correct in her observation that the academic study of grammar is a descriptive rather than an explicitly evaluative project: corpus-informed grammatical description is, above all, an account of what people do. Grammarians tend to resist stating explicitly what people should do, and yet, as Wordsworth complains, they nevertheless imply that language education must be based on data that represent common practice, rather than on, say, aesthetic criteria developed by a middle-class elite. There is a long history of elite commentary on popular language usage, and indeed the American journalist William Safire coined the term 'language maven', that is, 'language expert' as an ironic depiction of himself and other lay observers. Like Wordsworth, Safire and fellow journalist, Lynne Truss, the author of *Eats, Shoots and Leaves* (2003), many language mavens would agree that grammar is 'a question of manners, practically of morals' (Wordsworth 2006). Those who explore grammar using a corpus are less concerned with dismissing certain features as the fashionable foibles of the young, or alternatively as the quaint dialect of the rural elderly. Corpus-informed grammarians are more concerned with the way language is used – and the way in which usages change (another key text in this respect is Biber et al. 1999). However, the issue of whether those conventional practices that *can* be described using a corpus *should* then be adopted as an educational standard is still a matter for debate.

TASK 4.1   Attitudes to grammar

1. What are your own views about the purpose of studying grammar: to describe how people use language or to prescribe how they *should* use language?
2. Do any current features of contemporary speech irritate you? If so, why? Do you associate them with particular groups of speakers?
3. Are the descriptions that you give to features of speech that you dislike technical or moral in nature? (For example, people tend to characterise features they dislike as *lazy, uncouth, vulgar, faddish, uneducated. . .*)

What is grammar?

Debates, however, are all the better for being informed. To understand the debate, it is useful to have a clear idea of what grammar is. Although grammarians dispute some fundamental aspects of the nature and purpose of grammatical analysis, they generally agree that the study of grammar involves relating (a) the form of words, phrases and clauses to (b) the function they perform when combined and (c) the meanings they express. Let us take, for example, the word *blame* from the BNC and consider some of the contexts in which this word appears. A search for the first ten examples of this word comes up with the following results:

1. which rings with applause, and with **blame**. By the end of the novel Jaromil has
2. without incurring moral **blame** provided they made the decision in a reflective and
3. had been quick to fix the **blame** on him. The Carabinieri chief had left at once with a
4. she didn't really **blame** all the women Henry Phipps had conquered for succumbing
5. hoping to lay the **blame** elsewhere. Or it could have been brought in and
6. and can't say as I **blame** 'er." He inhaled sourly and broke into a glutinous cough
7. I don't mind saying I don't **blame** him a bit! I always did say Mr Merrivale was a
8. I couldn't, and don't, **blame** her. Anne is abroad at the moment, doing some
9. took place much, much later. **Blame** me for becoming poor if you like –; I admit, I
10. if you are just visiting, you **blame** her if the person you have come to see isn't

---

TASK 4.2(a)   Nouns and verbs

1. Look at the list of ten concordance lines given above.
2. Sort the uses of *blame* into two groups: (a) nouns and (b) verbs.
3. Think of the criteria that you used to make that classification.

If you look at the examples, you can see that *blame* falls into two general groupings:

Group A

1. which rings with applause, and with **blame**. By the end of the novel Jaromil has
2. without incurring moral **blame** provided they made the decision in a reflective and
3. had been quick to fix the **blame** on him. The Carabinieri chief had left at once with a
5. hoping to lay the **blame** elsewhere. Or it could have been brought in and

Group B

4. she didn't really **blame** all the women Henry Phipps had conquered for succumbing
6. and can't say as I **blame** 'er." He inhaled sourly and broke into a glutinous cough
7. I don't mind saying I don't **blame** him a bit! I always did say Mr Merrivale was a
8. I couldn't, and don't, **blame** her. Anne is abroad at the moment, doing some
9. took place much, much later. **Blame** me for becoming poor if you like –; I admit, I
10. if you are just visiting, you **blame** her if the person you have come to see isn't

In Group A, the word *blame* expresses a thing that can be *fixed* or *laid*. This thing can be identified by words like *the*, described by words like *moral* and can combine with words like *with*. Our classification of *blame* as a noun in these sentences is based, then, on a consideration of its meaning, and its function, that is, the way it combines with other words like *with, moral* and *the*.

In Group B, however, *blame* is functioning differently. We cannot use the combinations in B that we used in A; that is to say, we cannot say things like:

*she didn't really *the* blame all the women
*can't say as I *moral* blame 'er'
*I don't *with* blame him a bit!

In Group B, *blame* is not a noun but a verb. It combines with words like *I, you, she*; it can be intensified in combination with words like *really*, and its meaning can be modified by words like *didn't, can't, don't*. Rather than expressing a thing, it now expresses an act.

TASK 4.2(b)   Nouns and verbs (Continued)

1. Go to the BYU-BNC at http://corpus.byu.edu/bnc/.
2. In the word/phrase box, enter another word that can be either a noun or a verb, e.g. *love, hate, table, print, book.*
3. Look at the first 20 concordance lines and sort the uses into nouns and verbs.

Nouns and verbs, of course are basic grammatical categories. As corpora very quickly show us, nouns and verbs combine with different kinds of words and mean different things. In short, they perform different functions in sentences. Grammar is the investigation of grammatical categories, their function and their meaning. Descriptive grammarians tell us how people use words and how they combine them into phrases and larger grammatical units like clauses and sentences. They are less inclined to venture explicit opinions about which combinations of words, phrases and clauses are preferable to others. This territory is left to the aesthetic judgment of prescriptive grammarians – and language mavens.

Word categories

When we start exploring grammar using a corpus, it is useful to gather words into two general groups – lexical items and grammatical items. Lexical items carry most of the meaning of sentences, and they are distinguished by the fact that we daily invent new lexical items to express new meanings. Four types of word are lexical in nature:

- nouns, e.g. *girl, concept, nation, success*
- verbs, e.g. *give, take, think, sleep*
- adjectives, which are used to describe things, e.g. *hopeful, luminous, big, ugly*
- adverbs, which are used to describe actions, e.g. *angrily, noisily, furiously, soundly*

New technology constantly demands the invention of new lexical items to express novel concepts, e.g. *iPod* (noun), *download* (verb) or *geeky* (a mildly derisive adjective to describe someone who spends too much time with computers). Grammatical items, in contrast, are those categories of word that cannot easily be added to. We can easily think of a relatively new noun or verb, but it is difficult to think of a new preposition like *in, out, with, under*. It is also difficult to persuade people to adopt a new pronoun beyond a finite set that includes *I, you, he, she, it, we, they, something, nothing, anything*, and a few others. Grammatical words include the following:

- determiners, which are used in combination with nouns to identify them, e.g. *a, the, this, these, that, those, my, your*, etc.
- pronouns, which replace lexical nouns or noun phrases e.g. *I, you, he, she, it, we, they, someone, anyone, nothing*, etc.
- prepositions, which are used with nouns and noun phrases, usually to indicate things like position, direction, location, accompaniment, and so on, e.g. *in, on, under, with, up, beyond*, etc.
- auxiliary verbs, which are used with verbs to indicate concepts like time, duration, possibility and necessity, e.g. *be, have, can, could, must, should*, etc.
- conjunctions, which link words, phrases and clauses in different ways, e.g. *and, or, but, because, since, although, if*, etc.
- interjections, which are used particularly in spoken English to indicate hesitation, surprise, agreement, pain, and so on, e.g. *erm, uh, oh, ah, ouch*, etc.

Exploring lexical items with a corpus

We have already looked briefly at the lexical item *blame* with the BNC. If we look again at Groups A and B above, we can see that *blame* functions as a noun, in combination with the determiner *the* and the adjective *moral*. It can also be expanded by using the preposition *with*. If we return to the BYU-BNC website, we can limit our search to instances of *blame* as a noun by choosing to reveal the part-of-speech (POS) tags and then displaying only certain subsets of the results.

TASK 4.3   Restricting a search by grammatical category

1. Go to the BYU-BNC at http://corpus.byu.edu/bnc/.
2. In the word/phrase box, enter 'blame'.
3. At the bottom of the Search column, select 'yes' for 'See POS tag'.
4. Click Search. This will give you a set of results on the right of your screen.
5. Click on *BLAME (NN1)* to view examples of *blame* as a noun.

A further selection from the 645 examples of *blame* as a noun that were available at the time of our search shows different possible patterns. If we focus on uses of the noun with or without an article, we can see patterns such as the following:

(i) use in combination with the determiner *the,* often when the specific nature of the blame is either known by the speakers, or self-evident, as in:

> ... although he is not prepared to take the **blame** entirely. "If the mistakes had been ...
> ... his assassin did not hesitate to put the **blame** on the "big men". By this time ...

or specified after the word, as in *the blame for the low status*:

> She basically lays the **blame** for the low status retailing enjoys today at the door of ...
> The bulk of the **blame** for all that is placed on British Rail, which knowingly permitted ...
> The **blame** for his "characteristic errors, since they were ... his normal. ...
> At first they pinned most of the **blame** for the loss of jobs on the trade unions and the ...

(ii) use in combination with the determiner *a* when the sense is 'an unspecified member of a set of things':

> ... for a beleaguered Prime Minister a power shared is a **blame** shared.

(iii) use in combination with no determiner when the sense is general, indefinite or unspecific:

> "**Blame**, blame. No matter what you do. Blame is all you get in this family."
> ...it's almost impossible for the outsider to apportion **blame** for the success or failure of...
> ...giving credit, or distributing **blame**, is a reasonably simple matter. Just pluck the...

We can then return to the BNC results and select *BLAME (VVI)* in order to consider some of the 1798 examples of *blame* as a verb, e.g.:

> You could hardly **blame** them, though, for feeling bewildered from time to time.
> ...and I didn't **blame** her. After all, the Germans were still not far off

Other patterns quickly emerge. For example, it is evident that verbal uses of *blame* often occur in the infinitive (*to blame*) in expressions like:

> ...allowing them to **blame** all their ills on the Government." The safety net is...
> Jackson may well have the spirit of punk to **blame** for the misunderstanding.
> ...pre-empting a distracting row about who was to **blame**, leaving the Prime Minister...
> ...conceded it might be partly to **blame**. "But the hints of such things as "travel...
> ...they are at least partly to **blame** for the fact that Yorkshire cricket is in a mess."
> ...the government might be to **blame**. Although the move was hailed as sensational at...
> ...it is to **blame** everyone but herself when things are going wrong and to make...
> ...the huge shortage of sleepers were mainly to **blame**. Railway officials, like their...
> ...poor distribution was often to **blame**. The nation-wide state publishing...

Furthermore, it is clear that *blame*, whether it is used as a noun or a verb, is often followed by phrases introduced by the prepositions *on* and *for*, that is, prepositional phrases:

> She basically lays the **blame** *for the low status* retailing enjoys today at the door of...
> At first they pinned most of the **blame** for the loss of jobs *on the trade unions*...
> ...allowing them to **blame** all their ills *on the Government*." The safety net is...
> Jackson may well have the spirit of punk to **blame** *for the misunderstanding*.

To explore these combinations in more detail, we can revisit the BYU-BNC and enter *blame on*, and then *blame for* in the word/phrase box. The following examples have been selected from the results:

...he is determined to take the **blame for the controversy** it provoked. "It was my own...

...REAGAN'S ability to escape **blame for his frequent lapses** from even basic...

Jackson may well have the spirit of punk to **blame for the misunderstanding.**

...they are at least partly **to blame for the fact that Yorkshire cricket is in a mess.**"

...he and his players had to accept the **blame for a defeat which jeopardises Scotland's** ...

As for apportioning **blame for the £215 m fraud at International Signal and Control** ...

...had been quick to fix the **blame on him**. The Carabinieri chief had left at once with a...

...assassin did not hesitate to put the **blame on the "big men"**. By this time Odinga had...

...government tried to lay part of the **blame on Pakistan**, saying that Khalistan terrorists...

...an Egyptian engineering consultant, lays the **blame on the lack of unleaded fuel and** ...

The government puts particular **blame on car makers and pharmaceutical companies** ...

When the examples are grouped and examined in detail it becomes clear that English users combine the noun/verb and prepositional phrase as follows:

blame + *for* + EFFECT
blame + *on* + CAUSE

To sum up our exploration of the grammatical properties of *blame*, corpus-informed analysis shows us that we can use *blame* as a noun or a verb, in various combinations with prepositional phrases beginning with *for* and *on*. In other words, we can conceptualise *blame* as an act, as in *She/he blames CAUSE for EFFECT*, or *She/he blames EFFECT on CAUSE*. Or we can conceptualise *blame* as a thing that can be *fixed, laid, pinned* or *put*, as in *The blame for EFFECT was fixed on CAUSE*. Furthermore, if we continue to examine our corpus data, we will see other ways in which *blame* can combine with other words, e.g. the noun can be put before other nouns to indicate the type of thing that the main noun (which is sometimes referred to as the 'headword') is, e.g. *blame game*.

Adjectives and adverbs can also be explored using a corpus. A simple example would be to compare two words like *total* and *totally*. If we choose to reveal the part-of-speech tags in the BNC results, we can see that *total* is usually labelled as an adjective, in phrases like *your total income*; less frequently it is a noun, as in *40 per cent of the total*; and even less frequently it is a verb, as in *your savings must total less than £6000*. By contrast, *totally* is labelled solely as an adverb. As such, it intensifies other adverbs, adjectives and prepositional phrases (*totally unexpectedly, totally happy, totally beyond criticism*), or it can occur as the main or head word in a phrase that describes the extent of the action expressed by the verb (*totally endorse, rely totally*).

A more complicated example would be to compare the words *good* and *well*.

TASK 4.4   Comparing the use of adjectives and adverbs

1. Go to the BYU-BNC at http://corpus.byu.edu/bnc/.
2. In the word/phrase box, enter 'good'. Note down some of the results.
3. Repeat the search, this time entering 'well'. Note down some of the results.
4. Compare your results. How many parts of speech can *good* and *well* be classified under? How does the meaning of each change according to its grammatical category?
5. Repeat the search, this time entering 'did good'.
6. Repeat the search, this time entering 'did well'.
7. Compare the results you have noted down. In which instances are *good* and *well* interchangeable? In what circumstances can you not exchange *good* for *well*?

Although a traditional guide to standard English grammar might suggest that *good* and *well* have an adjective–adverb relationship, much like *total* and *totally*, a glance at the BNC data for each word tells us a different story. For a start, *good* can indeed be an adjective, as in *a good cause; they're good at it*. Like *total* it occurs less frequently as a noun, as in *the common good of all; the good of the state*. In informal, spoken English, it is even used as an adverb, for example *I did good enough to win*.

Well is more complicated than *totally*, appearing, as expected, as an adverb, in grammatical combinations similar to *totally* (*well known; well up; well beyond the maximum; well remember; write well*). However, it also appears as an adjective and a noun in its own right, albeit with very different meanings (*perfectly well; the well of loneliness*) as well as an interjection or hesitation marker (*well, well*). The range of uses of *good* and *well* leads to some interesting points of comparison, for example when each is used with the past tense of *do*, for example:

> . . . only when the entire class **did well**. "My son is quite a bright little boy," Villa's central defenders, Paul McGrath and Mountfield, **did well** to defend a . . .
> "I thought I **did well**," the European Footballer of the Year said . . .
> Nevertheless, the yacht **did well** on the first leg, finishing sixth.

... lightweight from Middlesex in his first major international, **did well** to take ...

"You **did good** there," he said, admiringly, meaning what he said. . .
... the Harlem Globetrotters did more damage racially than they **did good**,
... because they who would judge us and reward us if we **did good** and punish us if we did evil.
... until he broke me at 5–3, but I **did good** enough to win," said the 24-year-old . . .

The first group, featuring *did well*, is relatively easy to understand: the adverb *well* is used to evaluate the quality of the verb *do*, which, in these examples, refers to some kind of performance, often sporting or competitive.

In the second group, featuring *did good*, there is a split between those sentences that use *good* as a noun, referring to unspecific, general 'good things', and those sentences that seem to use *good* in a similar way to *well*, that is, to evaluate performance. In the case of *you did good there*, it is unclear from the limited context available whether *good* is being used as a non-specific noun or an evaluative adverb. If the latter, this is the kind of change in grammatical category that offends language mavens and prescriptive grammarians.

Exploring grammatical items with a corpus

As with lexical items, online corpora can be used to explore the patterns into which the closed set of grammatical items fall. Among the more interesting of the grammatical items are prepositions, those little items like *in, to, at, up* and *with*. As we have seen, they can be attached to nouns to make prepositional phrases that give a sense of direction, location, accompaniment and so on. However, many of these words can also be attached to verbs to make combinations, sometimes referred to as phrasal verbs or multiword verbs, that often differ in meaning from that of the verb alone. Compare:

... if you wish to **give** another £600 or more ... (*give = donate*)
... many inmates want to **give up** their appeals ... (*give up = abandon*)
Should she **give in** to her love for another woman? (*give in = surrender*)

A selection of examples from a BNC search for *give in* shows instances in which *in* is used as the start of a prepositional phrase and as part of a multiword verb:

1. Finally we **give in** and rent the movie we ignored a few months ago
2. Such knowledge will be the basis of the advice we **give in** the next chapter
3. to choose their own government, and we shouldn't **give in** to dictatorships
4. Nigel of course didn't **give in** to blackmail
5. the help that they may **give in** the identification of other portraits
6. Do not **give in** and take your puppy to bed with you
7. The psychic reasons for this solidarity I have tried to **give in** this essay

> ### TASK 4.5   Prepositional phrase or multiword verb?
>
> 1. Look at the selection of seven examples of the sequence *give in* above, taken from the BNC data.
> 2. In which examples does *in* combine with the preceding verb, *give*?
> 3. In which examples does *in* combine with the noun phrase that follows?
> 4. Go to the BYU-BNC at http://corpus.byu.edu/bnc/
> 5. Enter another sequence of verb + preposition (e.g. *put off*) and again sort some of your results into the categories of multiword verb and verb + prepositional phrase.

If you consider the relationship between the words in the seven examples of *give + in*, it should be clear that the combinations *give + in the next chapter, give + in the identification of other portraits* and *give + in this essay* are instances of *give* plus prepositional phrases; all the other examples of *give in* are multiword verbs, e.g. *give in + to blackmail.*

> ### TASK 4.6   Gender-specific and gender-neutral pronouns
>
> Which of the following utterances would you say? Would you write the same thing?
>
> *Everyone should do as he likes.*
> *Everyone should do as she likes.*
> *Everyone should do as he/she likes.*
> *Everyone should do as they like.*

Corpus-based analysis can be used to demonstrate the limitations imposed upon English speech and writing by having a finite set of pronouns. The English personal pronoun system is marked for gender in the third person singular (*he, she* and *it* expressing masculine, feminine and neuter subjects, respectively). However, in the third person plural, there is only a single item *they*, indicating all three genders. The corresponding object pronouns are of course *him, her, it* and *them*. What English lacks is a singular pronoun that means *he or she*, or *him or her*. This causes problems in situations in which the non-specific pronouns *everybody* and *everyone* are used. Technically, these pronouns are also singular in number, as can be seen when we look at the form of the verb that is used in combination with the pronoun: we have *everyone wonders* and *what is everyone going to start thinking*, not *everyone wonder*, and *what are everyone going to start thinking*. Consequently, speakers should theoretically maintain a consistency of number in sentences like *everyone should do what he/she likes*. However, the clumsiness of writing *he/she* or *he or she*, alongside anxiety about using one gender-specific pronoun (either *he* or *she*) to substitute for a non-gender specific pronoun (*everyone*), has prompted the frequent use of *everyone . . . they* in sentences such as the following:

This is something **everyone** wonders when starting out, even if **they** are not intending . . .

... **everyone** would look at that noticeboard and **they** would all understand ...

What is **everyone** going to start thinking when **they** see how you've cut the ...

Examples like this might again irritate prescriptive grammarians who value logical consistency over economy of expression; however, there is undoubtedly an awkwardness in expressions like *What is everyone going to start thinking when he or she sees how you've* ...

As the examples above show, corpora can allow us quickly to explore large quantities of data and see how different types of word, namely, lexical items and grammatical items, work in actual utterances and written sentences.

Exploring phrases with a corpus

Grammatical analysis extends beyond the classification of individual words. Traditionally, parsing involves the consideration of how words expand into one of five types of phrase, namely *noun phrase, prepositional phrase, verb phrase, adverb phrase* and *adjective phrase.* To illustrate these types of phrase, we can search a corpus and consider the kinds of pattern that individual words – nouns, prepositions, verbs, adjectives and adverbs – conventionally form. Instead, however, of looking at the actual lexical or grammatical items that cluster around the word in question, we consider the *type* of items that cluster together. In other words, we would look not only at which words cluster with the noun *tree* (for example *an ornamental tree, a giant tree, my apple tree, that chestnut tree,* etc.) but also at the type of words that cluster with *tree.* In these examples, the grammatical categories are as follow:

- *DETERMINER + ADJECTIVE + tree*
- *DETERMINER + NOUN + tree*

By focusing on grammatical categories rather than the words themselves, we can say something useful about the general structure of noun phrases, for example, that they commonly begin with a determiner (*a, an, my, that*) and that the headword (*tree*) can be modified by a descriptive adjective (*ornamental, giant*) or a noun that tells us its type (*apple, chestnut*).

Noun phrases

Let us continue to explore different structures that have *tree* as the main noun or head word. The following examples are taken from the MICASE corpus:

a tree	Det + N
this big tree	Det + Aj + N
a coconut tree	Det + N + N
the tall pine tree	Det + Aj + N + N

These patterns show the main variations in the structure of the noun phrase in English. Noun phrases often begin with a determiner that identifies the noun in some way. For example, *a* or *an* indicates that the tree is an unspecified member of a particular set of trees; *this* and *that* indicate that the tree is identifiable by its distance to or from the speaker; *the* indicates that it is a specific member of a particular set of trees; *my, his* and so on would indicate that it is identified by possession. After the determiner, the noun might be modified by a descriptive adjective (*big, tall*), or it might be classified using another noun (*coconut, pine*). Where all these options are chosen, the noun phrase usually has the pattern *Determiner + Adjective(s) + Noun + Noun.*

TASK 4.7   The structure of the noun phrase

1. Go to MICASE at http://quod.lib.umich.edu/m/micase/ and click to Search the corpus.
2. Choose another common noun, such as *water*, and look at the variations in the structure of the noun phrases in which it appears as the headword.
3. Be sure to look only at those phrases where the noun is the most important item. That is, in the expression *cool water*, the adjective is describing the noun, which is therefore the headword. By contrast, in the phrase *water quality*, the noun *water* is classifying another noun, and therefore the second noun *(quality)* is the headword.
4. Note down the most common NP structures that you find, e.g. *Determiner + Noun.*

Prepositional phrases

Noun phrases are often preceded by a preposition, such as *at, in, under, over, across, behind, to, from, of,* etc. – these small words that often express concepts like location, direction and possession. A glance at the concordances from MICASE for *water* shows us a range of possible prepositional phrases:

of water	Prep + N
into the water	Prep + Det + N
in hot water	Prep + Aj + N
from your tap water	Prep + Det + N + N

As you can see, the structure of prepositional phrases is fairly simple: the preposition precedes the noun phrase (which is in fact what *pre-position* literally means). The complexity of structure arises from the noun phrase, which can consist of a simple noun or a more complex structure.

Verb phrases

As we have just seen, nouns cluster into phrases with determiners, adjectives and other nouns. In addition, noun phrases can be transformed into prepositional phrases with the addition of a preceding preposition. Verbs take different partners, as we can see by looking at those words that modify an expression like *grow*.

TASK 4.8(a)   The structure of the verb phrase

1. Go to the SCOTS corpus at www.scottishcorpus.ac.uk.
2. Click on Advanced Search.
3. Click on General, then Word Search, then Word/Phrase Concordance.
4. Enter 'grow*' in the Search box and press Return.
5. Scroll down the page to find the concordance of results.
6. Click on the word *Left*, to the left of the word *Node* to order your results.
7. Do not consider those results which are nouns (*growth*) or those results in which *growing* and *grown* are used as adjectives, e.g. *a growing boy; a grown man*.
8. How many different auxiliary verbs can you find, modifying the various forms of the verb *grow*?

A search of SCOTS for *grow** will retrieve different forms of the verb – *grow, growing* and *grown* – as well as other, non-standard variants (such as *growed, growen, growin*) that we can ignore for the moment:

grow	V
might (not) grow	aux + (n) + V
must grow	aux + V
will grow	aux + V
am/is/were growing	aux + V
have been growing	aux + aux + V
has/had grown	aux + V
be/are grown	aux + V
have been grown	aux + aux + V
can be grown	aux + aux + V

To arrive at this list, we have restricted our selection to those clusters in which the form of *grow* is the headword. Looking only at those expressions in which *grow, growing* and *grown* are headwords, we can see from the above sample that the form of the verb phrase is quite restricted. Verbs can only be modified by one or more auxiliary verbs, the primary auxiliaries *be* and *have* and the modal auxiliaries *may, will, can*:

• The primary auxiliaries mainly give information about time and duration, although the verb *be* plus the past participle *grown* changes the voice of the phrase from active to passive (*we can grow them → they can be grown*).
• The modal auxiliary verbs add a sense of possibility or prediction (*can grow, might grow, will grow*) and obligation (*must grow*).

TASK 4.8(b)   The structure of the verb phrase

1. Go to the BYU-BNC at http://corpus.byu.edu/bnc/.
2. Search for a verb of your own choice in the corpus and try to find the maximum number of auxiliary verbs that can modify that verb. For example, can you find anything longer than *I may have been being a bit selfish* (Aux + Aux + Aux + V)?
3. From looking at longer verb phrases, what can you say about the usual order of the auxiliary verbs found in them (i.e. what is the usual order of modal and primary auxiliaries)?

Adjective and adverb phrases

Adjectives are those descriptive words that modify nouns, like *tasty, fat, ugly*. adverbs, you will recall, include those words that describe actions, such as *quickly, angrily, noisily, fast, greedily*, as in the following:

She *ate up* the spaghetti	*quickly*
	angrily
	noisily
	fast
	greedily

It will come as no surprise to discover that adjective phrases have adjectives as head words (e.g. *really tasty*) while adverb phrases have adverbs as head words (e.g. *really quickly*). In each case, the head adjective or adverb can be modified by a different type of adverb – one that either intensifies or softens their meaning. These adverbs include *really, totally, wholly, very, considerably, quite* and so on. Examples of these uses are as follows:

	Adjective phrases		*Adverb phrases*
The spaghetti was	*really* tasty.	She ate it	*really* quickly.
	very		*very*
	quite		*quite*

The typical structure of the adjective phrase is therefore ADVERB + ADJEC-TIVE, while the typical structure of the adverb phrase is ADVERB + ADVERB. Looking at the SCOTS corpus, we can run a concordance search on adjectives and adverbs, and again order them according to the closest word to the left of the key word or node, so that we can easily see how they are modified. For example, the adjective *beautiful* combines with a number of adverbs to give adjective phrases such as:

Adverb	*Adjective*
absolutely	beautiful
achingly	

exotically
fabulously
outstandingly
quite
really
so
very

In a similar fashion, the adverb *slowly* combines with a number of modifying adverbs to give adverb phrases such as:

Adverb	*Adverb*
extremely	slowly
rather	
r-e-a-l-l-y	
sae/so	
very	

Corpus searches also turn up exceptions to the general rule that adjectives and adverbs are modified by adverbs. Colours are examples of adjectives that can be modified by other adjectives, e.g. *bright blue.* Corpus searches show that *pretty slowly* is also possible, as is *pretty tasty*; however, in this case the adjective *pretty* is being used exceptionally to modify other adjectives and adverbs, usually in spoken contexts. It is not generally the case that adjectives do this. And although it is less common, it is entirely possible for adjectives and adverbs to be modified by more than one adverb, as in *really very beautiful* or *so very slowly.*

TASK 4.9   The structure of adjective and adverb phrases

1. Go to the BYU-BNC at http://corpus.byu.edu/bnc/ or the SCOTS corpus at www.scottishcorpus.ac.uk.
2. Using the BNC or SCOTS, look at the structure of phrases with adjectives or adverbs as the headword. Remember to distinguish between those words that are actually modifying the headword and those words that are simply added together in a list of equal items. That is, distinguish between phrases such as:

a clean tidy garden	Det + Aj + Aj + N
the *immaculately tidy* house	Det + AjP [Av + Aj] + N

The second example is of a noun modified by a determiner and two adjectives. The second example is of a noun modified by a determiner and an adjective phrase that, in turn, consists of a modifying adverb and an adjective. The structure shows that in the first example the garden is *clean* and *tidy*, while in the second example the house is *immaculately tidy*.
3. What is the longest adjective or adverb phrase that you can find? What is its structure?

From phrase to clause

In the previous section, we used corpora to explore the structure of phrases, that is, we considered which words cluster together to make a phrase, and we considered the relationships between them. Within each phrase, an individual word can function as a modifier or a headword, as we have seen. In the noun phrase *blue sky*, the noun is the headword and the adjective is the modifier, describing the noun. In the adjective phrase, *sky blue*, the adjective is the headword and the noun is the modifier, classifying the adjective.

Phrases have their own set of functions in the sentence as a whole. They combine in a variety of ways to make up clauses, which in turn combine to form complete sentences. In written language in particular, these sentences can become quite complex.

The clause centres on the verb phrase (that is, a main verb plus one or more auxiliary verbs). Noun, preposition, adjective and adverb phrases orbit around the verb phrase in a number of ways, depending primarily on the kind of verb phrase selected. Depending on their function in the clause, we classify the phrases as *subject* (usually a noun phrase), *predicator* (verb phrase), *object* (noun phrase), *complement* (noun phrase or adjective phrase) and *adverbial* (adverb phrase or prepositional phrase). These five constituents (known as SPOCA, from their initial letters) are the building bricks from which clauses are constructed.

TASK 4.10   Clause structure

Identify the phrases that are functioning as SPOCA in these examples, taken from the children's story *Katie Morag and the Two Grandmothers* by Mairi Hedderwick [SCOTS Document 832]:

1. One sunny Wednesday morning Mrs McColl woke Katie Morag early.
2. Here comes the boat.
3. Granma Mainland lived far away in the big city.
4. My, you're still a smart wee Bobby Dazzler.
5. Grannie Island revved the engine very loudly.
6. Show Day was always a big event on the Island of Struay.
7. Alecina was Grannie Island's prize sheep.
8. But all ended well.

Most corpora do not automatically tag phrases according to their clause function, although some corpora that are not yet widely available online do (such as the Penn Treebank Project, at www.cis.upenn.edu/~treebank/home.html). Some grammarians who have used corpus materials extensively are sceptical about the value of parsing above the level of the phrase or above set sequences that they describe as 'patterns' (e.g. Hunston and Francis 2000). However, traditionally, most grammarians pay attention to levels of structure above the phrase, so here we look at ways of exploring clause structure by examining some typical clause structures that four basic types of verbs enter into:

- *copular verbs*, i.e. verbs of being or perception, like *be, become, taste, feel*
- *transitive verbs*, i.e. verbs that are followed by an object, like *push, read*
- *ditransitive verbs*, i.e. verbs that can be followed by two objects, like *give, tell*
- *intransitive verbs*, i.e. verbs that are not followed by an object, like *sleep, snore*

Clauses with copular verbs

Copular verbs link a subject with a complement. They include verbs of being such as *be* and *become* and some verbs of perception, such as *feel, taste, look,* etc. Copular verbs are usually preceded by a noun phrase (the subject of the clause) that 'agrees' with the verb in person and number, and is followed by an adjective phrase or another noun phrase (the complement) that gives information about the subject. A search of the BNC for *become* and *taste* yields the following examples of clauses, excerpted from longer sentences:

Subject	Predicator	Complement
my flat	had become	*pretty run down*
the ability to sing and dance	has become	*increasingly important*
Kundera	has become	*a common name*
you	've become	*the thing you are*
some of the wilder wheat beers	might taste	*odd*
the food . . .	didn't taste	*too different*

Note again that the subject agrees with the predicator (i.e. the verb phrase) in person and number. That is, the form of the verb depends on the subject: *the ability. . .*has *become, you* have *become* and so on. And note that there is a clear relationship between the subject and the complement: the complement either describes the subject (*my flat. . .pretty run down*) or the complement has a relationship of identity with the subject (*you. . .the thing you are*).

It will also be clear from the corpus searches that *taste* in particular combines with phrases in different ways from those shown above; for example, in the clause *you can taste food*, there is no relationship of identity between *you* and *food*. *Food* is therefore not a complement in this instance, and so it follows that *taste* is not always a copular verb.

TASK 4.11   Copular verbs

1. Go to the BYU-BNC at http://corpus.byu.edu/bnc/ or the SCOTS corpus at www.scottishcorpus.ac.uk.
2. Do a corpus search for another verb of perception, such as *look*, and pick out five examples in which it is used as a copular verb with a complement, and five examples in which it is not.

Transitive verbs

Transitive verbs are normally followed by an object, that is, a noun phrase that does not have a relationship of identity with the subject. In the example *you can taste food, food* is the object, and *taste* is a transitive verb. Given the similarity between clauses like *the food tastes good* and *you can taste food*, sometimes it is difficult to distinguish between complements and objects. One test of this is to change the sentence from active to passive:

*good is tasted by the food...
food can be tasted (by you)...

Objects of sentences can generally be turned into the subject of a passive clause, while complements cannot. A good dictionary will identify a verb as transitive; examples include *find, trust, push*. The meaning of all these verbs implies that there is something that is found, trusted and pushed. A selection of clauses from the BNC that include these words is:

Subject	Predicator	Object
Robert	found	*peace and assurance*
the team	found	*no reliable evidence*
I	trust	*Marie*
I	trust	*the leadership of India*

Often in the corpus examples, these verbs are found in the imperative form associated with commands or suggestions (*Trust me; push the opponent over your flexed knee*). Here the clause has a predicator and an object, but no subject. A common feature of the verb *push* is that the object is followed by an object complement. This kind of complement describes or has a relationship of identity with the object rather than the subject:

Subject	Predicator	Object	Object Complement
I	push	*the hat*	*back*
The banks	push	*prices*	*high*

TASK 4.12 Transitive verbs

1. Go to the BYU-BNC at http://corpus.byu.edu/bnc/ or the SCOTS corpus at www.scottishcorpus.ac.uk.
2. Do a corpus search for the verb *call*. Identify two examples in which it is used (a) without an object, (b) with an object and (c) with both an object and an object complement.

Ditransitive verbs

As their name suggests, ditransitive verbs can take two objects, usually labelled as direct and indirect objects, e.g.:

Subject	Predicator	Indirect Object	Direct Object
they	give	students. . .	an opportunity. . .
they	give	you	the feeling that. . .
Libet's experiments	tell	us	something about
My . . . colleagues	tell	me	one of the main
			dangers. . .

Either of the noun phrases that follows the verb can become the subject of a passive clause; that is, we could transform the first example by saying either *students are given an opportunity (by them)*, or *An opportunity is given to students (by them)*. Both noun phrases therefore pass the test of 'object-ness' noted in the previous section. The indirect object can be distinguished from the direct object by the fact that the former can be expanded into a prepositional phrase by changing its position in the sentence: *they give an opportunity to your students, Libet's experiments tell something to us.* Only the indirect object can be so expanded.

TASK 4.13   Ditransitive verbs

1. Go to the BYU-BNC at http://corpus.byu.edu/bnc/ or go to the SCOTS corpus at www.scottishcorpus.ac.uk.
2. Do a corpus search for a ditransitive verb such as *make* or *promise*. Identify two examples of the verb being used with (a) one object and (b) two objects.
3. When the verb has two objects, identify the *indirect* object.

Intransitive verbs

Intransitive verbs are usually followed by neither a complement nor an object. This type of verb often expresses physical behaviour, such as *walking, sleeping, snoring, sneezing*, where such behaviour does not extend towards another participant in the action. Examples include the following:

Subject	Predicator
Lachlan	sneezed
Phillis	snored
I	walked

One advantage of exploring the relationship between verb type and clause structure is that it quickly becomes clear how creatively users of language defy norms and expectations. Just as transitive verbs can be used without objects (as in the simple command, *push*), so also can intransitive verbs be used with objects, as in the following:

Subject	Predicator	Object	Object complement
He	sneezed	himself	back to life

TASK 4.14   Intransitive verbs

1. Go to the BYU-BNC at http://corpus.byu.edu/bnc/.
2. Do a corpus search for an intransitive verb such as *laugh, sing*. Identify four examples of the verb being used (unusually) with an object.
3. Is there any pattern that emerges about the nature of the objects that normally intransitive verbs take?

Adverbials

So far our survey of clause structure has focused on the basic elements of Subject, Predicator, Complement and Object. The final constituent, Adverbial, can be added to any sentence type. Adverbials, which are realised by adverbial or prepositional phrases, give extra information about time, location, direction, manner and so on. Examples with some of the verb types given above include the following:

Subject	Predicator	Object	Complement	Adverbial
I	became		free	by some secret action
He	pushed	the pad		aside
I	walked			out of the village

Adverbials are also identifiable partly by their relative mobility in the clause; it is easy, for example, to change the above examples to *By some secret action, I became free; I pushed aside the pad; Out of the village I walked.*

TASK 4.15   Two types of adverbial

1. Go to the BYU-BNC at http://corpus.byu.edu/bnc/.
2. Search for ten examples each of the Adverbials *quite often* (an adverb phrase) and *in particular*. Pay attention to the position they take in the clause (i.e. front, end or mid position) and the meanings they have. What patterns can you see emerging?

TASK 4.16   Familiarising yourself with clause types

1. Using a good dictionary, choose four verbs, making sure that you have a selection of verb types – copular, transitive, ditransitive and intransitive.
2. Go to the BYU-BNC at http://corpus.byu.edu/bnc/.
3. Search for each of your four verbs in turn, and note down the typical structure of a sample of the clauses in which they are found. Bear in mind that some of the clauses you will find will be more complex than those we have dealt with so far, so choose relatively straightforward examples until your confidence increases.

Complex sentences

Complete sentences are built up of one or more clauses in a sequence that can be linked in a number of ways, for example, by using the following:

- a coordinating conjunction, usually *and, or/nor, but*
- a subordinating conjunction such as *if, because, unless, although*, etc.
- a relative clause, beginning with *who, which, that*
- a non-finite clause, beginning with an infinitive verb or a participle.

Coordinate clauses: coordinating conjunctions

Using tagged corpora such as the BNC, we can quickly and easily obtain many examples of sentences constructed using these four methods. However, a word of caution is appropriate before proceeding. Because manual tagging takes so long, most large corpora, like the BNC, are tagged using automatic part-of-speech parsers. Automatic tagging is far from perfect, and it is often the case that you will find errors in the part-of-speech labels given to particular words. However, used with due care, tagged corpora are still useful for finding general tendencies and for identifying certain grammatical features quickly. For example, we can search the BNC for examples of coordinating conjunctions by inserting [cjc] in the WORD/PHRASE box. The results show many examples of these conjunctions linking phrases, but they also link entire clauses, such as the following two clauses, which have been numbered:

1 [There was clearly a need to adapt my lifestyle], **but** 2 [playing the role of victim was never among my plans.]

Coordinating conjunctions link equal clauses, shown above by square brackets; *but* acts as a signal that the second clause qualifies the first clause, or that it expresses unexpected information, in the context given by the first clause. Note that each clause has at its centre a main verb, here *was* in each case, around which the other constituents are arranged. The phrase structure of the other constituents is quite complex and includes one clause that post-modifies a phrase, in the noun phrase *a need [to adapt my lifestyle]*, and another clause that substitutes for an entire phrase, as in the clause *[playing the role of victim]*, which takes the place of a noun phrase. These complex structures are discussed in more detail below.

Subordinate clauses: subordinating conjunctions

We can search the BNC for subordinating conjunctions by entering [cjs] in the word/phrase box. The BNC gives a large number of possible subordinating conjunctions, though if you scroll down the page you will see from the frequencies that some are marginal, and indeed several are non-standard spellings of more frequent items, e.g. *'cept, accordin'*. Still, around sixty subordinating conjunctions have a frequency of over 100 in the 100 million words of the BNC. One of the thousands of examples of sentences including a subordinate clause is the following:

[You can stay here [**until** we close up for the night]]

Again, note that each clause is centred on a verb phrase: *can stay* and *close up*, respectively. The difference between this kind of complex sentence and a sentence made up of coordinate clauses is that here one clause is embedded *inside* the other. *Until we close up for the night* is an adverbial clause, since it functions as an adverbial, just like an adverb phrase or a prepositional phrase. And, like other adverbials, it can be moved around the sentence: *Until we close up for the night, you can stay here.* Clauses beginning with subordinating conjunctions are often adverbials in the main clause.

TASK 4.17   The function of subordinate clauses

1. Go to the BYU-BNC at http://corpus.byu.edu/bnc/.
2. From the drop-down menu given at *Insert Tag* choose conj.SUB, or simply type [cjs] into the word/phrase box.
3. The website will then display a list of subordinating conjunctions in the BNC. Click on one or two to see them in context. Remember to distinguish between those conjunctions that introduce a phrase (which would have no verb phrase) and those that introduce a clause (in which there is a verb phrase).
4. What kind of information does the subordinate clause contribute to the main clause?

Subordinate clauses: non-finite verbs

When we looked earlier at an example of a sentence that was made up of two coordinate clauses, we noted in passing that each of the equal clauses also contained subordinate clauses. Each of the subordinate clauses was introduced by a non-finite verb (that is, the form of a verb that is not marked for tense): the infinitive *to adapt* and the participle *playing*. The sentence is shown again below, with the subordinate clauses italicised:

[There was clearly a need *to adapt my lifestyle*], but [*playing the role of victim was never among my plans.*]

These examples illustrate two other functions of the subordinate clause. The first, *to adapt my lifestyle* is embedded inside a noun phrase, and its function is to elaborate upon the headword, which is the main noun, *need (a need [to adapt my lifestyle])*. We can therefore say that the subordinate clause *post-modifies* the noun. In the second case, *playing the role of the victim* functions, like an entire noun phrase, as the subject of the main clause. We can indeed replace the whole subordinate clause with a single pronoun: ***this** was never among my plans.* We therefore say that this subordinate clause is a noun clause, since it functions in exactly the same way as a noun phrase.

TASK 4.18   Non-finite subordinate clauses

1. Go to the BYU-BNC at http://corpus.byu.edu/bnc/.
2. Enter the infinitive form of the verb *to account* in the word/phrase box.
3. Restrict your search further by asking the search program to select only examples following a singular or plural noun – do this by modifying your word/phrase search to include the tag *[n*] to account.*
4. Under *OPTIONS* select *SEE POS TAGS* to 'yes'. Identify the examples in the results where the infinitive form introduces a post-modifying subordinate clause. What kind of nouns are post-modified by subordinate clauses beginning with *to account*? Is there a pattern of meanings?
5. Then run a word/phrase search for the present participle form of the verb (i.e. *accounting*). Identify examples where the participle introduces a subordinate clause. Look particularly at those examples tagged VVG (i.e. the participle form of the verb).
6. Can you replace the entire subordinate clause with a pronoun like *this* or *something*? If so, you have identified a subordinate noun clause.
7. Repeat this series of searches with one or more verbs of your own choosing.

Subordinate clauses: relative clauses

Relative clauses are a little like those post-modifying subordinate clauses mentioned above, in that they are usually embedded into noun phrases or prepositional phrases, and they tell us more about the preceding noun. Instead of being introduced by non-finite verbs, however, they are introduced by relative pronouns, such as *who, which* and *that*. In the following example, the relative clause is embedded inside a prepositional phrase, and it refers back to the preceding noun *courts*.

[However the case was passed (to the military courts [***who** revoked the arrest order*])].

Relative clauses that refer back to human beings or institutions are introduced by the personal relative pronoun *who*. Non-human referents are introduced by *which* or *that*. Often the difference in choice is purely one of register – *which* is felt to be more formal than *that*. However, some word-processing programs, like Microsoft Word, prompt writers to reserve *which* for those relative clauses that give optional information about the noun, so-called 'non-defining relative clauses'. In turn, *that* is reserved for relative clauses that give essential, or defining, information about the preceding noun. Examples of each type of relative clause are, respectively:

[It is a beautiful country [***which*** *is being devastated by a disease which can be stopped*]]
[This is one lesson [***that*** *could save their lives*]]

One further type of relative clause, the comment clause, does not refer back to an individual noun; rather, as its name suggests, it comments on the previous proposition as a whole:

[First of all, he knew how to listen –; [*which is very rare*]]

TASK 4.19   Types of relative clause

1. Go to the BYU-BNC at http://corpus.byu.edu/bnc/.
2. Search for *that* and *which*, discarding instances in which they do not introduce relative clauses.
3. Choose some examples of the relative clauses from your search and sort them into (a) non-defining relative clauses, (b) defining relative clauses and (c) comment clauses.

The grammar of speech and writing

The preceding sections have used corpora to illustrate a traditional model of grammar, a model that conceives of language as organised into sentences, which are in turn combinations of clauses, phrases and words. This traditional model of grammar is, of course, very much based on written language. In the early days of large-scale digitised language corpora, the model of grammar based on written language was not greatly challenged, for the simple reason that it is easier to collect large quantities of already-written text than to record and transcribe speech. Only in recent years, have substantial corpora of relatively spontaneous spoken interaction become available, and accounts of English grammar are beginning to focus on evidence from everyday speech. As we saw at the beginning of this chapter, this shift in emphasis from the analysis of carefully turned written English text to spontaneous, interactive spoken discourse is not without its critics. However, one of the strengths of corpus-informed language study is that we can now look in detail at how conversational English is constructed. For example, the BNC data can easily be restricted to particular registers, which include 'spoken' or, defining more narrowly, 'courtroom speech', 'interview', 'sermon', 'conversation' and so on, by selecting from a pull-down menu on the BYU-BNC page, and the SCOTS data can be restricted to the spoken documents only by selecting 'spoken' in the Standard or Advanced Search options. By limiting our searches to spoken documents, we can begin to explore aspects of the grammar of speech. Here we focus on one common feature of speech to which the availability of corpora has drawn our attention, namely delexicalised verbs.

Delexicalised verbs

In the discussion of clause structure above, we assumed that clauses with transitive verbs typically involved a subject, a verbal process and an object through which the process was realised. So, for example a typical written clause might be as follows:

If you simply **take** cuttings from an apple tree they will grow vigorously...

Here, the subject of the first clause is *you*, the object is *cuttings* and the verbal process is *take*, which has its basic dictionary meaning of moving something or someone from one place to another. However, if we search for the sequence *take a* in the spoken section of the SCOTS corpus, we find other possible uses of *take* (Figure 4.1):

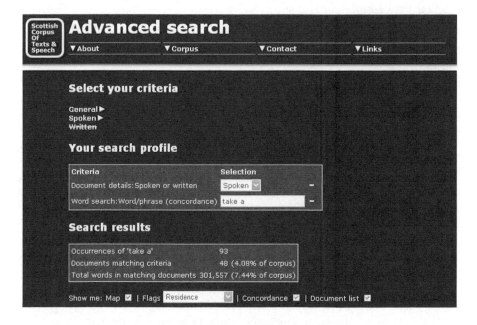

Figure 4.1   SCOTS' advanced search page

These uses include the following:

I **take** a drink
Do they **take** a big jump at the top
Before you had to **take** a breath
maybe you can just also **take** a look at this one
ye just **take** a nap or a kip yeah
just **take** a wee sippie at a time

In these examples, *take* has lost its meaning of moving something from one place to another – in other words it has become delexicalised. What seems to be happening here is that the delexicalised verb substitutes for a verb that has been turned into a noun and put in the object position in the clause (*drink, jump, breathe, look, nap/kip, sip*). The reason for this is possibly that the action that would have been expressed as a verb can more easily be modified when it has been turned into a noun (*big jump, wee sippie*). Delexicalised verbs are also a relatively common feature of written English, but they seem particularly useful in spoken language, where there is perhaps greater emphasis on evaluating events and actions. Other common delexicalised verbs are *have* and *give*, as in the following examples, also from the SCOTS data:

lie doon and **have** a wee bit relax
if you want to **have** a wee blether with him
can we just **have** a wee look at this
I'd like to **give** an especial welcome
so I **give** another wave as I'm going over
I think she'll **give** me a wee phone when she gets it

TASK 4.20　Delexicalised verbs

1. Go to the BYU-BNC at http://corpus.byu.edu/bnc/.
2. Search for delexicalised verbs plus adjectives plus nominalised verbs by entering a sequence like *have a [aj*] [vvb]* in the word/phrase box.
3. When you get the results, click the number in the DISTRIB column to check if they are more common in speech or in written registers. If the register is written, consider the register (fictional prose, for example, often mimics the conventions of speech).

Colligation

The availability of language corpora has allowed linguists to turn their attention more fully to *colligation*, that is, the grammatical relationships that words and phrases form. Hoey (2005, p. 43) defines colligation as follows:

1. the grammatical company a word or word sequence keeps (or avoids keeping) either within its own group or at a higher rank

2. the grammatical functions preferred or avoided by the group in which the word or word sequence participates
3. the place in a sequence that a word or word sequence prefers (or avoids)

In other words, to explore the colligation of a word or phrase, we would consider the following questions:

- how is the word or phrase modified, and/or what does it modify?
- does the word or phrase typically appear as part of the subject, predicator, object, complement or adverbial in a clause?
- does the word or phrase typically function as the head or modifier in a phrase?

In this fashion, we build up a profile of the grammatical behaviour of the word or phrase in question. To explore colligation, let us consider a fairly rare lexical item, *eco-friendly*. In the 100 million words of the BNC, *eco-friendly* occurs only 15 times, in the following contexts:

1. It's more **eco-friendly**, as (a) the plants are a replaceable resource, and (b) burning ethanol distilled from them doesn't add to atmospheric CO_2.
2. . . . I would like to be allowed to put my faith in wine merchants such as the Kendricks or Simon Loftus of Adnams when they tell me which of their wines are **eco-friendly**.
3. The play is a musical about **eco-friendly** aliens whose mission is to save our planet.
4. Muji's own make of **eco-friendly** transport follows sturdy, basic designs. . .
5. **Eco-friendly** collectives such as Catweasle Press, Conscious Earthwear and No Lo Go (a label and an Oxfam shop in London's Marylebone High Street) are embracing unbleached cotton, old bedspreads and jumble sale clothes.
6. And it may be a comforting thought to some that an Australian company is experimenting with **eco-friendly** coffins made of newspapers, which are cheap and biodegradable.
7. . . . that salted peanuts are a killer for birds; that **eco-friendly** insecticides are a contradiction in terms.
8. In Japan and traditionally **eco-friendly** European countries such as Switzerland and Denmark, it has never been popular.
9. . . . a wing of guest rooms in every hotel converted to an **eco-friendly** environment, to be monitored over two years to see how energy consumption compares with standard rooms.
10. Will my hon. friend look at the work being done in Austria and France to make an **eco-friendly** diesel fuel from oilseed rape and other oil crops?
11. Enter Goldfinger, the **eco-friendly** banana.
12. The initiative, based on ideas introduced by the Inter-Continental group, focuses on areas such as energy-saving heating, recycling waste and buying **eco-friendly** products.
13. Do you want to know how easy it is to affect the environment of the world by planting trees or buying **eco-friendly** products?

14. **Eco-friendly** power plant planned for capital's centre...
15. They were impressed by the **eco-friendly** solvent spinning operation, which starts with harvested woodpulp and uses chemicals which can be totally recycled.

On the basis of the 15 examples from the data provided by the BNC, then, we can make the following tentative suggestions about the colligation of *eco-friendly.*

How is the word modified, and/or what does it modify?

Eco-friendly modifies nouns. More specifically, it modifies nouns expressing human or human-like beings and institutions (*aliens, collectives, European countries*), products (*ethanol, wines, (make of) transport, coffins, insecticides, diesel fuel, banana, products* (x2)), industrial plant or processes (*power plant, solvent spinning operation*) and ambience (*environment*). The most common type of headword is product. *Eco-friendly* can in turn be modified by the intensifying adverb *more,* indicating that it is a quality.

Does the word or phrase typically appear as part of the subject, predicator, object, complement or adverbial in a clause?

If for the sake of argument we look mainly at the function of the phrase in which *eco-friendly* appears in the clause or subordinate clause, then we find the following results:

Subject of clause	Object	Complement	Adverbial
5	3	2	5

There is a fairly even distribution of phrases amongst the clause functions. In the subject position, people and things that are described as *eco-friendly* engage in actions (*embrace, enter, follow*), are described (*are a contradiction in terms*) and are subject to action in passive constructions (*are planned*). They also participate as objects in other clauses, in which they are *made* and *bought* (x2). Alternatively, things such as *ethanol* and *wine* are described as *eco-friendly,* and those things and people that are *eco-friendly* are present in different kinds of Adverbial (*about eco-friendly aliens, with eco-friendly coffins, in...eco-friendly countries, to an eco-friendly environment, by the eco-friendly solvent spinning operation*).

Does the word or phrase typically function as the head or modifier in a phrase?

In the overwhelming majority of instances (13 of the 15), *eco-friendly* is a modifier, preceding a noun. In two instances, it is the head of its own phrase, and once it is modified by *more.*

The above profile confirms – if confirmation were needed – that *eco-friendly* is an adjective that enters into particular kinds of relationship with nouns and adverbs – as we would expect from our discussion of adjectives earlier. However, the colligational profile tells us more than this – it shows the grammatical and semantic preferences in the use of the adjective: its use as a modifier rather than a headword, for example, or its extensive use with different kinds of products. This kind of information is particularly useful to dictionary-makers and learners of English as a foreign language.

TASK 4.21   Colligation

Eco-friendly is of course a fairly straightforward word, which yields sufficient examples to provide a quick and fairly rough analysis. Using the BNC data, you might wish to attempt a colligational profile of another word – a more frequent and variable one, like *baby*.

1. Go to the BYU-BNC at http://corpus.byu.edu/bnc/.
2. Search for the sequences 'baby [n*]' and 'baby [aj*]'. Your results will give you insights into the use of the word in phrases like *baby boom* and *baby fresh*.
3. Then search for '[n*] baby' and '[aj*] baby'. Your results will show you instances of *baby* as a headword.
4. Since there are over 8000 instances of *baby* in the BNC, take a sample of perhaps 100 instances, and track the use of phrases with *baby* as subject, predicator, object, complement and adverbial. One question that such an analysis would answer is how much *agency* babies tend to be given in Anglophone culture – do they tend to be the subject or the object of active clauses?

Verb systems

The verb phrase is the heart of the grammar of the clause. The other constituents (subject, object, complement, adverbial) are all related to the verb phrase. In this section, we turn our attention to the forms and meanings of the verb itself.

Grammarians talk about different verb systems when they attempt to relate the different forms of verb phrases to their meanings. Verb systems include tense and aspect (whereby the verb form usually changes to express meanings related to time and duration). Other verb systems include mood (the distinction between statements, questions and commands), modality (the use of modal auxiliaries to express concepts like possibility and obligation, e.g. *might work, should work*), voice (the distinction between active and passive uses, e.g. *he has remodelled the house, the house has been remodelled*) and finiteness (the capacity of the verb phrase to signal tense, as in *is/was working*, or not to signal tense, as in *working*). Here we will touch briefly on the use of corpora to explore two features of verb systems, namely, aspect and voice.

Verb aspect

The tense of the verb in English gives us a basic two-part distinction between present and past tense, with futurity being expressed by a variety of means including the modal auxiliaries *will/shall.* The combination of tense with aspect offers English speakers the option of expressing the occurrence of events in a fairly nuanced fashion with respect to time and duration (see Figure 4.2). For example, if I am referring to a habitual action that may or may not be happening at the moment of utterance, I can say *I work in a chemist's shop.* If I am referring to an action that *is* happening at the moment of utterance, and that has duration, I can say *I'm working right now, can you call back?* If I am referring to something that occurred at some unspecified point in the past, I can use the present perfect aspect to express it (e.g. *I've worked occasionally*). If I want to add the notion of duration to the sense of 'sometime in the past', I can say *I've been working on and off for years* (see Figure 4.2).

One of the features often taught to learners of English as a foreign language is that certain types of verb, namely, verbs of perception and affect, like *see* and *love* tend to be expressed using the simple aspect, even though the actions the verbs refer to have duration and may be happening at the moment of utterance. That is, learners are taught that *I see* is preferable to *I'm seeing,* and that *I love you* is preferable to *I'm loving you.*

A corpus can help us investigate exactly how these verbs behave with respect to tense and aspect. For example, we can run a search for 'see*' in the BNC, restricting the search to spoken data. First of all, we can note that the instances of *see* (14,270 as a verb) far outnumber the instances of *seeing* (614 as a participle or verbal noun). Many of the instances of *see* can be accounted for by the common discourse marker, *I see.* Even so, it is revealing to compare the uses of *see/seeing* in oral presentations, e.g.:

Here we **see** an advertisement for Eyesilmar make up.
So again we **see** a split in the er in in in amongst the great powers . . .
We **see** the creation of of of the confederation of the Rhine.

And we are **seeing** in eighteen thirty a significant gap . . .
But we are **seeing** a widening gap . . .
. . . what we're **seeing** here is oxygen being utilized by respiration . . .

	Present tense	**Past tense**
Simple aspect	I work	I worked
Continuous aspect	I am working	I was working
Perfect aspect	I have worked	I had worked
Perfect & continuous	I have been working	I had been working

Figure 4.2 Combination of tense and aspect

We can observe that there is an option in English to choose *either* the simple or continuous aspect in this kind of context – but there is a subtle change in meaning. The first group of utterances treat *see* as an uncontested *fact* – something has presented itself to our sight or our understanding. In the second set of utterances, the emphasis is on *seeing* as a *process* of perception or understanding – the process is what is at stake in these utterances, and it might be more easily contested than in the first group of utterances.

TASK 4.22   Verbs of perception in the simple and continuous aspect

1. Go to the BYU-BNC at http://corpus.byu.edu/bnc/.
2. Select *Spoken* from the box labelled *Register 1*.
3. In the word/phrase box, search in the spoken data for a verb of perception or affect, like *hear, love, feel, know*.
4. Consider the distribution of your chosen verb's uses in the simple and continuous aspects.
5. Then look more closely at the options in context, and consider if the choice of aspect changes the meaning of the utterance in any way.

Formal and informal passive constructions

O'Keeffe, McCarthy and Carter (2007, pp. 106–114) analyse and discuss the meanings of *be*-passives and the less formal *get*-passive, as in

> He was arrested.
> He got arrested.

They conclude that the *get*-passive is used more in informal contexts when 'speakers are marking attitude, most probably that attitude denoting concern, problematicity in some way, or, at the very least, noteworthiness of the event *as judged by the speaker*, beyond its simple fact of occurring' (ibid, pp. 113–114; emphasis in original).

Their observations can be tested by running a search on the spoken data in the BNC for *was *ed* and *got *ed* and comparing the 'neutrality' or otherwise of the speaker's stance in the results. Some of the results might support the suggestions made by O'Keeffe, McCarthy and Carter; in other cases the stance of the speaker using the informal *get*-passive is more difficult to gauge. Compare the following examples:

> My wedding wasn't an ordinary wedding, I **was married** on top of Arthur's Seat. . .
> I mean, my father **was killed** ten weeks after the war started.
> Yes, I **was involved** in the nineteen twenty six strike. . .

Er well there was none of them **got married** during the time that I was there. Er my biggest downfall was that the guy that employed me who was the eldest brother of the two that owned the company **got killed** in a bloody erm riding accident. . .

And eleven of them **got involved** in a fist fight in the middle of one of those New York streets.

Arguably, in the view of O'Keeffe, McCarthy and Carter, the use of the *get*-passive by the second group of speakers problematises the actions of being married, killed or involved more explicitly than does the use of the *be*-passive in the first, although in some instances the use of the *get*-passive simply signals that the event is 'noteworthy or of some significance to the speaker' (ibid, p. 111). An alternative theory is that, more explicitly than the *be*-passive, the *get*-passive assigns responsibility for the action to those affected by it. Thus, if the speaker says *I was involved in the 1926 strike,* the speaker's agency is not explicitly expressed; he or she might have been involved by accident. But if the speaker says *I got involved in the 1926 strike,* then his or her agency, or carelessness, is more explicitly expressed. If those affected by an action bear some of the responsibility for it, and the speaker expresses this, then the situations are probably more likely also to be those that problematise the action in question.

Data-driven grammar versus intuition

The general issues raised by the discussion of *be* and *get*-passives cast light on a key topic of debate amongst grammarians, namely, the value of using corpus data at all. Until the widespread availability of automatically searchable, digitised, language corpora, linguists had to rely for their observations on more limited language data, manually collected and analysed, or alternatively, they had to rely on intuition, their reflections on their own knowledge of language and their feelings about what is acceptable and unacceptable, and what particular constructions mean. The view that grammarians should rely on intuition was strengthened, from the 1950s on, by the prominent linguist Noam Chomsky's distinction between *competence*, an individual's knowledge about language, and *performance*, the spoken and written language that an individual actually produces (see Chomsky 1965). Chomsky made the description of competence, or knowledge of grammar, the goal of linguistic scholarship and played down the value of performance. For grammarians following in Chomsky's footsteps, intuition is the key to eliciting generalisations about language structure and to formulating rules that show the relationship between one structure and another. In generalising about the structures of language and the relationships between these structures, they attempt to model knowledge about grammar. Performance, as represented by corpora, plays little or no part in this project. Corpus grammarians, therefore, have had to engage in restating the value of analysing performance. They claim that the study of language data on a large scale brings to light structures and behaviour that are not available to intuition alone. At their most extreme, corpus linguists argue that their models of grammar are 'data-driven', that they emerge from a study of the language behaviour of thousands of people.

Given the proven insights that corpus data has given us into the behaviour of words and phrases, it is now difficult for any grammarian to dispense with the immensely powerful tools that corpora represent for the study of language. Performance is back on the linguistic agenda. However, it is an indisputable fact that data does not automatically give rise to theories that explain it; we still use our intuition to search corpora for features that we think might be interesting: we construct hypotheses based on our intuition or a partial analysis of the data, and we test those hypotheses against further data. There is therefore a continuous interaction between our intuitions and our data-based analyses. For example, the authors of this book, as people brought up in Scotland, might feel that the distribution and meanings of modal auxiliary verbs in the Scottish speech community vary from those that are current south of the border. We might feel on the basis of our intuitions about our own and our fellow Scots' practice that certain modals were avoided, others used and yet others had meanings particular to the Scottish community. We could then form a hypothesis based on our intuitions, test them against corpus data and refine them in the light of our findings.

Summary

The methodology of corpus-informed grammatical study involves, then, both intuition and data analysis, and the data itself does not guarantee the theory that attempts to explain it. Moreover, what the corpus grammarian hopes to achieve at the end of the day is an account of the linguistic behaviour of a community; such an account is as far from a model of *individual* knowledge of grammar as it is from the prescription of linguistic etiquette desired by commentators such as Dot Wordsworth. In the end, then, what intuition-led grammarians and corpus-informed grammarians are arguing about is not so much the validity of evidence, as the ultimate goals of grammatical study.

FURTHER READING

Biber, D., Conrad, S. and Reppen, R. (1998). *Corpus Linguistics: Investigating Language Structure and Use.* Cambridge: Cambridge University Press.

Biber, D., Finegan, E., Johansson, S., Conrad, S. and Leech, G. (1999). *The Longman Grammar of Spoken and Written English.* London: Longman.

Biber, D., Leech, G. and Conrad, S. (2002). *The Longman Student Grammar of Spoken and Written English: Workbook.* London: Longman.

Carter, R. and McCarthy, M. (2006). *Cambridge Grammar of English: A Comprehensive Guide to Spoken and Written English Grammar and Usage.* Cambridge: Cambridge University Press.

Hunston, S. and Francis, G. (2000). *Pattern Grammar: A Corpus-Driven Approach to the Lexical Grammar of English.* Amsterdam: John Benjamins.

Exploring Discourse with Corpora

5

Linguists organise language into different levels. For example, grammarians explore how individual words are formed and how different words are combined into phrases and sentences, while phonologists focus on the complexities of pronunciation. In each case, linguists look for patterns and systems in the midst of the everyday complexity of language use. So far in this book, we have looked at units of language smaller than the sentence and used corpora to allow us to see patterning in language at these levels. In this chapter, we turn from lexical items and grammatical constructions to consider the extent to which it is possible to study larger units of linguistic organisation, or *discourse*, through corpora. Discourse has been defined in very different ways over time, and within the context of various disciplines, so we shall begin by explaining what we mean by the term in the context of linguistics and corpora, before demonstrating the sorts of analyses that can be carried out with online corpora.

Some of the questions considered in this chapter are as follows:

- What is discourse?
- How can we obtain information about discourse from a corpus?
- What features characterise the discourse structure of spoken language? / What features characterise the discourse structure of written language?
- What are the strengths and limitations of using corpora to explore units of linguistic organisation above the sentence?

What is discourse?

The term 'discourse' has different meanings for different scholars. For some, discourse refers to particular ways of talking and writing in a given social context: they talk of the discourse of education, religion, the marketplace, politics and so on. These scholars explore the conventions of discourse within these contexts – what, for example, distinguishes a sermon from a political speech? What happens if a politician begins to adopt some of the conventions of a sermon into his or her speeches – or if a minister of religion begins to adopt practices more closely associated with politicians? Some scholars are interested in issues of power and inequality and how these are maintained and challenged through different kinds of communication. They explore, for example, the ways that politicians and political interviewers contest topics in broadcast discussions. These two concepts of discourse – discourse related to particular social domains and discourse as a means of maintaining and challenging power – influence linguists' understanding of discourse, and we shall return to them later in the chapter.

For many linguists, however, 'discourse' simply means the organisation of language above the level of the sentence. A crucial distinction is between speech and writing: some linguists restrict the term 'discourse' to the organisation of speech of different kinds, including conversational interaction. Spoken discourse is itself a major topic of linguistic exploration, and particular methods have been developed to study it, such as conversation analysis and pragmatics. Many linguists are equally interested in studying the nature of patterning above the sentence in written texts and consider this a legitimate aspect of discourse analysis too. Complementary methods of analysis have developed to deal with written discourse, such as the study of textual cohesion, clause relations and genre analysis. While it is fair to say that many of the techniques of analysis, such as the study of pragmatics or cohesion, can be applied both to spoken discourse and written text, the differences between certain types of speech and writing have meant that linguists tend to use some methods to analyse one channel of communication and other methods to analyse the other. Two brief excerpts from the SCOTS corpus illustrate why this might be. The first example is a conversation between four students, the second is an essay, originally handwritten, and written when its author was in her twenties.

Example 1   Conversation 16: Four students on memories and music festivals

F813: //Aw!// //I had this doll//
F814: //[laugh]//
F813: and you cranked up its arm and its hair grew, it went mmm
F814: //Aw yeah!//
M811: //[laugh]//
F814: //I remember them!//
F813: //And then you cranked it back up it went// mmm and back in and, like, you can make its hair grow longer.
F814: I just had loads of dolls that you filled them with water so they could pee. //[inaudible]//
M811: //[laugh]//
F813: //I had// //that, I had//
F814: //like, you just// just cause it was meant to be dead //natural so you fed her with a bottle then you just squeezed it and it peed. [laugh]//
M811: //[laugh]//

F812: //[laugh]//
F813: //[laugh]// What did you have?
M811: I had //He-Man was the best thing//

Example 2   'Where are the songs of spring?' by Christian Kay

When my American friends learned that I proposed to leave the clammy cosiness of central heating and return to Scotland in March, they were quite concerned.

'You'll freeze to death', they cried, picturing me wrapping my plaidie around me and struggling back to my comfortless clachan over the windswept moors.

Having spent the larger part of three Massachusetts winters surreptitiously turning off radiators and opening windows, I did not share their fears. 'When I get back, it will be spring', I boasted. With their minds full of sad tales of American tourists returning frozen from British summers, they seemed to think this small consolation.

Spurred on by such obvious scepticism, I held forth on the subtle delights of a Scottish spring, describing the gentle blossoming of tree and flower, the pale but cheerful sunshine, the fresh sweet smell of the awakening earth. In my ecstasies, I paused to pity them, for in New England spring scarcely exists.

It is clear from the above examples that speech and writing can be quite different. The conversation is interactive, spontaneous, characterised by false starts, overlaps, fillers (*like*), hesitations, non-verbal features such as laughter, indicators of vagueness (*loads of*) and exclamations (*aw yeah!*). The essay is monologic, organised into complete sentences and paragraphs characterised by consistency of topic. Compared to the conversation, the descriptive vocabulary in particular is rich in adjectives (*clammy cosiness, comfortless clachan, windswept moors, sad tales, small consolation, obvious scepticism, subtle delights, gentle blossoming, pale but cheerful sunshine, fresh sweet smell, awakening earth* versus *dead natural*). In lexis, grammar and – above all – discourse organisation, then, speech can be quite different from written English.

The examples given above, of course, are quite extreme. Features of spoken text can appear in some written texts, and vice versa. Email exchanges, for example, capture some of the interaction of spoken conversation. Example 3, an email exchange between two university professors (one being the author of the handwritten essay, some decades later) shows some features associated with speech, such as shorter sentences (often omitting subjects) and the conversational filler, *well*. One author also shifts into a mode of writing that imitates the sound of Scottish speech: *awrabest* ('all the best'). In general, too, the emails contain a high degree of content that a wider readership probably finds obscure: the authors were at the time working on a language awareness project financed by the Scottish Education Department and references to aspects of that project will be transparent to the email authors, while they remain opaque to those outside the correspondence.

Example 3   Email correspondence 1 – C Kay & J McGonigal

From: Christian

To: Jim

Subject: Re: welcome back?

Date sent: Tue, 24 Oct 2000 17:43:05 GMT

Dear Jim

Hope you had a nice break and are feeling refreshed. No doubt you are catching up on stirring times here.

The Language Games proved a doddle to scan, so I attach a copy for you to play with in your stray moments. Stylistics is done and semantics is on its way.

See you ere long, I expect.

Christian

Date sent: Wed, 08 Nov 2000 16:45:48 + 0000

Subject: Re: Various

To: Christian

Copies to: Jim

From: Jim

Hi Christian—

Well, I've been the silent one with marking deadlines for Monday and then being observed by HMI at my teaching for 4 hours today, and then another couple of hours discussion on what we think we are achieving! Not so bad, really, but tiring enough.

My contact in LATS is is a 'Development Fellow'—but working more on the writing and project side rather than the technical arm. I have phoned her just now and left a message for a contact.

This is for the production and marketing dimensions, sending out Envelopes and production of cds—is that correct? And possible later joint conference locally, bringing in some of their Scots stuff (grammar broonie etc—I mean, an a' that).

She'll phone me the morn's morn.

Awrabest—

Jim

While we can think about organisation of speech and writing as requiring different approaches to discourse analysis, then, it is best to think of the characteristics associated with one or other of the two modes of communication as forming the ends of a continuum. Written texts can sometimes move towards the end of the continuum associated with spoken utterances and vice versa. The corpus linguist Douglas Biber (e.g. Biber 1988) has shown that it can be misleading to polarise speech and writing, that is, to assume that all spoken language is more akin to other types of spoken language than it is to written language. Rather, some types of spoken language are similar in many respects to some types of written language – consider speeches which have typically been thoroughly prepared before being delivered, for example, such as presidential addresses or church sermons. However, when beginning an exploration of discourse in English, it can be useful to focus on speech and writing separately.

To sum up what we have covered so far, then, 'discourse' can be defined as that level of linguistic organisation that operates above the level of the sentence. Given the different characteristics of face-to-face spoken interaction, and considered written production, the methods of analysing this level of organisation differ as we move from an exploration of speech to an exploration of written texts. However, there are often areas of overlap, when someone will 'speak like a book' or someone will write in a colloquial manner. The exploration of linguistic organisation at the level of discourse is clearly sensitive to context, and scholars of discourse include people interested in the ways in which people use language to indicate membership of particular social groups (discourse communities), how people use particular genres of language to accomplish communicative goals within those social groups and how people use language to establish, maintain and resist relationships of power in and between those social groups.

Using corpora to explore discourse

The use of corpora in the exploration of discourse is still in its infancy, though Baker (2006) provides a useful introduction to various strategies. One issue facing corpus linguists is the sheer range of ways in which discourse analysts approach their data. For example, in the analysis of the organisation of speech and writing, researchers might focus on the following:

- The structure and management of conversational turns
- How particular words make explicit semantic relations across sentences
- The conventional 'moves' or 'stages' expected in particular text types
- The assumptions that participants refer to in order to make sense of utterances or sentences

Our first challenge as corpus analysts of discourse is therefore to decide (a) what kind of spoken or written exchanges we wish to analyse and (b) what kind of approach we wish to take to the analysis of those exchanges. Let us say for the sake of argument that we wish to analyse hesitation phenomena in conversational interaction, and we choose the spoken part of the BYU Corpus of Contemporary American English. At this point, two options present themselves. We can:

- Annotate the corpus
- Investigate discourse from a starting point of surface features of language

The first solution, annotating the corpus, would mean going through the spoken part of the corpus and adding a 'tag' every time a hesitation occurred, whether that hesitation is signalled by a pause, the repetition of a word or a non-verbal filler like *uh, ehm*. However, this solution is not practical for most online corpora analysed through integrated search tools, although it may be an option for a home-made corpus, or one that can be downloaded and manipulated. The Advanced Search facility of the SCOTS corpus, for example, allows you to select documents and download them (permissions have been cleared for all texts for educational use). You can then annotate them as required.

TASK 5.1   Downloading documents for annotation

1. Go to the SCOTS corpus at www.scottishcorpus.ac.uk
2. Click on Advanced Search
3. Scroll down the page. You will see a full list of spoken and written documents in the SCOTS corpus. On the left-hand side of each title, there is a box that can be ticked to select items for download. Select two or three items, scroll down to the bottom of the page, and click 'Bulk Download'. (Note that you can vary the criteria for selection on the Advanced Search page to focus on particular types of text: for example, you can choose to select from spoken documents only, written documents only, documents composed in a particular decade and so on.)
4. The documents you have selected will then be downloaded as a zip file to a folder of your choice. When you open the zip file, you will see various files, including 'Plain Text' files that can be opened and their contents annotated.

Annotation involves adding information to a corpus so that features which lie below the surface of language, like hesitation, can be found by automatic means. POS tagging is common, but other forms of tagging, such as semantic tagging, prosodic tagging and discourse tagging are rare, partly because there are many possible ways of tagging such features, and automating the tagging process is far from straightforward. To tag for something like hesitation phenomena you would have first to decide that it was important, secondly figure out the surface phenomena which identify hesitation, thirdly be confident that your corpus allows you to identify something like a significant pause, and then either go through the corpus and tag it manually or devise a computer program to tag the phenomena that you had identified as relevant to your study.

This is no mean challenge, and, consequently, discourse tagging is not available in any existing online corpora of which we are aware.

The second solution, starting from the surface features of the language, provides a much more straightforward starting point for the study of discourse through corpora and is the one which the tasks and examples in the remainder of the chapter adopt. This solution involves using surface features of language, such as lexical items, as a starting point for the study of discourse. While this does necessarily limit what it is possible to do, with a little ingenuity, we can still go quite a long way.

For example, rather than annotating a corpus for hesitation phenomena, we might consider the use in spoken discourse of the two surface markers *ah* and *erm*. These are clearly features of conversational interaction; however, they are neither words nor grammatical items. Does their patterning in spoken discourse suggest anything about their function?

TASK 5.2   Exploring discourse markers

1. Go to the BYU-BNC at http://corpus.byu.edu/bnc/.
2. Click on 'Compare Words' and type 'ah' and 'erm' in the two 'Word(s)' boxes.
3. Click on 'Search'.
4. Look at the kinds of words that frequently combine with *ah* and *erm*. What patterns can you find in their use?

As the discussions in this book often demonstrate, raw statistics in corpus searches need to be approached with caution (see Chapter 2 for more on interpreting corpus statistics). However, the results for *ah* and *erm* are suggestive of their use in discourse. To begin with, *ah* appears in the BNC less frequently than *erm*: only 13.5 per cent of the instances are of *ah*, while the remaining 86.5 per cent of instances are of *erm*. Secondly, *ah* collocates more frequently with verbs like *nodded* and *smiled*, at least in reported speech as it is represented in prose fiction. Typical instances, then, include:

The Doctor **nodded**. "**Ah**," he said hurriedly.
"**Ah** yes." Myles **smiled**.

Though it appears in other contexts too, one possible function of *ah* is clearly to signal agreement, or a positive stance towards the matter being discussed. This is not the case with *erm*. Its most frequent collocates are nouns, like *government, flats, points, settlement*. Typical incidences include these, from discussion genres:

the **Government**, unlike your **erm** Local District Council
Well **erm** it was actually **erm** trying to **erm** eliminate **erm** the **erm** dangers of the war

Here *erm* is much more evidently a hesitation phenomenon, indicating that the speaker is trying to be precise about the exact phrase to use and is

Table 5.1   Discourse markers

Discourse markers	Typical function
Hey; listen; look. . .	Focusing attention
Well. . .	Shifting the expected direction of the discourse; or signalling a response that might not have been anticipated
So; anyway; oh yeah	Resuming an interrupted or diverted topic

Source: Based on Carter and McCarthy (2006, pp. 219–220)

pausing and 'filling' the silence while he or she comes up with the desired wording.

One possible use of corpora, then, is to bring together a range of surface markers and allow analysts to sift through the many examples in order to identify patterns of usage. Certain discourse markers function to 'organise the talk and monitor its progress' (O'Keeffe, McCarthy and Carter 2007, p. 39), that is to say that they have little semantic weight and convey little *ideational* meaning, that is, information content, and instead have a strongly *textual* function. They include some of the most common expressions in spoken language: O'Keeffe, McCarthy and Carter (ibid, p. 39) list *you know, I mean, right, well, so, good, anyway* as all occurring among the most frequent words (or two-word expressions) in spoken text. The authors of the *Cambridge Grammar of English* have analysed the CANCODE corpus to arrive at a number of features more commonly associated with spoken discourse than with grammar *per se*. For example, they associate discourse markers with typical functions, as in Table 5.1.

These and other surface discourse markers can be explored by sifting through the vast amount of data that corpora can provide us with.

TASK 5.3   Discourse markers in speech and writing

Compare the frequency and use of *hey, listen, look, well, so, anyway, oh yeah* across the different textual registers available in the BYU-BNC and Corpus of Contemporary American English. You can do this by entering, for example, *oh yeah* as a search string, displaying the results as a chart and then choosing to 'Show all sections' on the resulting chart. In which register is the expression most frequent? Is the expression most frequent in spoken or written genres as a whole? In what registers does it not occur at all? Look at examples of these registers and try to explain why this is, in linguistic and non-linguistic terms.

As we have seen in this section, corpora allow us to investigate patterns and tendencies in language. However, because they can be used for many different ends, corpora are many things to many people. For example, a corpus may be used as follows:

- a repository of whole texts and/or excerpts
- a source of comparative data
- a representative body of texts for analysis as a whole

Let us consider these in turn.

A repository of whole texts and/or excerpts

First, a corpus may be used in a straightforward fashion as a repository of a variety of texts. It can be a good source of data which is otherwise difficult to obtain, particularly, but not limited to, spoken language. For example, you might be interested in the language of courtrooms but not be able to access such texts, or you might want to compare the English spoken in New Zealand with that spoken in Scotland but not be able to travel to carry out fieldwork. In these situations, you can turn to a ready-made collection, a corpus, for such data and benefit from material collected by other researchers. The role of the corpus in such scenarios is essentially that of a text archive.

In one respect in particular, some newer online corpora have an advantage over some of the earlier ones as far as discourse analysis is concerned. Most corpora nowadays adopt a whole-text policy as standard, that is, corpus builders consider it preferable for corpora to contain complete texts rather than extracts. This has not always been the case: the Brown Corpus, which was first made available in 1964 and contains texts published three years earlier, as well as later corpora which have mirrored its size and composition for comparative purposes, all contain 2000-word samples from each of 500 texts. The various national corpora which form the International Corpus of English (ICE) also contain 500 texts of 2000 words each, and some samples are composite, that is, they are made up of more than one short text. A design like this makes it more straightforward to control the relative sizes of different textual genres within the corpus, which is particularly important when comparability across corpora is crucial. However, while the design of ICE and Brown is neat, its value is more limited for research into features of discourse, which emerge from, or have an effect on, the complete text. Besides, advances in technology and more affordable computer hardware mean that corpus builders are no longer tightly restricted by computer memory capabilities and processing power.

While many online corpora have adopted a whole-text policy in their design, it is not always possible for reasons of copyright for the complete texts to be accessible through the online version of the corpus. This is a particular issue for corpora containing texts produced in the recent past, and is the case, for example, with the BNC, although whole texts are accessible with the commercially available version. The BNC adopted a general policy of including shorter texts in their entirety, but selected 45,000-word extracts of longer texts, so a study of discourse must exercise some caution. The Corpus of Contemporary American English contains nearly 150,000 texts; however, as with the BNC, through its own site and through the BYU-BNC interface, for copyright reasons only small extracts can be viewed online. Generally speaking, the SCOTS corpus and the MICASE corpus are exceptions from this tendency as they were intended from the outset to be freely available on the internet, and so full copyright permissions for texts were obtained at the time of creating the corpus. Even so, for a few texts, such as published novels, the SCOTS corpus includes only selected chapters rather than the entire text.

TASK 5.4 Sequencers in whole texts/excerpts

1. Go to an online corpus that allows you to view texts in their entirety, e.g. MICASE or SCOTS.
2. Search for a series of words that organise the sequence of information in a text, e.g. *first, firstly, first of all, in the first place, for a start, what's more, besides, on top of that, in addition, to sum up, in sum, finally, to conclude.*
3. For each word, indicate if it appears in the first third, second third or final third of the text.
4. Repeat your search using an online corpus in which you can only view partial context, e.g. the BYU-BNC, Corpus of Contemporary American English or TIME corpus.
5. Can you identify in which part of the text the search item occurs?

From the results of your searches, how important do you think it is to have whole or partial texts available to the corpus explorer?

A source of comparative data

Secondly, a corpus may provide a source of comparative data, that is, it may act as a background against which to analyse the language of a single text, extract or genre. A researcher who finds a particular word, grammatical construction, or pattern of interaction in a small language sample (such as a recording of a family conversation, a newspaper article, a lecture) can then turn to a corpus to see whether the word or construction is common, whether it tends to be used by a particular sort of person or whether it is being used in an unusual way in the smaller sample. In this case, a corpus is being used as a more or less representative sample to give a general picture of language use, against which the typicality of smaller amounts of data can be assessed.

A representative body of texts

However, the most typical use of a corpus, and the use generally intended by the term corpus linguistics, involves the use of the corpus as a representative sample of texts to find out about language, often by doing some sort of quantitative or statistical analysis. What we are doing in this case, therefore, is using the corpus (a body of naturally occurring language data on computer), and the methods of corpus analysis (using computer software to manipulate the data in various ways), to look at patterns in the data, which in turn allow us to understand how language is structured, at all levels.

TASK 5.5   Tag questions

The following examples of tag questions all come from recordings made in the north-east of Scotland contained in the SCOTS corpus:

1. You were playing Play-Doh today, were you?
2. It's not really broken, is it?
3. You need your towel to get dry, don't you?
4. It's a birdie, up in that nest, is it?

Fit these examples into the following table, according to whether the main part of the sentence (the *anchor*) and the tag question (in these cases made up of an auxiliary plus pronoun) are positive or negative:

	Tag question +	Tag question −
Anchor +		
Anchor −		

Which pattern do you think is most common? Use the SCOTS corpus to carry out a small quantitative study, selecting one form of the tag question and its polar opposite (e.g. *are you?* and *aren't you?, does she?* and *doesn't she?*).

Can you find any examples of negative anchors followed by negative tag questions? Try using the BYU-BNC, the Corpus of Contemporary American English, and WebCorp.

Take a sample of examples of tag questions from another online corpus. Can you find tag questions of each type from the table above? In each case, what does the tag question contribute to the discourse it is part of? Does it function to express the speaker's opinions; to seek confirmation; to prompt another speaker; to challenge; to emphasise?

For a detailed corpus study of tag questions, see Tottie and Hoffman (2006).

Analysing spoken discourse

It will be clear from this chapter so far that patterns of organisation in spoken and written text vary considerably. Patterns of discourse organisation in speech are typically much less clearly defined than those at lower levels, such as phrase and sentence grammar; nonetheless various types of patterns can be found. Even in spontaneous conversation, some predictable patterns occur, as suggested by Gadamer (2003, p. 383):

> We say that we 'conduct' a conversation, but the more genuine a conversation is, the less its conduct lies within the will of either partner. [. . .] The way one word follows another, with the conversation taking its own twists and reaching its own conclusion, may well be conducted in some way, but the partners conversing are far less the leaders of it than the led.

Gadamer is talking here about the way in which language enables us to come to an understanding with other people, but the observation is also very relevant to the study of the forms which spoken discourse takes. The way in which one word follows another in conversation, and the processes of turn-taking between participants in a conversation, are just two of the concerns of discourse analysis.

Adjacency pairs

This predictability in spoken discourse is at its most extreme in the case of *adjacency pairs* (see for example Stenström 1994; Levinson 1983). Adjacency pairs are mutually relevant turns which are normally found together in discourse: for example a question is typically followed by a response; an offer is typically followed by an acceptance or refusal of that offer. Consider the following exchange, between a mother (F1103) and her young daughter (F1104) in the north-east of Scotland (n.b. *moo* is a Scots form of *mouth*):

> F1103: Ah! Dinna even think aboot pittin that in your moo. I saw you just
> noo, didn't I? You're nae gonna dae that again, are ye? No.
> F1104: I'm sorry Mum.
> F1103: Aye, that's okay, just dinna do it again. I telt ye nae to eat your toys.
> [SCOTS document 1629]

Stripped down, this exchange consists of a reprimand (quite a complex one made up of an interjection, a command and two questions, one of which is answered by the mother herself), followed by a common adjacency pair of an apology (*I'm sorry Mum*) and a 'smoother', that is, an acceptance of the apology (*Aye, that's okay, just dinna do it again*). Task 5.6 asks you to think about other common types of exchange where we are conditioned to expect a particular type of response.

In actual examples of interaction, it is clear that some discourse sequences like adjacency pairs can be more complicated than the simple table in this task suggests. For example, this Question/Answer sequence from the MICASE corpus falls somewhere in between a preferred and dispreferred response:

> S1: yeah well what i'm trying well yeah (xx) th- what happened is that in
> Castilian and only in Castilian, what was the /f/ in Latin, or what is
> believed to have been a /f/ in Latin, cuz i'm gonna have to sort of
> uh, nuance a little later something i'm saying, but what traditionally is
> believed to be an F sound in Latin a /f/ sound, in other words a labioden-
> tal fricative, as Castilian evolved, that /f/ became a /x/. alright? whereas
> in all the other varieties of Romance that didn't occur.
> S2: how do you know that that's the case or that maybe they were using, um
> a letter which we used for something else to represent, the labiodental,
> fricative?
> S1: because we have the living evidence of all the other Romance languages.
> moreover the fact the other point is cuz here i'm giving you just lim-
> ited data, uh there are lots of exceptions to this rule. okay there are a

numb- there, are a fair number of exceptions. okay? **i'm afraid** to really answer your question thoroughly i would have to go off on such a tangent, it would lead us much too far afield your question is perfectly legitimate and i don't want to give you the impression i'm just trying to deke it or duck it rather, so if you want to discuss it with me further i'd be more than happy but i don't want to take up class time with that okay? [S2: okay]
[MICASE Transcript ID LES355SU009]

Here S2 asks a question that S1 answers before acknowledging that the answer is an inadequate one. The discourse marker *I'm afraid* signals the speaker's acknowledgement that the answer to the question is not a sufficient one and that there is no time available to offer a detailed and adequate response. Instead the sequence moves into another adjacency pair, an offer (*if you want to discuss it with me further i'd be more than happy but i don't want to take up class time with that okay?*) which S2 follows with a preferred response, acceptance (*okay*).

TASK 5.6   Adjacency pairs

1. What sort of response do you expect to follow the utterances below? Think about the response you expect and then search in a corpus which includes spoken language (for example MICASE, the BYU-BNC, Corpus of Contemporary American English, SCOTS) to find examples where these expressions or similar ones are the first part of an adjacency pair. Can you identify both preferred and dispreferred responses? What happens in the discourse when the response given is different from the preferred response?

		Preferred response	Dispreferred response
Hello!	Greeting	Greeting	No greeting
Can you help me?	Request	Compliance	Non-compliance
How are you?	Question	Answer	No answer
Cup of tea?	Offer	Acceptance	Refusal
I like your shoes.	Compliment	Acceptance	Downgrade

2. Some discourse markers are associated with dispreferred responses. Search for examples of *I'm afraid* in the spoken section of an online corpus and investigate how many types of adjacency pairs it appears in.

Pragmatic meaning

One approach to the study of spoken discourse, as we have seen, involves looking at units of language larger than the single utterance, such as adjacency pairs.

A complementary approach derives from pragmatics, or the study of speaker meaning, a discipline that grew out of semantics, the study of word and sentence meaning. Adolphs notes (2006, p. 119): 'The areas of pragmatics and discourse analysis have traditionally focused on short extracts of texts, rather than on extracting patterns from multi-million word corpora'. This is partly because speaker meaning is very closely connected with the particular context in which an utterance takes place: so again we need to find an entry point into a corpus from a surface feature of language, that is to say a place where speaker meaning and the non-literal use of a lexical item go hand in hand.

This is the case, for example, with the familiar Scots word *wee*, which means *small*. In this first set of examples below, we can read *wee* literally, to indicate small size.

tripping ower a ginger cat an a **wee** spaniel dog
naebody's goin to get rich oot o **wee** books o poems
that sonsie sorta face that **wee** babies have in their pram
There's enough public spirit in this **wee** community.
But I had a **wee** flash-licht in my pocket.

Compare these with the second set of examples, below, again from the SCOTS corpus. Here it is difficult to interpret *wee* purely literally. This fact suggests that the speaker is using *wee* to indicate some other kind of non-literal meaning and that the speaker is using the expression to manage a relationship with the hearer or hearers. Consider these examples, and reflect on the impact that the use of *wee* might have on the relationship between speakers and hearers.

While he's snoring, ah huv a **wee** can.
You huv a **wee** seat, hen.
I mean, ring a bell or somethin, gie a **wee** cough.
I'm down the pub the night, couple of gills and a **wee** shufty at the talent.
She was gorgeous, she was like a **wee** Shirley Temple, only blonde
Oh, that's a **wee** shame.
You can help wi some o the **wee** particularities

It should be apparent that *wee* here creates a sense of intimacy among speakers (see further Douglas and Corbett 2006). Commenting that something which has happened is a *wee shame* rather than just a *shame* shows the speaker's genuine concern by reducing the social distance between speaker and hearer. Offering someone a *wee seat*, especially in combination with the familiar *hen*, shows the speaker's kindness. By suggesting that the time spent sitting will be small, the expression also functions to maintain the speaker's *face*, that is his or her interpersonal image, and, conversely, for the speaker to help the hearer maintain his or her self image (see for example Brown and Levinson 1987). Compare the difference between asking someone to *ring a bell or something, gie a wee cough*, rather than *ring a bell or cough*. The latter is a very blunt order, whereas the former wording serves to lessen the imposition of the order. And in the case of the last example above, reducing the apparent burden of *helping with particularities* allows the speaker not to impose too much on the hearer's generosity.

This interpretation, that *wee* adds a connotation of familiarity or intimacy, is supported by the fact that it often occurs alongside another adjective meaning *small*. Consider these examples:

> His complexion revealed the beers he usually drank from mid-
> morning until the **wee small** hours.
> Oh there'd be a **tiny wee** sort of kitchen area.
> **Wee totty** chihuahuas that'll fit in your pocket
> she aye yaised tae jump at the **least wee** noise
> oh, this is a **little wee baby** ain!
> keep it on for another **little wee** while.

If these near-synonyms conveyed only literal meaning, the use of more than one in sequence would be redundant. The use of several together suggests that different kinds of meaning are being signalled.

TASK 5.7   Speaker meaning: intensifying adverbs in speech

The following short passage is taken from an informal conversation in the SCOTS corpus, between two young females who live in Glasgow. They are talking about weddings and specifically here about the custom of collecting money at the bride's hen night.

F689: //[laugh] Just go about, just **totally**// blaggin it, //intae like pubs an clubs,//
F631: //[laugh] No!//
F689: with buckets, saying "Right, I'm getting married, give us cash, give generously," //and all that.//
F631: //Right.// Oh, I'm gonna be even more suspicious of it now. I just think, I mean you can **totally** see why people would have done it long ago, you know, when //people//
F689: //Mmhm//
F631: like wouldn't have had any money an //needed money to sort//
F689: //I know.//
F631: o set themselves up, but, ehm, sometimes when you're out, you know, you see groups of women goin around and they're all **totally** dressed to the nines and they're sort of asking for money from me in my sort of scruffy //jeans and [laugh] I think "No, you've//
F689: //[laugh]//
F631: probably got more than I do,"
        [SCOTS document 1384]

Look at these speakers' use of the adverb *totally* (highlighted in the passage). What does *totally* mean here? In other words, what does it add to the utterance? How

⇨

TASK 5.7   (Continued)

does this usage compare to the meaning of *totally* in the following examples, also drawn from the SCOTS corpus?

- But there are words that mean **totally** different things. [SCOTS document 1428]
- the running of the health service is **totally** devolved to the Scottish Executive [SCOTS document 1129]
- he's erm an obsessive who gets **totally** involved in a case, makes him a very good cop [SCOTS document 1383]

Explore the spoken sections of several online corpora, such as the BNC, Corpus of Contemporary American English, MICASE and SCOTS, to see the different ways in which *totally* is used. Can you identify examples similar to those in the passage above? What patterns of usage can you spot?

Try the same search with other intensifying adverbs, such as *utterly, definitely, completely*.

Analysing written discourse

Linguists who have been interested in spoken discourse have concentrated much of their attention on the micro-management of conversational interaction; that is, how adjacency pairs contribute to the conversation, how turns are organised, how particular pragmatic markers indicate the stance that the speaker is taking with respect to the hearer(s). In contrast, linguists who have been interested in written discourse analysis have been more concerned with how writers give explicit signals that their sentences combine to form a coherent text, rather than, say, a series of disconnected propositions. The claim that sentences are organised into coherent texts seems almost too obvious to require elaboration: we recognise odd-sounding sequences, we can finish other people's sentences, distinguish between an unordered list of sentences and a text, and we can recognise texts as belonging to particular genres or isolated extracts as being, for example, an introduction or a conclusion to a longer text.

The signals of the connectedness (as opposed to the randomness) of texts are various. In a classic study, Halliday and Hasan (1976) identified various 'cohesive ties' that contribute to what they called the 'texture' of written discourse. These cohesive ties include the following:

- the ways that pronouns and other referring expressions link one part of a text to the next
- substitutions and ellipses that stand in for and presuppose the existence of content elsewhere in a text
- conjunctions and connecting adverbs such as *because, if, although, however, otherwise*, etc., that signal semantic relations such as cause-result, condition-consequence, statement-qualification and so on

- patterning of vocabulary according to semantic relationships such as synonymy, antonymy and hyponymy (that is, the relationship between co-members of any given category, such as *knife, fork* and *spoon*).

While the presence of cohesive signals does not guarantee that sentences will combine into a coherent text, cohesive ties give the reader a strong steer as to how to interpret a written text.

TASK 5.8   Text cohesion and coherence

Below you will see all the sentences from a short letter in the SCOTS corpus, jumbled up and numbered. Try to put them in their original order.

Dear Joan and Arthur

1. Carole's parents will be coming and us yins [ones] that's about all.
2. My wee budgie died, I fairly miss him.
3. Its on the 16th March at 10.45 a quiet affair, and a wee tea in their house later on.
4. Jimmy is redundant.
5. How are you both keeping.
6. Just a wee note to say that Willie would like you, if you could, to come to his wedding.
7. I heard on T.V. that they caught the rascal who was stabbing the people in your district.
8. It's been a terrible winter.
9. Well, that's all my news.
10. I have had flu, better now.
11. See you soon if you can manage.
12. Isa's not too well with her asthma.
13. Hope they put him away for a long time.
14. I have not been able to see Peggy & family for 3 weeks but maybe I'll get there this week.
15. Arthur will not be getting about on his bike much.
16. All the rest are fine.

Cheers for now,
Chrissie

You can check the original order by going to the SCOTS corpus at www.scottishcorpus.ac.uk and searching for the Biggam Collection Letter: 16. Even if you did not reproduce the original sequence exactly, it is likely that you produced a text that was fairly close or at least made sense on its own terms.

Now think about how you managed to put the sixteen sentences in a coherent order. What features of the language gave clues to the order (all features contributing to the *cohesion* of the text)? Think about the development of the information presented (the *coherence* of the text).

There are some sequences of sentences in the letter used in Task 5.8 that will have been signalled by the reference between a pronoun and a likely noun phrase, for instance: *I heard on T.V. that they caught **the rascal who was stabbing the people in your district***. *I hope they put **him** away for a long time.* Other sequences will have been signalled by the later sentence's dependence on information explicitly expressed in an earlier sentence: *Just a wee note to say that Willie would like you, if you could, to come **to his wedding**. Carole's parents will be coming [**to his wedding**] and us yins that's about all.* As a whole, the letter is partly tied together by a network of lexis relating to health and illness: *asthma, flu, died, fine, how are you keeping?*

As noted above, a corpus can act as a repository for a wealth of everyday texts such as this one, and they can be analysed on a text-by-text basis. However, some of the features noted above are difficult to search for automatically across different texts. Searches for pronouns, for example, will not tell the searcher what noun phrase they relate to. And it is impossible to search for elided elements such as *to his wedding* in sentence six of the jumbled up letter.

Two aspects of textual cohesion do lay themselves more readily open to corpus searches online – conjunctive and lexical cohesion. In the first case, we can look at the way that a set of lexical markers such as conjunctions and adverbs signal the relationship between clauses and sentences. In the second we can look at ways in which networks of words are systematically patterned in a text.

Conjunctive cohesion

Halliday and Hasan (1976) identified two grammatical classes of word that have the discourse function of signalling different types of semantic relationship between stretches of text. Conjunctions proper always appear at the start of a subordinate clause; conjunctive adverbs often appear in the same position, but are generally more mobile, appearing in the middle or at the end of clauses, as a concordance search on the conjunction *if* and the adverb *nevertheless* in SCOTS quickly demonstrates:

I'm in for a sleepless night	**if** I can't creep closer to Fiona
We all need her sleep	**if** she's to be herself in the morning
this prison, of fragrant fresh air	**if** I may say so
I just feel happier	**if** you have me as an escort

Nevertheless, questions arise.

It has to be asked, **nevertheless**, if such long-term sufferers are best

The village was **nevertheless** bordered by a large tourist market

Winter (1977, 1994), in work developed by Jordan (1984), Tadros (1985) and Hoey (1983, 1991, 2005), latterly with reference to corpus data, introduced the notion of what he called 'vocabulary 3', that is lexical items such as nouns and verbs that performed signalling functions in discourse. A noun that sometimes performs a similar discourse signalling function to *because* would be *consequence*, as in the following excerpt from the written record of a debate from the Scottish Parliament:

> I also apologise for my short absence earlier. That was a **consequence** of a weak bladder – something that is not confined to the old.

Winter and his followers argue that the vocabulary 3 item *consequence* explicitly signals the semantic relationship between the second sentence and the first, a discourse function that might equally be performed by a conjunction and rephrased as: *I also apologise for my short absence earlier **because** I suffer from a weak bladder, something that is not confined to the old.*

One issue that arises when we look at text in bulk is how vocabulary 3 items actually work in large quantities of text. We can explore this question by looking, for example, at a verb like *assume* that sometimes functions as a vocabulary 3 item, signalling a semantic relationship of 'hypothesis + affirmation/denial'.

TASK 5.9   Lexical signals

1. Go to the SCOTS corpus at www.scottishcorpus.ac.uk.
2. Click on Advanced Search.
3. Click on General.
4. Choose Document details.
5. Choose Spoken or Written.
6. Choose Written and click on General again.
7. Choose: Word search, and Word or phrase (concordance).
8. Type in 'assume*', using an asterisk as a wildcard character.
9. Scroll down the page and examine the concordance.
10. Click on a key word to see the full text around the word.
11. Decide whether the verb *assume* functions as a vocabulary 3 item or not.

Not all of the instances of *assume* fall into a pattern of 'hypothesis + affirmation/denial'. Some occurrences, for example, are synonymous with 'took upon himself' as in 'he assumed power'. However, many examples do signal a semantic relationship that organises part of the written discourse, as in this excerpt from *The Loss of the Princess Victoria*, an account of a tragedy that struck a Scottish-Irish ferry in 1953, resulting in 133 deaths:

> The coastguard officers organising the search **assumed** from that statement that the Victoria had lost all engine power and was drifting before the north-westerly gale down onto the Wigtownshire coast between Corsewall Point and Portpatrick. Consequently the two rescue ships involved were directed to the ship's last stated position off Corsewall Point, the lighthouse keepers at Corsewall and Killantringan were asked to look out for her, and preparations

were made to receive survivors on shore. **In fact** the ship was heading at approximately five knots for the Irish coast, every turn of her screws taking her away from the area where the rescuers were converging, towards a coast where ships and lifeboats were available or, indeed, at sea but no one was expecting her. [SCOTS document 1372]

In this instance, the use of *assumed* in one sentence sets up the expectation that the assumption will be affirmed or denied later in the text. The assumption is denied, with the denial signalled by *in fact*. By sifting through the examples of *assume** in the corpus, we can begin to build up a set of lexical signals that signal the semantic relations between different parts of text:

Hypothesis   +   Affirmation   or   Denial

assume   *in fact*

Another way of building up an inventory of vocabulary 3 items to explore further is to use the synonym-finding facility provided by the BYU-BNC, or the Corpus of Contemporary American English. This facility refers to a thesaurus to suggest the distribution of synonyms of a term across different registers. So, for example, we can explore how synonyms of *assume* are distributed in speech and different written registers.

TASK 5.10   Finding synonyms in the BYU-BNC

1. Go to the BYU-BNC at http://corpus.byu.edu/bnc/.
2. Type 'assume' in the Word(s) box.
3. Choose SPOKEN for Section 1 and ACADEMIC for Section 2.
4. The results show the frequency of synonyms for *assume* in the spoken part of the BNC and in the academic written part. There is little difference between them, with *think, accept, believe* in the top five in each register.
5. Redo the previous task, with 'think*', 'accept*' or 'believe*' as the search item in turn. From the results, consider whether these partial synonyms can also work as lexical signals of 'hypothesis + affirmation/denial'. If so, modify your table of lexical signals accordingly.

These tasks, involving signals such as conjunctions, connective adverbs and those lexical signals that also help organise text, aid us in a qualitative exploration of how written texts are structured. They give us insights into the formal structure of written texts. However, other researchers are interested in the ways one text alludes to or even is 'colonised' by another set of texts. This kind of issue considers how texts exist in a network of relations that indicate cultural common ground and shifting power relations.

Intertextuality

Intertextuality is the study of the relationship between texts. The relationship between one set of texts and another is one aspect of their meaning. As Bazerman (2004, p. 94) observes:

> ...intertextuality is not just a matter of which other texts you refer to but how you use them, what you use them for, and ultimately how you position yourself as a writer to them to make your own statement. People can develop adeptly complex and subtly skilled ways of building on the words of others. Such complex intertextual performances are so familiar we hardly notice them.

We can begin to pay attention to intertextuality by looking at allusions to famous quotations in large corpora. Shakespearean quotations, for example, can lend authority to a text and present the writer or speaker as someone who commands cultural capital. This occurs in an article in *TIME* magazine from the 1970s, reporting on the Watergate scandal, which appears in the TIME Corpus:

> Sloan led the reporters onto the fact that funds for the burglary came from C.R.P. Among other sources who pepper the book's pages with their tips: "the Bookkeeper," a conscience-stricken woman who served C.R.P.'s finance chairman, Maurice Stans. **Something is rotten in Denmark** and I'm part of it," she tremblingly warned Bernstein in her home one night a few weeks after the breakin. [*TIME Magazine*, "Woodstein" Meets "Deep Throat", 22/04/1974]

The allusion to *Hamlet* is a complex one: it grandly aligns the corruption at the heart of the American government with the corruption in King Claudius' Elsinore. It also presents 'the Bookkeeper' as someone who, although tainted by this corruption, has a cultured perspective on the world and an anguished self-knowledge. Finally, the *TIME* article treats its readership as an equally cultured group that will recognise the allusion to a canonical literary text.

Often, as in Task 5.11, adopting an iterative approach can be very productive. Iteration involves carrying out a procedure repeatedly, each time modifying the query based on information obtained in the previous attempt, that is in response to 'feedback'. With the first example in the task above, *all is for the best in the best of all possible worlds*, it is likely that you adopted an iterative approach to find the most appropriate part of the quotation to search for. The whole quotation, in the form given in the task above, does not actually occur in the TIME corpus (at least at the time of writing), and, unlike the other examples, the individual words in the quotation are all highly frequent, so it is difficult to tell in advance which parts of it are most likely to occur in instances of intertextual reference. An iterative approach allows you to narrow the search, in order to locate as many of the instances of the allusion as possible, while minimising the effort needed to manually discard instances of the surface form which do not allude to Voltaire's *Candide* (or the formulation by the German philosopher Leibniz to whom Voltaire himself was alluding). In terms borrowed from information technology, gradually refining the query allows you to maximise both *recall* (the number of examples found) and *precision* (the number of relevant examples).

TASK 5.11   Intertextuality

Intertextuality involves discourse patterning above the level of the text, specifically *between* texts. Use the online TIME corpus, at http://corpus.byu.edu/time/, to find examples of the following quotations being used as intertextual allusions. [Tip: not all allusions will repeat the full expression, so you will find more results if you search for parts of the quotations and also variations on them.]

- all is for the best in the best of all possible worlds
- it is a truth universally acknowledged
- it was the best of times, it was the worst of times
- something rotten in the state of Denmark

In each case, what does the use of the allusion add to the text in which it occurs? How easy is it to identify the original source of the quotation? How often is the intertextual nature of the sequence made explicit? Do you notice a change in usage over time? Think of further intertextual references of your own.

Pick out a few examples of each and explain what the intertextual allusion contributes to the text or sentence in which it occurs.

Summary

A corpus approach to discourse offers a complementary approach to traditional discourse analysis. It cannot replace the detailed, qualitative analysis of single texts and individual genres, whether spoken or written, but it does offer new possibilities and a new perspective on large-scale patterning in texts. A caveat, however, is that while a corpus can point to patterns in discourse, these remain to be interpreted by the linguist. What is the significance of a particular finding? Is it fair to generalise from a sample of texts to a genre as a whole? A corpus will show a (small) sample of what has occurred in language, but cannot show what it means nor what does not occur.

Corpora allow us to build up a larger and more nuanced picture of patterns and exceptions in language, which only become evident in looking at large quantities of data. This is true not just of discourse patterns but also of patterns of lexis, grammar and so on. General corpora allow us to see a linguistic background against which isolated examples can be analysed and understood and to determine what are the features of the structure of a text which make it recognisable as an example of a particular genre. Discourse patterning, even more than lexical or grammatical patterning, is so ingrained that it is difficult to tell what is salient in language without quantitative evidence. Corpus evidence therefore reduces the researcher's bias and prejudices about language. The evidence from a large general corpus also enables us to investigate more thoroughly discourse patterning across genres and modes.

FURTHER READING

Baker, P. (2006). *Using Corpora in Discourse Analysis*. London, New York: Continuum.

Biber, D., Connor, U. and Upton, T. (2007). *Discourse on the Move: Using Corpus Analysis to Describe Discourse Structure*. Amsterdam: John Benjamins.

Biber, D., Conrad, S. and Reppen, R. (1998). *Corpus Linguistics: Investigating Language Structure and Use*. Cambridge: Cambridge University Press.

Nunan, D. (1993). *Introducing Discourse Analysis*. London: Penguin.

Schiffrin, D. (1994). *Approaches to Discourse*. Oxford: Blackwell.

Schiffrin, D., Tannen, D. and Hamilton, H. (eds) (2001). *The Handbook of Discourse Analysis*. Oxford: Blackwell.

Stenström, A.-B. (1994). *An Introduction to Spoken Interaction*. Harlow: Longman.

Stubbs, M. (1983). *Discourse Analysis: The Sociolinguistic Analysis of Natural Language*. Oxford: Blackwell.

ten Have, P. (1999). *Doing Conversation Analysis: A Practical Guide*. London: Sage.

Widdowson, H. (2004). *Text, Context, Pretext: Critical Issues in Discourse Analysis*. Oxford: Blackwell.

Exploring Pronunciation with Corpora

6

In this chapter, we look at how online corpora can illuminate the study of pronunciation. The contents of this chapter are intended to complement an introductory course in phonetics and phonology (such as Roach 2000); however, some of the earlier sections and tasks serve as a basic guide to the subject. The chapter investigates the following issues:

- How can pronunciation be described?
- In what way do accents differ?
- How do children acquire a range of pronunciations?
- How might we explore intonation using online corpora?

In this chapter, we consider several online resources, such as the Speech Accent Archive, which are specifically designed to support the teaching and learning of phonetics and phonology. At the time of writing, most accessible online corpora focus on the printed word, even if occasionally those words have been annotated to show their pronunciation. Exceptions include MICASE and BASE, which also allow users to download recordings of spoken academic English, American and British, respectively, and ELISA, the video corpus of interviews with native speakers of English. A particularly useful corpus for examining accent variation is the Scottish Corpus of Texts & Speech (SCOTS), partly because SCOTS contains a substantial number of recordings of transcribed speech that can be listened to online and downloaded as sound files.

SCOTS has the advantage of containing a substantial number of recordings of speakers, from within and outside Scotland, whose backgrounds are quite diverse in geographical origin and upbringing, in social class and in age. The recordings also represent more and less spontaneous language, from casual conversation to lectures, and they are available as high-quality transcribed audio or audio-visual documents. In this chapter, the analysis of these materials is at an introductory level; given the quality of the recordings, much more sophisticated analysis is also possible.

Describing different accents

Accents are systematically described according to the science of phonetics and phonology. Phonetics is concerned with how speakers articulate individual sounds. For example, some sounds are made by completely or partially blocking the airflow from the lungs through the mouth. These sounds are called *consonants*. Phoneticians describe consonants by considering *where* the complete or partial blockage occurs (for example, do the lips come together or does the tongue touch the ridge behind the teeth?); *how* the air ultimately escapes (in an explosive 'burst', in a hiss of friction, round the sides of the tongue, through the nose?); and whether or not the vocal cords are vibrating during this process. So the consonant /p/, for example, would be described as an *unvoiced bilabial plosive* because (a) there is no vibration of the vocal cords during articulation, (b) the airflow is completely blocked by the two lips coming together and (c) the air then escapes in an explosive burst.

Another set of sounds is articulated not by blocking the airflow from the lungs through the mouth but by altering the shape of the tongue as the air passes through the vocal space. These sounds are called *vowels* and, since there is no blockage of air, they have to be categorised differently from consonants. When describing vowels, phoneticians pay attention mainly to the point in the mouth where the tongue is at its closest to the roof of the mouth (front or back), how far the tongue is from the roof of the mouth at this point and whether or not the lips are rounded, spread or in a relaxed, neutral position. And so /i/ (the 'ee' sound, as in 'keep') is described as a *close front* vowel because, during its articulation, the highest point of the tongue is at the *front* of the vowel space and *close* to the roof of the mouth.

Every speaking person acquires through time a set – or *inventory* – of sounds that make up his or her accent. The set of sounds varies from person to person and from community to community. The study of how these consonants and vowel sounds combine and vary is called *phonology*. Students of pronunciation, then, may be interested in both phonetics (how speakers articulate individual sounds) and phonology (how and why these individual sounds combine in particular patterns).

TASK 6.1   Consonants and vowels

Look at the following words and identify the number of consonants and vowels in each word *as it is pronounced*. For example, *milk* is made up of three consonants and one vowel (CVCC); and *phone* is made up of two consonants separated by a single vowel (CVC).

1. sound	6. pair	11. nation
2. strike	7. quit	12. creative
3. shovel	8. quite	13. conference
4. through	9. pullover	14. hopeless
5. ought	10. gnat	15. television

The international phonetic alphabet

Individual segments of sound are described using a special alphabet, the first version of which was devised by the International Phonetic Association in 1888, and the most recent of which was published in 2005 (see www.arts.gla.ac.uk/IPA/ipa.html). A symbol is assigned to each consonant and vowel sound, and these symbols are used consistently across languages and language varieties. The tables below (adapted from MacMahon 2002, pp. 16, 32–33) show a possible inventory of phonetic symbols that might be used in three general accents: (1) Received Pronunciation, which historically has come to be a prestigious reference accent for English, although few modern speakers actually use it; (2) General American, a reference accent for the United States; and (3) Scots, the linguistic cousin of English, spoken throughout lowland Scotland and the northern islands of Orkney and Shetland. We usually place IPA symbols in slash brackets to distinguish them from ordinary spelling; and so, for example, /ŋ/ is the IPA symbol used to indicate the sound that is usually represented by two letters, *ng*, in ordinary spelling.

Consonant sounds

The inventory of consonants is generally shared by all three accents, though some consonants, such as /x/ (the final sound in *loch*) are found mainly in Scotland. The way in which other individual consonants, such as /r/, are pronounced across the three accents do differ, as we shall shortly see. Figure 6.1 shows different ordinary spellings for each IPA consonant symbol.

/p/	pin, appear	/ʒ/	vision, beige
/b/	ball, ebb	/x/	loch (Scottish)
/t/	tap, Thomas, betting	/h/	hat, who
/d/	do, ladder	/ʍ/	when (Scottish)
/k/	cat, account, chord, bouquet	/tʃ/	chin, watch
/g/	go, ghost, begging	/dʒ/	gin, jam, suggest, midget, adjacent
/f/	foot, phone, rough, off	/r/	red, hurry, write, rhythm
/v/	voice, of	/j/	yes, feud
/θ/	thigh	/w/	when (RP and Gen Am), win, one
/ð/	thy	/l/	let, silly
/s/	sit, science, miss, peace	/m/	mat, summer, bomb, autumn
/z/	zoo, dizzy, roses, scissors	/n/	not, knot, sunny, gnat, pneumatic
/ʃ/	shove, sure, machine, special	/ŋ/	sing, sunk

Figure 6.1   Consonant symbols
Source: From MacMahon (2002, p. 16)

Consonant symbols

The key words given above are intended to provide a reference point for the symbol; they are not intended to indicate the 'correct' way to pronounce a particular spelling. For example, the final <th> spelling in *with* is usually pronounced with a /ð/ in England and as a /θ/ in Scotland. However, among particular groups, this sound is pronounced as a /v/ or a /f/. It is pointless to argue that one of these realisations is or is not 'correct'; it is more useful to consider who produces these articulations, and how and, perhaps, even why the pronunciations vary.

TASK 6.2   Consonant symbols

Which of the above consonant symbols do *you* use to articulate the sounds represented by the underlined letters below?

1. bo<u>th</u>er	6. thi<u>n</u>k	11. <u>y</u>es
2. bi<u>tt</u>er	7. so<u>rr</u>ow	12. rea<u>ch</u>
3. mea<u>s</u>ure	8. day<u>s</u>	13. trou<u>gh</u>
4. ju<u>dge</u>	9. da<u>z</u>e	14. <u>wh</u>ich
5. thi<u>n</u>	10. <u>sh</u>oes	15. <u>w</u>itch

As noted above, when considering how and why pronunciations of consonants vary, it is important to consider three factors in their articulation: (1) where the blockage to the airflow occurs (*place of articulation*), (2) how the blockage is accomplished (*manner of articulation*) and (3) whether or not the vocal cords vibrate during articulation (*voicing*). For example, /ð/ and /θ/ are both pronounced by the tongue-tip blocking the airflow just behind the upper teeth. Both are pronounced by forcing the air through the blockage, causing friction. The main difference between the two sounds is that with /ð/ the vocal cords vibrate, while with /θ/ the air is pushed through the vocal space without vibration of the vocal cords. We therefore classify /ð/ as a *voiced* dental fricative, and /θ/ as an *unvoiced* dental fricative.

The difference between /ð/ and /v/, however, lies not in the voicing or the manner of articulation – in both cases the vocal cords vibrate, and in both cases air is pushed through the vocal space with friction. In this case, the difference between the consonants lies in the *place* of articulation:

- with /ð/ the obstruction to the airflow is caused by the tongue-tip touching behind the upper teeth,
- with /v/ the obstruction is caused by the upper teeth touching the lower lip – /v/ is a voiced *labio-dental* fricative.

	Bilabial	Labio-dental	Dental	Alveolar	Post-alveolar	Palato-alveolar	Palatal	Velar	Glottal
Plosive	p b			t d				k g	
Nasal	m			n				ŋ	
Tap or flap				ɾ					
Fricative		f v	θ ð	s z		ʃ ʒ			h
Affricate						tʃ dʒ			
Approximant					ɹ		j		
Lateral				l					

Figure 6.2 Consonants of British English
Source: Adapted from MacMahon (2002, p. 23)

What usually happens when one consonant substitutes for another – /θ/, /f/ and /v/ can be used as a substitute for /ð/ as the final consonant in *with* – is that one or two of the three factors involved in the articulation of a consonant remain stable, while the others change. For example, a voiced consonant can become unvoiced (e.g. /ð/ becomes /θ/), but the place and manner of articulation remain stable. Or, the manner of articulation remains stable, but the place of articulation or the voicing change (e.g. /ð/ becomes /v/ and then /f/; or /ð/ becomes /θ/ and then /f/).

Figure 6.2 shows a chart of the main consonant sounds of English, with place of articulation along the top and manner of articulation down the side. Where there is a pair of consonants in a box, the one on the left is unvoiced, and the one on the right is voiced.

Vowel sounds

Vowel sounds vary across accents more obviously than consonants, as the following table indicates. They are grouped generally as *stressed* vowels, that is, those that are pronounced with some force, and *unstressed* vowels, which are pronounced with less force, as shown in Figure 6.3.

Stressed vowels

Key word	RP	Gen Am	Scottish
seat	i	i	i
sit	ɪ	ɪ	ɪ
way	eɪ	eɪ	e
sever	ɛ	ɛ	ɛ
seven	ɛ	ɛ	ɛ or ɪ
pam	a	ɐ	ɑ
palm	ɑ	ɑ	a or ɑ
cot	ɒ	ɑ	ɔ
caught	ɔ	ɔ	ɔ
nose	əʊ	oʊ	o
cut	ʌ	ʌ	ʌ
full	ʊ	ʊ	u
fool	u	u	u
birth	ɜ	ɜr	ɪr

Figure 6.3   Stressed vowels
Source: Adapted from MacMahon (2002, pp. 32–33)

berth	ɜ	ɜr	ɛr
worth	ɜ	ɜr	ʌr
horse	ɔ	ɔr	ɔr
hoarse	ɔ	ɔr	or
tide	aɪ	aɪ	ʌɪ or ɪi
tied	aɪ	aɪ	ae
house	aʊ or ɑʊ	aʊ	ʌʊ
boy	ɔɪ	ɔɪ	ɔe
dear	ɪə	ɪr	ir
hair	ɛə	ɛr	er or ɛr
poor	ʊə or ɔ	ʊr	ur

Figure 6.3   (Continued)

The sheer variety of vowel sounds might at first seem bewildering; however, if you look closely at the table, you will see that a smaller, 'core group' of vowels recurs again and again, though the members of this group are distributed differently across the three accents. The best way to introduce yourself to the table is to pronounce the key word yourself and think about whether your accent most resembles the RP, General American or Scottish pronunciation – or if it is something different (e.g. Indian, Australian, Irish or Northern English). Try to imagine how a typical RP, General American or Scottish speaker would pronounce the key words in the table. You will shortly be able to check your intuitions by exploring online corpora.

Unstressed vowels

The symbols used in the international phonetic alphabet were devised for stressed vowels. Unstressed vowels are trickier to describe and assign symbols to, and there is considerable variation amongst individual speakers. However, Figure 6.4 is an attempt to show some likely articulations.

Key word	RP	Gen Am	Scottish
father	ə	ər	ɪr
ago	ə	ə	ʌ or ɪ
China	ə	ə	ʌ
pitted	ɪ or ə	ɪ or ə	ɪ or e
pitied	ɪ or ə	i	i
happy	ɪ or i	ɪ	e or i or ɪ

Figure 6.4   Unstressed vowels
Source: Adapted from MacMahon (2002, p. 33)

TASK 6.3 Familiarising yourself with the international phonetic alphabet

To begin to help you familiarise yourself with the IPA, identify the words written below. Bear in mind that some of the words might have different conventional spellings, depending on which accent you are using. Some words are in fact repeated; once you have identified them, group them together and figure out the accent.

1.	θɪŋkɪŋ	16.	smokɪr
2.	tʃiəz	17.	ʃur
3.	kerfɪl	18.	laɪtnɪŋ
4.	ʃʊə	19.	kampsaɪt
5.	ədʒʌdʒ	20.	niðər
6.	lʌitnɪŋ	21.	jɒt
7.	ʃɔ	22.	tʃirz
8.	bɪkam	23.	ʌlʌu
9.	sməʊkə	24.	laɪtnɪŋ
10.	əlaʊ	25.	kɛrfəl
11.	ʃor	26.	wɪslə
12.	jɑt	27.	ʃʊr
13.	kɜst	28.	əlaʊ
14.	kɛəfəl	29.	bəkɑm
15.	jɒt	30.	ʃɔr

If this book has given you your first systematic exposure to the international Phonetic Alphabet, you might need to take some more time to familiarise your-self with the symbols used to convey the 'units of sound' in language. Further information can be found at websites such as 'Omniglot', a survey of various writing systems around the world (www.omniglot.com/writing/english.htm). The brief review above is intended to refresh the memories of those with limited exposure to the systematic study of pronunciation. Those who have begun their studies in phonetics and phonology will know how useful the phonetic alphabet is for comparing and contrasting different pronunciations.

Using online corpora to explore pronunciation

Given a reasonable familiarity with the international phonetic alphabet, we can begin to use the spoken component of the SCOTS corpus, which also includes some examples of non-Scottish speakers, to see how articulations of particular words vary from accent to accent. The activities below illustrate some of the many ways in which the SCOTS corpus can be used to explore different pronunciations.

Most of the activities in the following sections make use of the Standard Search facility of the SCOTS corpus. This allows users to choose to look at Spoken Documents only. These documents are transcribed according to conventional English spelling, or, where appropriate, in a spelling that reflects a Scottish accent.

Accent variation

To begin, we can simply pay attention to certain sounds that distinguish different accents. A basic way of using the search facility of a corpus that includes audio recordings is to identify words that include these sounds and to listen to how different speakers articulate them. The following activities focus on two consonants and two sets of contrasting types of vowels.

Variation in the articulation of consonants

We begin our exploration of pronunciation by using online corpora to listen to the articulation – or lack of it – of two particular consonants: the sound /r/ as it sometimes appears before other consonants and at the end of words and the Scottish consonant /x/, which represents the sound normally represented graphically as 'ch' sound in words like *loch, Auchinleck* and so on.

We noted above that IPA symbols are often enclosed in slash brackets, e.g. /r/. More specifically, the slash brackets indicate that the enclosed IPA symbol represents a 'phoneme', that is, it stands for a *set* of similar sounds that have the same role in pronunciation. For example, as we shall see, the /r/ symbol represents different kinds of 'r' sounds which are articulated in slightly different ways. Each individual 'r' sound can be allocated a *phonetic* symbol of its own – conventionally enclosed in square brackets – to show exactly how each /r/ sound is pronounced; for instance by moving to the tongue-tip to the ridge just behind the teeth but not touching it [ɹ] or by tapping the tongue-tip rapidly against the ridge [ɾ]. Since these slightly different articulations have the same function in English speech, we will use the more general *phonemic* symbol /r/ which represents them all.

/r/ at the end of words and before consonants

One of the most variable features of English accents is the articulation of the consonant /r/, particularly at the ends of words like *car, near, floor* and so on, and before consonants in words such as *part, skirt, world, government*. English accents can in fact be divided into those that pronounce the /r/ in such contexts (rhotic accents) and those that now omit the /r/ in these contexts (non-rhotic accents). Most accents in England are non-rhotic; most accents in Scotland and North America are rhotic. However, even amongst the rhotic accents, the way of pronouncing /r/ differs quite markedly. As indicated above, some speakers hold the tongue very close to the small ridge behind the upper teeth, while others tap the tongue or even roll it against this ridge. Some speakers from certain ethnic communities might roll the tongue-tip back towards the central part of the vocal space. Many North American speakers pronounce /r/ by constricting the throat muscles at the end of a vowel sound.

TASK 6.4   Exploring different articulations of the consonant /r/

1. Go to the SCOTS corpus at www.scottishcorpus.ac.uk.
2. Go to Standard Search.
3. Look at Documents and click on 'Spoken' only.
4. Enter '*r' in the Search box. This will produce a number of documents that include words ending in *r*.
5. Click on the title of one of the documents to see it in its full context.
6. Scroll to the bottom of the page and click the loudspeaker icon to hear the recording.
7. Click on one of the numbers after *next* (at the bottom of your screen) to find segments of text that include a word ending in *r*; click on *prev* to return to earlier examples.
8. To listen to examples of words ending in *r*, click on the icon for 'play' at the bottom of your screen.

This activity allows you to listen to a number of articulations of final /r/ in the speech of different people. To find some words that have /r/ in the middle, you can repeat the activity, but this time search for '*r*'. These 'wildcard' searches are not perfect, since a word like *sincere*, which ends with an /r/ when pronounced but not when written, would fall into the '*r*' list. However, a rough initial search will generate a number of results that you can then refine. For example, a search for '*r*' includes *born* in the results. You can go back to Standard Search, choose *spoken documents only*, and then search specifically for *born*, which is a useful word as it occurs many times in the spoken documents.

You can then choose a sample of documents that feature *born* spoken by different speakers and in different accents, who will probably have articulations of /r/. In conversational contexts, the articulation of /r/ can be fast, and at first it will be difficult to hear whether a speaker misses out the sound completely or articulates it by approaching the ridge behind the upper teeth with his or her tongue, tapping the ridge, rolling the tongue against it or constricting the throat. However, practice will sensitise your perception.

For example, among the SCOTS data, Conversation 36 involves a woman (speaker ID F1077) who was born and raised in England before moving to Scotland as an adult. She retains her English accent, omitting the /r/ phoneme in contexts where it is followed by a consonant or a pause. These contexts are highlighted below in **bold** in her contributions to the conversation. If you go to 'Quick Search' and key in *appleringie*, and then click on the text, *next* and the icon for *play* (see the screenshot in Figure 6.5), you will be able to read and hear the following exchange:

> F718: //appleringie is what?// //Mmhm.//
> F1077: //Southernwood or artemesia.//
> M1078: //Southernwood.//
> F1077: And er the only time I'd ever heard it called appleringie was as a child. It was in the garden and it was always appleringie. //I always had this//
> F718: //It's very scented, isn't it, a-// //southernwood, yeah.//
> F1077: //aye, very sort of herbally smell, and I always used to have this//

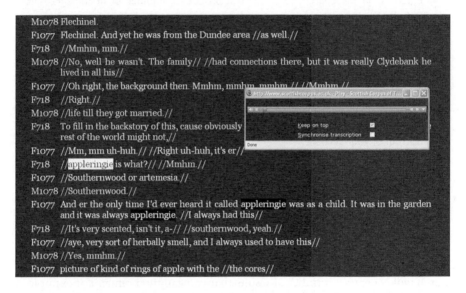

M1078 Flechinel.
F1077 Flechinel. And yet he was from the Dundee area //as well.//
F718 //Mmhm, mm.//
M1078 //No, well he wasn't. The family// //had connections there, but it was really Clydebank he lived in all his//
F1077 //Oh right, the background then. Mmhm, mmhm, mmhm // //Mmhm //
F718 //Right.//
M1078 //life till they got married.//
F718 To fill in the backstory of this, cause obviously rest of the world might not,//
F1077 //Mm, mm uh-huh.// //Right uh-huh, it's er//
F718 //appleringie is what?// //Mmhm.//
F1077 //Southernwood or artemesia.//
M1078 //Southernwood.//
F1077 And er the only time I'd ever heard it called appleringie was as a child. It was in the garden and it was always appleringie. //I always had this//
F718 //It's very scented, isn't it, a-// //southernwood, yeah.//
F1077 //aye, very sort of herbally smell, and I always used to have this//
M1078 //Yes, mmhm.//
F1077 picture of kind of rings of apple with the //the cores//

Figure 6.5 Screenshot for Conversation 36, featuring *appleringie*

Notice that the speaker does pronounce /r/ before vowels. Later in the conversation, you can hear her also pronounce /r/ when it occurs at the end of one word that is followed by another that begins with a vowel, as in the instances highlighted below:

> F1077: //It is, there is still a club there, I'm sure. It was on the the first floor of a building, [inaudible] entrance.// Erm mmhm. And we met there because we were both in the Young Conservatives; it was a Young Conservatives disco.

These distributions of /r/ are typical of English accents. Of course, many other accents can be heard in the SCOTS corpus. Conversations 27–29 involve two Scottish women conversing with a young American man. You can compare

Possible search item	RP	Gen Am	Scottish
bir̥th	ɜ	ɜr	ɪr
ear̥th	ɜ	ɜr	ɛr
wor̥th	ɜ	ɜr	ʌr

Figure 6.6   Vowel articulations before /r/

his articulation of words like *term, rockers, were* with his Scottish interlocutors' pronunciation of words like *sort, Ayr* and *heard*.

If you look at the vowel table shown earlier and reproduced in part as Figure 6.6, you will see that the articulation of certain vowels before /r/ varies quite considerably in Scottish accents compared to American and English accents. The kind of search performed in Task 6.4 can easily illustrate the variety of vowel articulations before /r/.

/x/ in Scottish accents

A conventional feature of the Scottish accent, particularly but not exclusively of older speakers, is the /x/ sound heard in words like *loch* and names such as *Auchenblae* or *Auchterarder*. This sound is disappearing amongst some Scottish speakers, particularly in urban Scottish centres. However, that other Scottish speakers associate this consonant with group identity is evident in some explicit comments on variation from conversations in SCOTS, such as this example of four secondary schoolgirls from the linguistically conservative North East (n.b.: the double slashes // indicate overlap):

F832: //I hate when, when people who're not Scottish they say "lock",//
F834: //Like when [inaudible]//
F832: //"Lock Ness" instead o "Loch, Loch//
F833: //Yeah, no, that annoys me.//
F835: //Like I live in//
F832: //Ness"//
F835: eh, I live in Tochhill Place //but everyone go//
F832: //uh-huh// //[laugh]//
F835: //"I live in Tochhill Place", that's like, no that'll be Toch-,ch//
F833: //[laugh]//
F834: //[laugh]//
F835: //[laugh]//
F832: //[laugh]//
F833: //[inaudible], I'm just jokin//
F832: An they can't say "Auchenblae" //It's "Auckenblae"//
F833: //Yeah, I know.//

TASK 6.5   Exploring alternations between /x/ and /k/ in Scottish accents

1. Go to the SCOTS corpus at www.scottishcorpus.ac.uk.
2. Go to Standard Search.
3. Look at Documents and click on 'Spoken' only.
4. Type 'loch*' or 'auch*' into the Search box.
5. Click on the title of one of the documents to see it in its full context.
6. Scroll to the bottom of the page and click the loudspeaker icon to hear the recording.
7. Click on one of the numbers after *next* (at the bottom of your screen) to find segments of text that include a word ending in *r*; click on *prev* to return to earlier examples.
8. To listen to examples of words including *ch,* click on the icon for 'play' at the bottom of your screen.

There is evidence from linguistic surveys that, as the schoolgirls from North East Scotland have noticed, the /x/ sound is indeed being replaced by /k/ amongst younger speakers in southern and urban Scotland. In fact, there is little evidence in the SCOTS recordings for that change; however, it must be remembered that the SCOTS data is a partial sample that does not represent the whole population of Scotland. By clicking on the *information* icon at the bottom of the SCOTS screen, you can see further information about the document and about the participants involved in the conversations. The information which is available in SCOTS tends to confirm that in the SCOTS recordings that include the sequences *loch* and *auch* the speakers concerned are either older Scots or from more rural Scottish locations.

Accents of English online

If you wish to hear speakers of other accents, native and non-native, you can go to the Speech Accent Archive developed at George Mason University. At this site, you can hear how a wide range of speakers pronounce the following paragraph, which is used to elicit the full inventory of sounds pronounced by English speakers.

> Please call Stella. Ask her to bring these things with her from the store: Six spoons of fresh snow peas, five thick slabs of blue cheese, and maybe a snack for her brother Bob. We also need a small plastic snake and a big toy frog for the kids. She can scoop these things into three red bags, and we will go meet her Wednesday at the train station. [Speech Accent Archive]

The Speech Accent Archive contains recordings of many people reading the above paragraph; it also contains very detailed phonetic transcriptions for each speaker. If you listen to the different accents – English, Scottish, American, Australian and others – you can compare transcriptions and begin to familiarise yourself with the different possible articulations.

TASK 6.6   Focusing on your own accent

Try reading the elicitation paragraph yourself and – if possible – record your performance. Try identifying some key features of your pronunciation; for example:

- Do you have a rhotic or non-rhotic accent?
- What kind of /r/ sound do you produce and where?
- When do you use /s/ and when do you use /z/ at the end of words?
- When do you pronounce 'th' as unvoiced /θ/, and when as voiced /ð/?

Exploring vowels online

As we have already noted, the phonemes of a language are classified as either consonants or vowels. The difference between consonants and vowels is that the latter are articulated not by blocking the stream of air that is pushed through the vocal space but by changing the shape of the tongue as the air-stream passes through the mouth. And so, in the articulation of /i/ in words like *teeth* and *speed*, the tongue is close to the roof of the mouth, and the narrowest passage of air is at the front of the mouth. The vowel /i/ is accordingly described as a close front vowel. By contrast, /a/ in words like *can't* and *bar* is an open back vowel, since the tongue is kept low, and the narrowest passage of air is at the back of the vocal space.

Listen again to the elicitation passage read by different speakers in the Speech Accent Archive. Places where /i/ and /a/ might be pronounced have been highlighted in the passage below:

Pl**ea**se call Stella. **A**sk her to bring th**e**se things with her from the store: Six spoons of fresh snow p**ea**s, five thick sl**a**bs of blue ch**ee**se, and maybe a sn**a**ck for her brother Bob. We also n**ee**d a small pl**a**stic snake and a big toy frog for the kids. She can scoop th**e**se things into thr**ee** red b**a**gs, and we will go m**ee**t her Wednesday at the train station.

If you listen to several recordings in the Speech Accent Archive, and look in particular at the vowel realisations, you will notice a large degree of variation. For example, many speakers who pronounce *snack* with an /a/ have a rather different sound in *bags, /æ/*. When articulating the latter vowel, the tongue is near-open, and the narrowest passage of the air-stream is towards the front, not the back of the mouth.

TASK 6.7   Comparing Scottish and English vowel articulations

1. Go to the Speech Accent Archive at http://accent.gmu.edu
2. Click on *browse*.
3. Click on *language/speakers*.
4. Scroll down the page and click on *English*.
5. Click on *english13* (Oxfordshire male), listen to the recording and look at the transcript. Using Table 6.1, note down the vowel symbols used for *ask, spoons, blue, snack, scoop, bags*.
6. Click on *english24* (Glasgow male), listen to the recording and look at the transcript. Again, note down the vowel symbols used for *ask, spoons, blue, snack, scoop, bags*.
7. Now choose another two speakers and note down how they articulate the vowel sounds. Are they closer to the English or Scottish speaker? Can you hear the difference in vowel sounds? Can you imitate them?

Table 6.1   Vowel articulations

	english13	*english24*	*Speaker 3:_____*	*Speaker 4:_____*
ask				
spoons				
blue				
snack				
scoop				
bags				

While the Speech Accent Archive is useful for comparing accents of speakers who are reading a single paragraph aloud, it tells us little about how people sound in more spontaneous conversation. Again, the SCOTS recordings give useful examples of conversational interaction. It is useful to search the spoken documents in order to listen to how some of the words that occur in the elicitation passage are pronounced in the SCOTS data, e.g.:

Key word	*Possible realisations*
please, peas, cheese, three	/i/
call, small	/ɔ/
Bob, frog	/ɒ/

All of these key words occur spontaneously in the SCOTS spoken data, and they can be compared with their various realisations in the Speech Accent Archive. For example, most Scottish speakers do not distinguish between the vowel sounds in *call* and *frog*, normally using the vowel /ɒ/ in both contexts; that is, they pronounce the vowels in these words and others, like *cot* and *caught*, in the same fashion. Identifying sounds and comparing pronunciations can help heighten your awareness of the many differences that go into each individual accent.

Monophthongs and diphthongs

Vowels can also be divided into two groups according to whether the tongue moves or not in the vocal space during their articulation. If the tongue stays still, the vowel is classed as a monophthong; if it glides, it is a diphthong. The distribution of monophthongs and diphthongs amongst Scottish, English and American speakers differs in some details, especially before /r/, as we have seen. Possible diphthongs are shown again below in Figure 6.7:

Key words	RP	Gen Am	Scottish
way	eɪ	eɪ	e
nose	əʊ	oʊ	o
tide	aɪ	aɪ	ʌɪ or ɪi
tied	aɪ	aɪ	ae
house	aʊ or ɑʊ	aʊ	ʌʊ
boy	ɔɪ	ɔɪ	ɔe
dear	ɪə	ɪr	ir
hair	ɛə	ɛr	er or ɛr
poor	ʊə or ɔ	ʊr	ur

Figure 6.7   Diphthongs

It is possible to explore the realisations of diphthongs in the pronunciation of three speakers in the SCOTS text archive:

F1077   Female speaker, English accent – Conversation 36
M964   Male speaker, American accent – Conversations 27–29
 F963   Female speaker, Scottish accent – Conversations 27–29

Conversations involving these speakers include various diphthongs in English, American and Scottish accents. Figure 6.8 shows a sample, alongside typical key words, some of which also appear in the elicitation text used in the Speech Accent Archive (shown in **bold**):

Key words	English accent	Scottish accent	American accent
down	/aʊ/	/ʌu/	/aʊ/
go, **snow**	/əʊ/	/o/	/oʊ/
may, **train**	/eɪ/	/e/	/eɪ/
boy, **toy**	/ɔɪ/ or /ɔi/	/ɔe/	/ɔɪ/ or /oɪ/
side, **five**	/ai/	/ʌi/ or /ai/	/aɪ/

Figure 6.8   Diphthongs in different accents

TASK 6.8   Exploring diphthongs in spontaneous speech

1. Go to the SCOTS corpus at www.scottishcorpus.ac.uk.
2. Click on Advanced Search.
3. Click on General and type *down* into the word/phrase search (concordance).
4. Click on Spoken and choose Participant details.
5. Choose Participant id and select = 1077. This search will give you examples of the word *down* as used by participants in the conversation involving F1077, a speaker with an English accent. You can listen to her articulation of this word, then repeat the process for participants F963 and M964, a female Scottish and male American speaker.
6. Now choose another key word, such as *go,* and listen to how the three speakers articulate this word. Finally, by listening to the articulations in the Speech Accent Archive of the key words shown above in **bold**, and looking at the transcriptions, you can consider how best to represent the different accents using the symbols of the international phonetic alphabet.

Vowel length

As we have seen, the articulation of vowels depends largely on the shape of the tongue and how rounded or spread the lips are. Vowels are also pronounced for a length of time, and the duration of time varies from context to context and accent to accent. For example, most speakers from England have a variety of short and long vowels, whereas in Scotland most speakers have relatively short vowels. The five main long vowels in southern English accents, and their Scottish equivalents, are shown below in Figure 6.9:

Key word	Long vowel (England)	Short vowel (Scotland)
peace	i	i
worth	ɜ	various, e.g. ʌ
half	ɑ	a
horse	ɔ	various, e.g. ɒ
spoon	u	ʊ

Figure 6.9   Long vowels and short vowels

To hear different accents realised, go to the Speech Accent Archive and listen to Scottish and southern English speakers pronouncing the highlighted words. A good contrast, for example, is between *english24* from Glasgow and *english11* from Staffordshire:

Please **call** Stella. Ask her to bring these things with her from the store: Six **spoons** of fresh snow peas, five thick **slabs** of blue cheese, and maybe a snack for her brother Bob. We also **need** a small plastic snake and a big toy frog for the kids. She can scoop these things into three red bags, and we will go meet her Wednesday at the train station. [Speech Accent Archive]

As expected, speakers from Scotland and southern England tend to pronounce these words with vowels of different lengths, as shown in Figure 6.10 below:

Word	Accent	Vowel	Duration
call	Scottish	ɔ	short
call	southern English	ɑ	long
spoons	Scottish	ʊ	short
spoons	southern English	u	long

Figure 6.10   Vowel length

Often long vowels are shown in transcription with a length mark, as /kɑːl/ *call* in the southern English pronunciation.

A glance at the detailed transcriptions in the Speech Accent Archive will show that it is too simplistic to argue that Scottish speakers pronounce all their words with short vowels in contexts where southern English speakers use longer ones. Both Scottish and English pronunciations are affected by systematic 'rules' of pronunciation:

- The 'voicing effect' (VE) claims that in most English accents, the length of a vowel is roughly 50 per cent greater when it occurs before a voiced consonant, compared to its occurrence before a voiceless consonant. Consider, for example, how you pronounce the vowel /i/ in *leaf* and *leave*.
- The 'Scottish Vowel Length Rule' (SVLR) argues that Scottish speakers lengthen their vowels when they occur in four places:
  - before /r/, which is of course spoken in Scottish accents; e.g. compare *bid* and *bird*
  - before voiced fricatives, /v, z, ʒ, ð/, e.g. compare *peace, peas,* or *teeth, teethe*
  - before grammatical boundaries within words, e.g. compare *mood* and *mooed (= moo + ed)*
  - at the end of an 'open syllable', that is, a syllable that concludes with a vowel, e.g. compare *seen* and *see*.

In all of the second items in the above pairs, the vowel in Scottish accents is lengthened.

TASK 6.9   Listening to vowel length

1. Go to the Speech Accent Archive, at http://accent.gmu.edu/.
2. Click *Browse*.
3. Click *language/speakers*.
4. Click *English*.
5. Click *english24*.
6. Click to play the recording. You can now listen to the recording and look at the IPA transcript. This speaker is from Glasgow; notice that his long vowels generally occur where the Scottish Vowel Length Rule predicts they should occur, i.e. before /r/ in *store*; before voiced fricatives in *peas, these* and *cheese* (but not, curiously, *please*); and at the end of 'open' syllables, *blue* and *three*. There are no examples here of vowels occurring before grammatical boundaries within a word.
7. Return to *Browse* and click on *atlas/regions*.
8. Click on the continent of Europe. You will then see a map of Britain with various speakers from England, Scotland, Wales and Ireland flagged. Click on each speaker in turn, and pay attention to where they articulate their long vowels. To what extent are their articulations predicted by the Voicing Effect Rule and the Scottish Vowel Length Rule?

Listening to different accents and considering how they have been transcribed trains you to perceive small, subtle changes in pronunciation that are important in distinguishing accents.

Once you have practised with the Speech Accent Archive, you can revisit the SCOTS spoken database and listen to different accents pronouncing long and short vowels. In the SCOTS texts, one possible activity is to use the Standard Search to locate pairs of words in the spoken part of the corpus that are subject to the Scottish Vowel Length Rule and those that are not. That is, you can identify and listen to different accents pronouncing the following words in which the vowels do not occur in SVLR contexts (that is, we would expect them to be short) and those words in which the vowels do occur in SVLR contexts (and so we would expect them to be lengthened). To begin with, you can listen to different realisations of /i/, as indicated below in Figure 6.11:

Non-SVLR contexts	**SVLR contexts**	**Why SVLR operates**
greed	agreed	grammatical boundary
peace	peas	before voiced fricative /z/
treat	tree	open syllable
beat	beer	before /r/

Figure 6.11   Realisations of /i/

As you listen to the accents in the SCOTS corpus, it might be difficult at first to distinguish between long and short vowels – and in spontaneous speech, speakers might not adhere to the rules consistently. However, studies such as Hewlett, Matthews and Scobbie (1999) suggest that in general 'voicing effect' and the Scottish Vowel Length Rule do operate fairly systematically in our everyday speech and do much to characterise different accents.

Fast talking

A consequence of spontaneous speech, as opposed to, say, reading aloud from a prepared list of words, is that many words change their pronunciation when spoken quickly, for example:

- some words have 'weak forms'
- the sounds in some other words change depending on the company they keep, in a process called 'assimilation'
- other sounds are simply dropped in a simplifying process called 'elision'

Weak forms are produced when frequently used words, usually grammatical words, are pronounced with an unstressed vowel. For instance, spoken in isolation, the words *of* and *was* would be pronounced with stress as /ɔv/ and /wɔz/. However, in the context of fast speech, the unstressed pronunciations of these words are likely to be, depending on the speaker, something like /əv/ or /ɪv/, and /wəz/ or /wɪz/. There are around sixty words in English that have strong and weak forms, depending on whether or not they are stressed (see, for example, Gimson 1980, pp. 261–263, for a list of common words).

In the spoken texts in the Speech Accent Archive the words highlighted are likely to be weak forms.

> Please call Stella. Ask her ***to*** bring these things with her ***from the*** store: Six spoons ***of*** fresh snow peas, five thick slabs ***of*** blue cheese, ***and*** maybe ***a*** snack ***for*** her brother Bob. [Speech Accent Archive]

TASK 6.10   Exploring weak forms

1. Go to the Speech Accent Archive, at http://accent.gmu.edu/.
2. Click *Browse*.
3. Click *language/speakers*.
4. Click *English*.
5. Play some of the recordings and pay particular attention to the pronunciation of the words shown in bold in the passage above. Are they weak forms or strong forms?

6. Then do an Advanced Search of a sample of the spoken documents in SCOTS for one or two of these words (e.g. *from, of, can*), using the concordance programme.
7. From the concordance results, try to find contexts where the words are likely to be stressed, and contexts where they are not likely to be stressed (the latter context is by far the more common).
8. Click on the key words to take you to the documents, where you can play the recordings and listen for weak and strong forms.

As an example, in SCOTS Document 1448 (BBC Voices Recording: Aberdeen), a group of adults can be heard talking about a childhood game called 'Kick the Cannie':

M1042: //That's kick the cannie, well you've got a ***can***, you put it on the floor,//
F1043: //[inaudible]//
M1042: an ye kick it as hard as ye ***can***, an then someone's got to go an chase that ***can***, meanwhile you all disappear. //It's like a hide-and-seek game.//

Here *can* is used both as a noun (*you've got a can*) and an auxiliary verb (*as hard as ye can*). Both pronunciations are stressed, and so they are strong forms. Compare the pronunciation of *can* here with the almost inaudible weak form in the rest of the conversation when *can* is used in questions such as:

F1054: ***Can*** you describe t- what Torry's like tae somebody say that's livin in England, in London.

The second key feature of fast speech is *assimilation*, which occurs when a sound changes in relation to the other sounds around it, that is, in relation to its phonetic environment. One common feature of assimilation is the change of /n/ to /ŋ/ before /k/. Thus we pronounce *think* as /θɪŋk/, not /θɪnk/. Depending on how careful Scottish speakers are, they might also pronounce phrases like *in Kent* as /ɪn kɛnt/ or /ɪŋ kɛnt/.

TASK 6.11   Exploring assimilation

1. Go to the SCOTS corpus, at www.scottishcorpus.ac.uk.
2. Click on Standard Search.
3. Choose Spoken Documents only.

4. Enter '*n k*' or '*n qu*' into the Word/Phrase box. This search will identify those words whose spellings end with *n* where the next word begins with *k* or *qu*. Remember, however, that spelling has a slippery relationship with sound and that not all words that start with *k* are pronounced with /k/ – *knife* being one of them!
5. Click on some of the documents and identify instances when the speaker assimilates /n/ to /ŋ/.
6. Other contexts where assimilation can occur include sequences in which /d/ is followed by /g/ or /b/ or in cases where /n/ follows /p/ in an unstressed syllable. You can therefore repeat this task, performing searches on the SCOTS spoken documents for '*d g*', '*d b*' and '*pen*'. Listen for instances of the /d/ becoming /g/ or /b/, and the /n/ becoming /m/.

One possible result for '*n qu*' is given below (from BBC Voices Recording: Portree). Listen to the speaker and try to decide if he says /bin kwʌit/ or /biŋ kwʌit/. Like other English speakers he certainly uses /ŋ/ in *think*:

M1007: Took a while to teach us the English but then when they did teach us the English we [inhale] we seemed to have grasped it and eh the accent has always **been quite** quite straightforward and I **think** when you've, when I find that particularly [inhale] eh pointed is when you meet some foreigners [inhale] and you start talking to them they say that our our ehm speech is much slower than that of people in the central belt and they can understand us a lot eh more clearly than they can

M1008: Mmhm.

M1007: eh in the rest of Scotland. An I, an I've often found that quite interesting.

In fast, connected speech, sounds do not simply change; they might well disappear completely. This feature of speech is called *elision*, and it happens in a number of instances, e.g.:

• clusters of consonants: in groups of three plosives, or two plosives and a fricative, the middle plosive might disappear, e.g. *facts* might be pronounced /faks/.
• Final /v/ is lost, e.g. in *of*, particularly before consonants.

TASK 6.12 Exploring Elision

1. Go to the SCOTS corpus, at www.scottishcorpus.ac.uk.
2. Click on Standard Search.
3. Choose Spoken Documents only.

TASK 6.12   (Continued)

4. Enter '*cts' into the Word/Phrase box.
5. Click on some of the documents and identify instances when the speaker simpli-
   fies this consonant cluster, e.g. by omitting the /t/. Using this as your starting
   point, listen to stretches of speech and identify other places where elision
   occurs.

For example, there is elision in the highlighted consonant clusters in the
following passage from SCOTS Document 354 (Conversation 07):

F643: ehm, when I was at R.G.I.T. I came across a book on colour therapy.
       I was, we had to give a presentation on, ehm, behavioural aspe***cts*** of
       management,
M608: mmhm
F643: and because I'd come from a design background I wanted to do some-
       thing that was easy. I'd written an article for a magazine on, on colour
       tre***nds*** and so forth, and I dug that out, doctored it a bit
M608: mmhm
F643: and ehm did a bit about colour in the workplace. So I'd studied the
       effe***cts*** of colour //for my//
M608: //mmhm//
F643: presentation.

The elision of /v/ in many words of Scottish speech has a long historical
precedent, and is reflected in the spellings used in the SCOTS transcription. To
listen to elision of /v/, search the following pairs of words: *of/o, have/hae, give/gie,
over/ower*. The following excerpt from a conversation between women working
in education in central Scotland shows elision of both /v/ and /θ/:

F1054: On the this series aboot weather on the TV and eh Matthew Fitt
        who's a super language guy eh came on an s- he gave all these words
        for eh for rain an he finished off and said a right good pish-oot.
        //[laugh]//
F1143: //[laugh]//
F1144: //[laugh]//
F1054: I thought, "You should ***hae*** started ***wi*** that Matthew, that was great".
        [SCOTS Document 1572: BBC Voices Recording: Stirling]

The features described in this section – weak forms, assimilation, and elision –
do much to give connected speech its character, a character quite different from
the pronunciation of words in isolation.

The acquisition of variation

Despite the gradual erosion of some Scottish features from the pronunciation of the middle classes and from some younger speakers, it is clear from the data in the SCOTS corpus that certain traditional Scottish pronunciations survive, particularly in areas such as the North East and the Borders. SCOTS is fortunate to have been donated a substantial body of recordings made by Jennifer Smith as part of a project to trace acquisition of those linguistic characteristics associated with the speech variety of Buckie in North East Scotland. These recordings are valuable in part because they provide data that help show how children acquire the continuum of speech patterns that extend from Broad Scots to standard Scottish English. The recordings are supplemented by other recordings in which parents interact with younger children, e.g. Conversations 15 and 37, in which fathers in Glasgow talk to their children. Given that the SCOTS data was largely collected in 2004–2007, a small corpus of recordings involving young children can be obtained by doing a restricted search (see Figure 6.12).

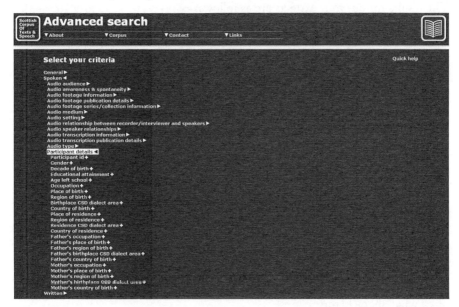

Figure 6.12   Restricting a SCOTS search

TASK 6.13   Restricting a Scots search to data from children

1. Go to the SCOTS corpus, at www.scottishcorpus.ac.uk.
2. Click on Advanced Search.
3. Under 'Select your criteria', click on 'Spoken'.
4. From the drop-down menu, click on 'Participant Details'.
5. From the next drop-down menu, click on 'Decade of Birth' and enter '= 2000'.

As you will see from your results, most of the available recordings are from Buckie, with the Glasgow data supplementing it. If you wish, you can further refine the corpus by using the Participant ID options to specify desired gender or place of birth – that is, you could focus on data concerning males or females, or narrow your search to either the North East or South West of Scotland. For our present purposes, however, we will consider four extracts from a recording made between a mother (F1121) and daughter (F1122) in the acts of making a jigsaw, drawing, baking, tidying the toybox and going for a walk (Conversation: Buckie – Mother and Child 01: Recordings 1–4).

When exploring the acquisition of the variety of pronunciations that we have been considering in this chapter, of particular interest is the way parents – or other adult care-givers – interact with the children and how the children respond verbally. For example, in the small corpus of data involving young children, the care-givers frequently make suggestions or elicit responses using *What/Fitt/How about/aboot . . . ?* These variables can be identified by clicking on 'Select your criteria' and entering *about* or *aboot* in the 'Word/phrase (concordance)' box. The results for our four extracts are as follows:

Mother (F1121)

What about pronunciations

what about, look . . .
what about if . . .
and what about if . . .
what about drawing . . .
what about chocolate crispies . . .
ehm, what about if we tidy . . .
what about we go through . . .
right, what about if I . . .
what about this one
what about them, look

What aboot pronunciations

okay, what aboot Liam?
what aboot if we co- cover
what aboot if we go and tidy . . .
what aboot these videos

Fitt aboot pronunciations

Fitt aboot Uncle Ian?
I think fitt aboot yellow . . .
Fitt aboot [forename]
Fitt aboot that plate there
Fitt aboot my chopping board
Right, fitt aboot [forename's] bottle?

Child (F1122)

What/How about pronunciations

how about every [inaudible]
what about this colour
how about a dog
Erm, how about the shape of a babywipe
how about if we put crispies on the plate
how about this
how about, how about to, to the, to the . . .
Mum, how about this?

A number of tentative observations can be made about these results. The first is that there is much more variation in the output of the mother: *what about, what aboot, fitt aboot* (but not *fitt about*, which is only found 10 times elsewhere in the corpus). The child varies between *how about/what about*. Elsewhere in SCOTS, mothers do use the *how about* form to children, but the contexts seem to be less directive or more conciliatory than when *what about/fitt aboot* are used (e.g. another mother in Buckie says to a sobbing child, *how about if ye go and get yer bath . . .*). Possibly the child has learned that *how about* is more suggestive than directive.

More pertinent to the topic of pronunciation is that the child does not use *fitt aboot*, or even *how aboot, what aboot,* even though she is clearly exposed to the variants. Elsewhere in the conversation she does use *aboot* (e.g. in the question *Is it aboot dry?*), but when making suggestions she confines herself to the *about* pronunciation.

More detailed work needs to be done on child-caregiver interactions for us to be able to propose firm and robust reasons for this variation in patterns of pronunciation between mother and child (see Smith, Durham and Fortune, 2007, for an extensive study); however, there is scope for speculation based on the evidence found here. One possibility is that the child is simply exposed to one variant (*about*) more frequently than another (*aboot*). However, in the conversations examined above, the *what/fitt aboot* forms are as frequent in the mother's output as the *what about* forms, though it is possible that a larger survey of the corpus would indicate a greater disparity. Another, perhaps more intriguing, possibility is that the child is articulating pronunciations based in part on her developing sense of what is appropriate to conversational interactions with her mother. It is possible that the child has begun to associate the *about* form with formality and so uses this variant when making suggestions that seek her mother's consent. If so, then the distribution of *about/aboot* forms will depend in part on the child's growing perception of what is and is not a formal situation. As she matures, her use of variants like *fitt* and *aboot* will be restricted to less formal contexts and domestic situations in which she (like her mother here) is the authority figure.

Lexicalisation

Corpus analysis can help us address a further issue, partly related to those covered in the previous section, of how and when variation in pronunciation gives rise over time to differences in meaning between variants. For example, Macafee (1994) argues that for many Scottish speakers for whom *home/hame* are available as variant pronunciations, the former can take on the distinctive meaning of an institutional home, for example, sheltered housing for the elderly. Effectively, we might argue that *home/hame* have at this point become two separate words, rather than two phonological variants of the same basic word; that is, we can argue that *home* has become lexicalised as a separate word with a restricted or different meaning. We can use the SCOTS corpus to explore this development, using the following procedure:

TASK 6.14(a)   Exploring lexicalisation

1. Go to the SCOTS corpus, at www.scottishcorpus.ac.uk.
2. Click on Advanced Search.
3. Click on 'General' and choose 'Document Details: Spoken or Written'.
4. Choose 'Spoken'.
5. Click on 'General' again and choose 'Word Search'.
6. From the drop-down menu, choose 'Word/Phrase concordance'.
7. Enter 'a home'.

In the documents available at the time of our search, there were eight instances of *a home*, in six of which *home* functions as a modifier for another noun, namely *a home help, a home language, a Home Economics teacher (three times)*. In the sixth instance one speaker is telling the other that he would not think of America as *a home*. Only in one instance is *home* used in its institutional sense, in this case to refer to an orphanage, in a recording made in Hawick by the BBC:

> M1012:   //Well the, the// the yin which maist folk wouldnae pick up on is 'The Holm' for Newcastleton, H.O.L.M. which is a low-lyin bi- eh beside the river where Newcastleton's situated, but The Holm I would, a teacher came here an he he'd been here months an he said, 'It it must be a very big orphanage at Newcastleton', //an he thought that aw the bairns fae Newcastleton were in a home

This particular speaker's use of the terms *home/hame* can be checked by doing a further Advanced Search.

TASK 6.14(b)   Exploring lexicalisation

1. Go to the SCOTS corpus, at www.scottishcorpus.ac.uk.
2. Click on Advanced Search.
3. Click on 'Spoken', scroll down to 'Participant ID' and enter '= 1012' in the box.
4. Click on 'General' again and choose 'Word Search'.
5. From the drop-down menu, choose 'Word/Phrase concordance'.
6. Enter 'hame'.

This search will give you instances of *hame* in conversations involving the male speaker with the identification number M1012. He uses *hame* in a piece of poetry that he recites to show Borders usages:

> M1012:   'Here in Hawick oor **hame** oo've lots to shout aboot . . .'

If these examples are representative, then this speaker has a distinction between *home* used for institutions such as orphanages, and *hame*, the place where he lives. However, it is well to be cautious from single incidences. Other speakers in the same conversation do use *home* and *hame* as synonyms. One of the females, for example, alternates between *hame* and *home* with little difference in meaning:

F1011: In the **hame** in they days as weel as at the scuil . . .
F1011: //[inaudible]// Mm, I was in New Zealand a number o years ago, my dad took me out there an when we were when we were comin **home** before we came **home** we were on a bus journey up tae Auckland for a flight ye see an we were in this hotel one night, an my dad was just along the corridor frae me an I could see he was havin difficulty gettin intae his room an there was a young manager comin along, an I heard my dad say, 'This kei winna wurk', //

More data would be needed to confirm the hypothesis, but from these recordings and from observations, it seems likely that while *hame/home* can be seen as two variant forms of the same concept, for some people the latter tends to be the form preferred for the concept of institutional home. However, a search of the full SCOTS corpus, written as well as spoken, for instances of *the hame* identifies one piece of literary fiction from the North East, in which *hame* is used in the institutional sense:

Bit o luck wis it nae, the skweel veesitin the *Hame* last wikk, an me findin oot that Syd Paterson, their newest pensioner, wis ma verra ain Granda! [From *Loon* by Sheena Blackhall]

Sheena Blackhall's use of *home* and *hame* can be further explored by doing a Standard Search, keying in her surname in the 'Author' box and searching for *home* and then *hame* in the 'Word/phrase' box. There are various instances of her use of one variant and the other; what patterns can you find in her usage of these forms?

The conclusion – as is often the case with linguistic studies of variation – is that the situation is complex. The presence of two phonological variants for the same concept can lead in some cases to one of those variants developing a restricted meaning – for speakers such as M1012, *home* might be the preferred pronunciation for rest home, orphanage and so on. However, for those such as F1011, who might also use *home* in this restricted sense, *home* and *hame* can still both be used as synonyms for the domestic home. And in some rare occasions, for example, in literature whose local features are strongly marked, *hame* can also be found in the institutional sense.

Phonological variants can co-exist for a considerable time; however, if enough people begin to use one form with a restricted or changed meaning, then gradually that new meaning may be diffused throughout the speech community (with only conservative speakers resisting the change), and ultimately two words with separate, if related, meanings evolve. Alternatively, one of the variants might simply be used less and less frequently until it disappears. Other pairs of Scots/English phonological forms that can be searched using the SCOTS text archive are *sair/sore* and *puir/poor*. From the evidence in the spoken corpus in particular, are these phonological variants used as arbitrary synonyms, or are they acquiring a distinctive set of meanings? Once you have checked the spoken documents, look at their uses in the written data.

Intonation

This chapter so far has focused largely on individual sounds – phonemes – and it has considered how they are described, how they differ across accents, how they change when combined in spontaneous speech, how variant pronunciations might be acquired by children and how variant pronunciations might relate to changes in meaning. In this concluding section, we look briefly at a topic which takes us beyond individual sounds or even sounds in combination – intonation.

When we speak, the frequency of the vibration of our vocal cords varies, producing changes in pitch that create the 'melody' of everyday conversation. The patterns of high and low pitch can carry certain types of meanings; researchers into intonation study the meaningful variation of pitch in conversational interaction. Such researchers look at the forms that intonation takes (put simply, falling tones, rising tones and level tones) and relate them to their function in spoken discourse.

There has been relatively little exploration of intonation using corpora for reasons that will be obvious, given a little thought. To use a corpus of spoken texts to its best advantage in the study of intonation, recordings have to be marked up, and even with some automation, it has been estimated that it takes three hours to transcribe and correct fifteen minutes of speech (Campione and Véronis [2001] 2004, p. 470).

An online resource that allows some limited exploration of intonation is the website of the University of Oxford's Intonational Variation in English and Oxigen projects. These projects make use of a tagged corpus of recordings of speakers of nine urban varieties of English, spoken in England, Wales and Ireland. Informants include bilingual Punjabi/English and Welsh/English speakers and speakers of Caribbean descent. The purpose of the IViE project was to investigate the under-researched issue of intonation variation across different English dialects, and its successor, the Oxigen project, made use of a revised version of the corpus to construct a statistical computational model of intonation. The revised corpus consists of 36 hours of speech made up of the following:

- Different sentence types read aloud. These include statements and questions that are grammatically marked (e.g. *May I lean on the railings?*) and not grammatically marked (e.g. *You remembered the lilies?*)
- A short text (*Cinderella*) read aloud
- Semi-spontaneous speech based on retellings of texts previously read
- Free conversations based on a task involving maps
- Spontaneous discussion on the topic of smoking

The IViE corpus can be downloaded free for research purposes, and the stimuli and map tasks used in the design of the corpus are available on the IViE website. The corpus can also be searched online, and users can listen to the recordings and view transcripts; however the documentation is quite technical in nature and difficult for the novice to decipher. More useful for the beginner is a page giving examples of the most common tunes in the IViE corpus, selected from the read sentences. These include the following:

- Falling tunes, used in statements and questions
- Fall + rises, used in questions
- Utterances with two rises, again used in statements and questions

In their research into variation amongst speakers of different urban varieties of English using IViE, Grabe and Post ([2002] 2004, p. 480) conclude that:

[...] the mapping between grammatical structures and intonational form is dialect specific also. A change in grammatical function can be associated with the production of a different pattern in one dialect but not another.

The situation with intonation is clearly complex, and much work is still to be done.

TASK 6.15   Listening to intonation patterns

1. Go to Intonational Variation in English, at www.phon.ox.ac.uk/IViE/tunes/.
2. Click on the sentences to hear the main intonation 'tunes' of English.
3. Go to www.phon.ox.ac.uk/IViE/download1.php. At this site, you can download IViE's audio files. These are freely available, but you must register in order to download the files. The audio files are recordings of scripted and spontaneous speech.
4. Listen to recordings such as the IViE audio files, the SCOTS spoken documents or the ELISA video interviews and pay attention to how the speakers divide their utterances into units characterised by falling, rising and level tones. Pay particular attention to how speakers map patterns of intonation onto statements, questions, exclamations, requests and demands.

Summary

This chapter has sought to introduce students to the study of pronunciation and offers insights into the ways that access to online resources such as corpora might be used in the exploration of different pronunciations of English. Currently there are limitations to the kind of exploration that is possible using online corpora. First of all, few corpora are available with transcriptions that are marked up for phonetic information, and those that are marked up (like the Speech Accent Archive) are often not searchable. The Speech Accent Archive makes up for this by having all its speakers read the same passage aloud – but what is gained in comparability is lost in spontaneity. The Intonational Variation in English corpus offers a range of speech events, from spontaneous through semi-spontaneous to scripted, but the marked-up text is again difficult to search. The SCOTS speech documents give orthographic transcripts (that is, transcripts in 'ordinary spelling', sometimes modified to convey particular accents) aligned to recordings of a range of spontaneous speech events. In the SCOTS data, all the participants were aware of being recorded, and so some level of modification of speech has to be assumed.

The danger of using orthographic transcription to make claims about particular articulations and intonation patterns is that it can be characterised, as it is by Leech, McEnery and Wynne (1997, p. 90), as 'a pseudo-procedure the only excuse for which is that it would be prohibitively expensive to attempt anything else'. However, allowing the reservations about using orthographic transcription as the basis for claims about speech, some tentative assertions can still be made about the dialectal variation in the SCOTS documents, which users can check over time against the actual recordings themselves.

The activities suggested in this chapter give an insight into the complexity involved in describing the pronunciation of different varieties of English. This very complexity makes the automated transcription of speech data an enormous intellectual and technical challenge, and despite advances in speech technology, reliable automated transcriptions are still far in the future. Until such time as they are available, online corpora will mainly be of use to the student of pronunciation principally as a source of examples that will continue to require careful manual analysis.

FURTHER READING

Gimson, A.C. (1980). *An Introduction to the Pronunciation of English*. London: Edward Arnold.

McEnery, T. and Wilson, A. (2001). *Corpus Linguistics: An Introduction*. Edinburgh: Edinburgh University Press.

Roach, P. (2000). *English Phonetics and Phonology: A Practical Course*. Third edition. Cambridge: Cambridge University Press.

Stenström, A.-B. (1994). *An Introduction to Spoken Interaction*. Harlow: Longman.

Contextualising
Corpus Texts

7

In this chapter we take a step back from the immediate co-text of language, and consider text as the product of a complex context. The principal issues considered here are as follows:

- What are the important features of the context of texts?
- How can we obtain contextual information from online corpora?
- How can online corpora help us draw correlations between features of language and features of context?

This chapter brings to the fore several of the issues which we have discussed earlier in the book. In Chapter 3 on word searches, we ended by looking at words in the context of their genre, mode, time period and geographical area. In Chapter 4, we studied, among other things, the grammars of different varieties of English, associated with different discourse communities. In Chapter 5, we looked at discourse markers and features characteristic of different types of speakers. Chapter 6, finally, showed how it is possible to draw correlations between features of pronunciation and sociolinguistic factors. The wider context of corpus texts has, therefore, rarely been far from view, even when the principal focus has been on describing features of the immediate co-text, or linguistic environment, of individual lexical items, grammatical constructions, phonological features and discourse structures. This chapter aims to illuminate more fully issues to do with the context of corpus texts.

The first Task, 7.1, highlights the connections between context and language. Some linguists argue that context is recoverable from language – using corpora, we can explore how far this claim is true.

Text and co-text

Linguists, especially corpus linguists, generally make a distinction between *co-text* and *context*. The co-text of a linguistic feature under investigation is the surrounding linguistic material, that is, the words, grammatical constructions,

---

TASK 7.1   The role of context

The following brief extract is taken from the ELISA corpus, at www.uni-tuebingen.de/elisa/html/elisa_index.html

'Sometimes if I need to talk to you real quick, and I blank out on your name, I'll just yell at your horse's name, okay? So you'll be a horse for just that couple of minutes, all right?'

Before you look at the text from which this has been taken, think about the assumptions you can make about:

- the mode of language (Is it spoken or written?)
- the speaker/writer (age, sex, nationality)
- what is happening in the extract
- the roles of the speaker (*I*) and listener (*you*) in the extract
- the level of formality of the text

In each case, what clues in the language of the extract have led you to make these assumptions?

Now use ELISA's concordancer to locate the complete text from which this is an extract. You can do this by searching for the word *yell* in the whole corpus, as this is the only occurrence of the word. Go to the complete text. Read the text, and the metadata at the foot of the page, to see how accurate your guesses were.

---

phonological or discourse features in its vicinity. It is by looking at co-text that we can make generalisations about the typical patterning of language and build up a picture of the use and meaning of linguistic items. Sometimes, it is the immediate co-text which is most significant: as we saw in Chapter 3, the collocates of *rugged* reveal that the word is used to describe both a landscape and, as an extension of this, male facial features. Sometimes, on the other hand, the relevant co-text is the complete text. Consider the words *yours faithfully*, which most commonly occur at the end of a letter: a linguistic explanation for the choice of this expression rather than its near equivalent *yours sincerely* would have to look right back to the start of the text (in this case the letter) to see whether actual practice in introductory greeting formulae in letters follows the recommendations of prescriptive style guides (by using a greeting such as *Dear Sirs, Dear Sir or Madam*) or flouts these recommendations (as with a greeting which includes the correspondent's name: *Dear Mrs Smith, Hi Peter*).

Most corpora nowadays consider a whole-text policy to be the ideal, that is, corpus builders believe it preferable for corpora to contain complete texts rather than extracts. This has not always been standard practice: the Brown Corpus, which was first made available in 1964 and contains texts published three years earlier, as well as later corpora which have mirrored its size and composition for comparative purposes (the 'family' of corpora including the Lancaster–Oslo/Bergen Corpus (LOB), Freiburg-Brown Corpus (FROWN), Freiburg-LOB Corpus (FLOB)), all contain 2000-word samples from 500 texts.

The various national corpora which form the International Corpus of English (ICE) also contain 500 texts of 2000 words each, and some samples are composite, that is, they are made up of more than one short text. A strict design of this sort makes it more straightforward to control the relative sizes of different textual genres within a corpus, which is particularly important when comparability across corpora is a main aim and means that users avoid problems arising from the normalisation of figures from corpora of vastly different sizes. Otherwise, for example, a single legal document of 40,000 words concentrating on a single topic might need to be counterbalanced by, say, 200 short newspaper articles of 200 words each, which would necessarily cover a much more heterogeneous range of subjects. However, while the composition of ICE and Brown is neat, the value of this design is more limited for research into features of discourse, that is, features which emerge from, or have an effect on, the complete text, as we saw in Chapter 5. Besides, advances in technology and more affordable hardware prices mean that corpus builders are no longer tightly restricted by computer memory specification and processing power.

While most of the corpora we have drawn on in this book have adopted a whole-text policy in their design, it is not always possible, for copyright reasons, for the complete texts to be accessible through the online version of the corpus. The issue of whether corpora contain whole texts or only parts of texts is an important one for the consideration of co-text. To return to our examples of *Dear X* and *yours sincerely/faithfully*, we would obviously require a full text to be able to recover from the corpus any rules that link the choice of closing salutation to the choice of opening salutation. Similar considerations hold for other texts – the linguistic patternings found in the introductions to academic research articles are likely to be different to those found at their conclusions. When making claims about the patterns of co-text that are evident in a particular corpus, then, we have to consider whether whole texts or samples have been used in its construction.

Text and context

Elena Tognini-Bonelli (2001, pp. 3–4) has remarked that:

> The corpus, in fact, is in a position to offer the analyst a privileged viewpoint on the evidence, made possible by the new possibility of accessing simultaneously the individual instance, which can be read and expanded on the horizontal axis of the concordance and the social practice retrievable in the repeated patterns of co-selection on the vertical axis of the concordance.

In other words, corpora allow us to see both the co-text, reading horizontally, and the typical context, reading vertically, of an instance of language use. A brief example of this dual vision can be seen in the SCOTS concordance for the search item *budge* below:

'This'll fix you, you'll no **budge**.
I would never **budge** till spring crept over
somethin never mair wid **budge**. Whaur leth and plester
naething, it seemed coud **budge**. But hinnerlie
They will not **budge** now: their stubborness

From a horizontal look at the co-text, it is clear that – as others have noted in the past – *budge* tends to occur in negative environments, *no budge, never budge, naethin . . . coud budge, will not budge*. Looking vertically down the concordance lines, it is clear that this negative *co-text* applies equally to *contexts* in which broad Scots and Standard English are being spoken or written.

Context is more abstract than co-text. In referring to the context of a linguistic item, whether it is a word, an instance of a grammatical construction or a complete text, we mean the totality of the features of its background which may affect the language used. This is also called the *context of situation*, a term first used by the anthropologist Bronislaw Malinowski (1923) and subsequently popularised by the British linguist J.R. Firth (1957b).

We saw briefly in Chapter 3 that it is sometimes objected that corpora present linguistic data out of context. Widdowson, in seeking to make clear where the value of corpus linguistics lies, describes the texts in a corpus as having a 'reflected reality' and notes that for language to be properly interpreted it must be recontextualised (Widdowson 2000, p. 7, and see also McEnery, Xiao and Tono 2006, pp. 131–144, for an extract and further discussion of this issue). Widdowson was concerned with the use of corpus data as a source of 'authentic' language in the EFL classroom; however, his point is no less relevant to linguists analysing corpus texts.

The context is made up of features concerning the author or speaker, such as his/her age, sex, social background, education, occupation, where he or she lives and was born and brought up, and other languages that he or she speaks. It also includes features of textual production, such as when the text was written (or whether it was drafted and redrafted over an extended period of time), whether it is a translation from another language (and if so, which), whether it has been published, or in the case of a spoken text, whether it was spontaneous or planned, whether the participants knew each other or the speaker knew the hearer(s) and so on. We shall see how it is possible to use such sociolinguistic and contextual variables in the examples and tasks in this chapter, but first let us consider how a number of online corpora present this kind of information.

Metadata

Some information about the context of texts may be ascertained from the text itself. For example, the genre of a letter may be clear from its layout on the page (if the text formatting preserves such information), or from set expressions such as *Yours sincerely* or *We acknowledge receipt of your letter of* [+ date], which all fluent or native speakers of a language will recognise as indicative of this particular type of text. Similarly, a poem is often, though not always, recognisable from its layout, and there may be clues in the metre or rhyme too. With a transcribed conversation, it may be possible to work out whether speakers are male or female from the names or pronouns that are used, and of course speakers may offer information such as their town of birth explicitly in the course of a conversation.

Much of the information that will aid sociolinguistic study, however, is not so readily established. 'Reading vertically', to adopt Tognini-Bonelli's term, is only possible if there is some way of relating the repeated patterns of co-selection to the social context. Expressed differently, if the research question requires you to know the location in which a conversation took place (on a bus, in the living room of one of the speakers, in a supermarket queue), the speakers' places of birth, or whether a talk was delivered extempore or was prepared in advanced and read from prompt cards, then you will need to use a corpus which makes such information available. This information is known as *metadata*. Metadata means data about data, that is, additional information about the corpus texts, which are themselves data for linguistic research. Different corpora naturally take different approaches to metadata: for example some hold metadata in a database which can be accessed from each text, while others include metadata in text header encoded in mark-up language.

Figures 7.1, 7.2 and 7.3 present samples of the metadata associated with three corpora: the first is the metadata accompanying a poem in the SCOTS corpus, the second the information relating to a television broadcast contained in the BNC and the third a search page from the MICASE corpus showing the different attributes of speakers and transcripts which have been recorded.

TASK 7.2   Corpora and metadata

Look at the BYU-BNC (http://corpus.byu.edu/), SCOTS (www.scottishcorpus. ac.uk) and MICASE (http://quod.lib.umich.edu/m/micase) and investigate how to access the metadata available with each corpus. In each case:

- Which details do you think are likely to be most valuable in investigating linguistic behaviour?
- Why do you think these details are most useful?
- In what ways do you think information such as the following might inform linguistic analysis: the speaker's father's occupation; the speaker's level of education; the level of interaction of speech; the speaker's first language?

Corpora and sociolinguistics

Context is of great importance in the field of sociolinguistics, which aims to relate variety in language to social and contextual factors, arguing that 'language exists in context, dependent on the speaker who is using it, and dependent on where it is being used and why' (Tagliamonte 2006, p. 3). Braun (2007, p. 32) has noted that a corpus is like a 'text museum'. That is, 'The exhibits are real

Author details ◄	
Author id	794
Title	
Forenames	
Initials	
Surname	
Gender	Female
Decade of birth	1930
Educational attainment	College
Age left school	15
Upbringing/religious beliefs	Protestantism
Occupation	Retired teacher
Place of birth	Glasgow
Region of birth	Glasgow
Birthplace CSD dialect area	Gsw
Country of birth	Scotland
Place of residence	Crieff
Region of residence	E & SE Perthshire
Residence CSD dialect area	Per
Country of residence	Scotland
Father's occupation	Stonemason
Father's place of birth	Lochgilphead
Father's region of birth	Argyll
Father's birthplace CSD dialect area	Arg
Father's country of birth	Scotland
Mother's occupation	Retail pharmacy

Figure 7.1   SCOTS screenshot showing extract of sociolinguistic metadata relating to an anonymous author

HV1 Central Weekend Live — part 1: television broadcast (Leisure). Recorded on 29 October 1993 with 10 participants, totalling 5626 words, 370 utterances (duration not recorded).
PS000 1261 words, 129 utterances.
PS3E3 ('Nicky Campbell', male, 30+, television presenter, Scottish): 323 words, 11 utterances.
PS3E4 ('Sue Jay', female, 40+, television presenter): 1153 words, 90 utterances.
PS3E5 ('Oliver James', male, 30+, consultant psychologist): 446 words, 26 utterances.
PS3E6 ('Dr Vernon Coleman', male, 40+, medical consultant/correspondent): 820 words, 47 utterances.
PS3E7 ('Dr Cosmo Hallstrom', male, 40+, medical consultant): 101 words, 1 utterance.
PS3E8 ('Donna', female, 40+, journalist): 681 words, 25 utterances.
PS3E9 ('Dr Simon Fradd', male, 40+, general practitioner): 546 words, 25 utterances.
PS3EA ('Graeme Wilson', male, 30+, representative of Citizens' Commission on Human Rights, Irish): 143 words, 9 utterances.
PS3EB ('Peter', male, 40+): 152 words, 7 utterances.

Figure 7.2   Screenshot from BNC website showing background information associated with text file HV1

(as real as e.g. historical artefacts) but, if you enter without preparation and appropriate background knowledge, your benefits will be limited.' Extending the analogy, if a corpus is like a text museum, then the metadata we discussed in the previous section is the equivalent of the small plaques which provide the appropriate background knowledge, giving information about the origin of each artefact, where it was found, when it dates from, who it might have been created by, whether it is part of a series of similar artefacts and so on.

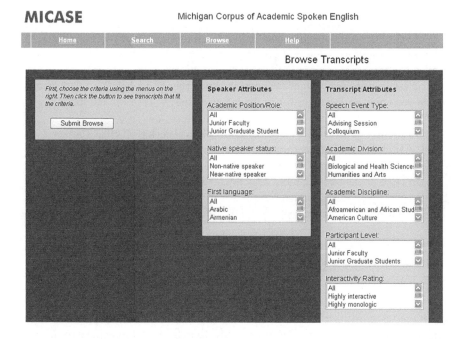

Figure 7.3   Screenshot of MICASE browse page showing metadata categories

Sociolinguistics has always relied on authentic data, rather than, say, introspective reflection on one's own language use. Because of the very nature of the field, specifically its concern with how language varies in relation to social factors, introspection about language can only take sociolinguists so far. Sociolinguistic data often take the form of small corpora of spoken material designed and built for the specific purpose of the research: quite typical, for example, are collections of 30–40 interviews or recorded conversations, which are relatively homogeneous in the sense that they have been recorded in similar circumstances or involve informants who share features of their background (e.g. similar age, same town of residence, similar occupations). It is important in sociolinguistics to limit the variables involved so that the generalisations which are drawn can be as robust as possible. Tagliamonte (2006) contains an informative discussion of the process of designing, collecting and analysing sociolinguistic corpora.

Corpora which are available online have so far been used relatively little in sociolinguistics (though see for example Anderwald (2001) for research which draws on the BNC), but they are a great resource to be tapped, as long as you bear a few issues in mind. To explore these, now complete Task 7.3.

In completing Task 7.3, you probably came up with a number of potential problems in using corpora to investigate sociolinguistic problems. Three important issues concern the nature of the corpus, the nature of the available metadata and, perhaps less obviously, the interactions between the two. First, several of the online corpora we have been using here are quite general in their scope and so contain quite heterogeneous collections of texts – everything from informal,

---

TASK 7.3   Corpora and sociolinguistics

Drawing on your experience of carrying out the tasks in this book and your knowledge of the online corpora used, what issues do you think arise in carrying out sociolinguistic analysis with online corpora? You might find it helpful to think about how you could go about answering the following specific research questions.

- Do younger speakers use more tag questions in speech than older speakers?
- Do students ask different sorts of questions in Arts and Humanities lectures compared with Science lectures?
- Do radio presenters use more adjectives than television presenters?
- Is seniority of position a significant factor in the choice of terms of address used by students to academic staff?

In each case, what sort of corpus would you use, what data would you need in addition to texts themselves and how would you carry out the analysis?

---

spontaneous conversation to carefully worded poetry. In order to turn these corpora to good use in sociolinguistic study, therefore, you may have to limit the texts you select, in order to create a more or less homogeneous subcorpus from a very heterogeneous corpus. For example, the paper cited above (Anderwald 2001) used a subset of the BNC made up of the spontaneous spoken data, which totalled about 5 million words of text, but still offered the regional variation required. While this represents only one-twentieth of the complete BNC, this is nevertheless a massive quantity of spoken data compared with the amount that a single researcher could collect and transcribe. So the first thing to bear in mind is that it is often possible to specify a relevant subset of a complete corpus. If you do choose to do this, however, remember to take it into account when you come to interpret your results.

Secondly, online corpora vary with respect to the quantity and nature of metadata which is provided alongside the texts. As we have seen, metadata is data about data, that is, background information regarding the corpus texts and authors/speakers. The ELISA corpus contains a number of metadata fields, and given the interview nature of the data, a great deal more can be established through reading the texts themselves. Similarly, it was an important decision in the planning of the SCOTS corpus that the team would collect a wide range of sociolinguistic metadata alongside each text: however, even this cannot hope to be comprehensive. Because spoken text participants and authors could choose not to provide information (or provide information only for those questions which they were comfortable answering), the full range of metadata is not available for all texts. Some participants were reluctant to provide information about their religious upbringing or affiliation, for example. Some issues that might turn out to be important – such as the marital status of the participants – might not have been anticipated by the corpus designers. The second thing to bear in mind, therefore, is any limitation of the chosen corpus in terms of metadata.

Some compromise might have been necessary or some useful bit of metadata might not be available.

Thirdly, it is not always possible to limit a search on the basis of particular metadata fields. Let us illustrate this with an example: the BNC gives information about the gender of speakers in the corpus' spoken texts, but it is not possible through the BNC's freely available web interface, or the BYU-BNC, to specify that you want to search for a particular word in the speech of only female or only male speakers. The gender of speakers can be checked *post hoc* and possible correlations can be investigated at that stage, but this is more time-consuming. This then highlights the importance of getting to know how best to exploit the available corpora. In time, you may decide to build your own corpus. Both Adolphs (2006) and McEnery, Xiao and Tono (2006) give excellent advice on this daunting but immensely satisfying solution.

If sociolinguists have not yet exploited online corpora as fully as they might, this is largely because of the special requirements of sociolinguistic analysis. McEnery, Xiao and Tono (2006, p. 108) have recently commented that:

> The expansion of corpus work in sociolinguistics appears to have been hampered by three problems: the operationalization of sociolinguistic theory into measurable categories suitable for corpus research, the lack of sociolinguistic metadata encoded in currently available corpora and the lack of sociolinguistically rigorous sampling in corpus construction.

Rigorous sampling is necessary for a study which takes a quantitative as well as a qualitative approach to analysis. A quantitative analysis, as we have seen in this book, is one which seeks to make generalisations, based for example on relative frequencies of linguistic items in the corpus, regarding the distribution of such items in the language as a whole (or the subset of language which the corpus seeks to represent). A qualitative analysis on the other hand need not concern itself with the frequency of items but rather with providing an in-depth description of a linguistic item. Often, both types of analysis will contribute to a study, and it is normally true that a predominantly quantitative analysis also requires some qualitative input, in order, for example, to establish the wider implications of a statistical finding.

McEnery, Xiao and Tono conclude, however, that 'With the increasing availability of corpora which encode rich sociolinguistic metadata (e.g. the BNC), the corpus-based approach is expected to play a more important role in sociolinguistics.' (ibid, p. 110). Already, online corpora can act as an excellent testing ground for intuitions regarding sociolinguistic variables. In the tasks in this chapter, we concentrate on the ELISA corpus, the BNC and the SCOTS corpus, all of which contain metadata, although it is presented in different ways. Indeed, Braun, one of the creators of the ELISA corpus, comments that 'the common overall theme of the interviews [in ELISA] creates a high degree of "intertextual coherence" (i.e. the homogeneity), which makes discourse construction and situational embedding even easier' (Braun 2007, p. 32). More such corpora are likely to be made available in the near future, so we recommend that you keep an eye on Internet portal sites for information on these.

Task 7.4 concentrates on identifying the clues available in a corpus to help you account for patterns or regularities in language.

TASK 7.4   Supporting evidence

1. Go to the SCOTS corpus at www.scottishcorpus.ac.uk.
2. Search for the word 'soccer' in the SCOTS corpus, using Quick Search.
3. Are you surprised to find examples of 'soccer' in a corpus of Scottish English and Scots varieties? If so, why is this? What does your intuition tell you about the word 'soccer'?
4. Click on the title of each text in which the word occurs to be taken to the complete text and access the associated metadata.
5. Using the information you can gain from the titles of the texts, the immediate context (concordance lines), the fuller context (i.e. whole text) and sociolinguistic metadata, can you account for each of the occurrences?
6. Repeat the search for *football* and *fitba / fitba'*.

TASK 7.5   Audio and video data

Use the SCOTS Standard Search facility to retrieve a list of all of the spoken documents in the corpus. (You can do this by unchecking 'written' in the Document section of the search box before hitting 'Search'.) Reorder the resulting list according to the type of media, by clicking on the 'Multimedia' heading in the list of retrieved documents. This will bring all of the video texts to the top of the list. Select one video text at random and listen to the audio without watching the accompanying video. (You may have to turn away from your computer screen!)

As you listen to the beginning of the audio file, jot down what you imagine to be the situational context of the speech event, and note any clues you are drawing on, for example:

- how many people are involved?
- roughly how old are the speakers?
- where is it taking place?
- if there is more than one speaker, how are the participants sitting or standing in relation to each other?

Now run the multimedia file again, and this time watch the video. Did the actual context, as far as you can establish it from the video, match your expectations? Do some questions remain unanswerable even with the additional clues from the video?

As you will easily see, some features of the context of a text can be ascertained from the linguistic content of a text and from background information which has been explicitly provided. With spoken texts, further information could have been recovered, if we had been present at the time of the recording. Before you try Task 7.5, make a list of the additional types of information you would expect to be aware of, if you were in the room while a recording took place, compared with simply listening to the recording after the event.

This chapter so far has related corpus data to the wider context of use. The second half of this chapter focuses on particular aspects of the context of texts. We begin with variables related to the speaker or writer, looking at the effect of age, and place of birth or residence on language. Then, we will examine some of the parameters of variation related to the situational characteristics of texts, that is, their use in context – textual mode, degree of informality and subject matter.

User-related variables

We can tell a lot about a speaker from what he or she says and how he or she says it. Conversely, some background information about a person can help us predict, to a greater or lesser degree, how he or she will use language. Read the following brief extracts from spoken texts in the SCOTS corpus, and think about your expectations of the speakers. Roughly how old are they? What sex are they? Can you tell where they come from? Do you have preconceptions regarding their level of education or occupation? In each case, note down the linguistic clues you find – these may form the basis of your own study later.

1. They make you be strong and when you eat, eat, eat, eat so much you get stronger and stronger and stronger and stronger and stronger! [SCOTS document 798]
2. [. . .] she pays a fortune and we were like, "Yvonne, you do know it's gonna be fake?" And she was like, "It's not!", and I was like, "You're not gonna get a bag, a Gucci bag for fifty quid!" [SCOTS document 804]
3. So I'll say a little bit about the background just in case, and highlight the key points there that we've been trying to address. I'll say a little bit about the language curriculum review group, how it was set up and what our main discussions so far have been, and then I'll focus in mainly on the three phases of the programme [. . .] [SCOTS document 1382]

You might have guessed that extract 1 is from the speech of a young child, and if so then the most obvious clues were most likely the lexical repetitions of *eat* and *strong*, or the unnecessary copula *be*. In fact, it is from a conversation involving a young boy who was about five at the time of the recording. He is talking about the function of muscles in the human body and in super-heroes' bodies. Extract 2 is easily recognisable as a conversation between friendly acquaintances. This time the speaker is female (the topic matter, designer hand-bags, suggests but does not of course confirm this) and in her early twenties at the time of the recording in 2005. Perhaps the repeated use of *like* to introduce quotations was the best clue to the speaker's age here. Extract 3, finally, is from a presentation given by a professional, a university-educated lecturer. Here it is probably the subject matter, and the explicit signalling of the different parts of the speech, a presentation to colleagues, which reveals the most about the speaker.

TASK 7.6   Sociolinguistic indicators

Drawing on your knowledge of language and familiarity with different sectors of society, make a list of lexical items or other linguistic features which you would expect to find in the speech of the following speakers.

- a judge
- an airline steward
- a first-year student
- a final-year student
- the mother of a young child
- a professor of linguistics

What was your reasoning for the words you noted for each speaker?

Did you consider each speaker in a context obviously linked to his or her occupation or status (e.g. a judge passing a verdict in a courtroom, an airline steward instructing passengers on how to use the emergency equipment on a plane, a mother taking her child to nursery, the professor giving a lecture to a class of students)? What happens if you consider them in a less obvious context (e.g. the judge walking in the park with her grandchildren, the mother speaking to customers in the hairdresser's shop she works in, the professor having Christmas dinner with her parents)? Would you still expect to find any of the linguistic features you suggested? To what extent are your words dependent on the context in which the speech is taking place and to what extent are they dependent on demographic features of the speaker?

It is often the case that it is not individual linguistic items which allow you to identify user-related features of a speaker: for example, while children commonly use diminutives such as *doggy*, *kitty*, *dolly* and so on, all of these items may also be found in the speech of adults, perhaps while speaking to children, or to pets, or in informal settings with other adults. Rather, combinations of items will act as indicators of contextual features. Therefore, a qualitative, rather than a quantitative, approach will serve us better here.

Here is an extract from a text in the SCOTS corpus, involving the word *pink*. What can you infer about the speakers, and the situation, from this extract?

F1117:   Are you doing a nice job? // You like yellow. How about doing a bit of red? You usually like red, don't you? //
F1118:   //Ca- I can't. // This is pink.

F1117: Is that pink?
F1118: Yeah.
F1117: What's your favourite colour?
F1118: Pink.
F1117: Pink? Pink to make the boys wink!
        [SCOTS document 1559]

TASK 7.7   User-related variables

Here is another extract from the transcription of a spoken text in the SCOTS corpus.

F1155: // I've heard of it then. // Oh, cause the people, there's girls that live upstairs from us, two of them always wear // army costumes,//
F1154: //[sniff]//
F1155: like, [laugh] I think they're in that TA thing.// And they always//
F1154: //No.//
F1155: wear that and then there's this other one who's kind of Gothic looking. I thought that she was a bit kind of Gothic looking but //she's not//
F1154: //Yeah.// //Oh.//
F1155: //fat so, can't be her.// [laugh] //She's quite skinny.//
F1154: //No.// No this, [CENSORED: forename], she's
F1155: So but erm [CENSORED: forename] // thought she saw her.//
F1154: //But the one that has// white, she has wh- like pretty much white peroxide hair the now, and er she's pretty chunky at the minute. //And she's got a really ugly boyfriend who looks like Marilyn Manson,//
F1155: //Well,//
F1154: and she looks like Courtney Love. [laugh] //[laugh]//
        [SCOTS document 1577]

What, for you, are the linguistic features which stand out in this short extract? Think about both what is being communicated and the language used.

Listen to the audio file. Do your answers change when you hear the intonation?

Now look at the accompanying metadata for this text. Which are the demographic factors which you think contribute most to the features of language used here: age, sex, geographical origin, occupation?

Choose another online corpus and investigate the typical semantic and lexical environment of some of the salient linguistic features exemplified here, for example:

• Is *chunky* often used to describe people? Does the co-text suggest that it is flattering or not?
• What sorts of words appear in the grammatical framework *that* [noun] *thing*, exemplified here as *that TA thing* [=Territorial Army]?
• Can you characterise the context in which expressions like *the now* and *at the minute* most commonly occur?

The speaker ID codes indicate that both speakers are female. Their utterances in conversation might indicate other sociolinguistic information, including the following:

- their age (are they adults or children?)
- their respective status (why does F1117 ask a lot of questions?)

If a pattern is sociolinguistically interesting then it should be generalisable. If you find patterns of interaction in one set of data between, say, an adult and a young child in the SCOTS corpus, you should check it against other similar interactions.

For example, you can compare this exchange against other extracts involving young children talking about colours. Can you see any tendencies in the way children use colour terms in speech, and the sorts of things that are described by the different colours? You can use the SCOTS Advanced Search to find colour terms being used by older speakers and ask the following questions:

- Are there different patterns of language use here?
- What other speaker variables or features of context might be affecting the use of colour terms?

Finally in this section, one real advantage of online corpora for analysis of the correlations between user-related variables and language is the accessibility of varieties of English from around the world. Through the Internet, we have immediate access to transcriptions, audio files, video files, analysis tools – and multimedia corpora – in a way that could scarcely have been dreamed of a couple of decades ago.

TASK 7.8   User-related variables

Working in small groups, take turns to play each other extracts from the ELISA corpus, which contains interviews with native speakers of English from around the world. How much footage do you have to listen to before you can guess correctly:

- where the speaker is from (how precise can you be?)
- roughly how old the speaker is
- the speaker's occupation?

Note down the linguistic clues which lead you to your responses – are these phonological, lexical, grammatical, discoursal?

As before, it is useful to check one set of data against another. Pick a few of the lexical 'diagnostic' items that you searched for using the SCOTS corpus. Using WebCorp search for further examples.

Use-related variables

The form which language takes is also affected by factors relating to the use to which it is put. Through language, most of us are perfectly capable of handling large numbers of different situations without a second thought. Think about the different ways you might speak or write in the following circumstances:

1(a) on the telephone to an elderly female relative to thank her for your recent birthday present
1(b) on the telephone to your best friend to arrange a night out
2(a) in an interview for a job you really want
2(b) giving a talk to brief a group of Scouts before a camping trip
3(a) in a letter to your French penfriend whom you've never met
3(b) in a letter to your bank to request a raise on your overdraft limit

In each response, you may have found yourself describing each pair of hypothetical situations with reference to three types of variables: the *mode* of discourse, that is, the role of language in the situation, including the channel it takes, for example, whether it is spoken or written; the *tenor* of discourse, which concerns the relationship between the participants and includes the level of formality expected for this relationship; and the *field* of discourse, in short, what is being spoken or written about and what is happening in the language event. In the systemic functional approach to language, developed by Michael Halliday (see for example Halliday 1978, Halliday and Hasan 1985), these three types of variables in the context of situation combine to define the *register* of language.

The first two situations clearly have some features of their register in common. In both, the mode of language is spoken – more precisely they are both telephone conversations, a particular type of situation where there are usually only two speakers and they are not visible to each other. Also, in both, you, as one participant, would know the other speaker well; however, there is likely to be a rather more formal tenor in the first of the pair, as most people would show more overt politeness to an elderly female relative than to their best friend, especially when she's bought them a present! Finally, the field or subject matter of the two telephone conversations will differ: the first may focus on the present received, the birthday itself, although of course there may be other topics of conversation such as the weather, your relative's health and so on as well. The second may typically also begin with general enquiries before focusing on all aspects of planning a night out.

In terms of mode, the second pair of situations are also both examples of spoken language – a talk and a face-to-face interview are both spoken genres. Indeed, they also share aspects of their tenor: there is a difference in power between the two parties in each situation. In 2(a) you, the interviewee, are in a position of little power and are expected to show deference to the other party, the interviewer(s). In 2(b) on the other hand, it is you who are in charge of the situation, and you will show control over your listeners through the language you use. Of course, the respective fields will differ greatly too: whereas in 2(a) the interview is likely to cover the nature of the job, your skills and qualifications, why you want the job and so on, in 2(b) topics such as safety, itineraries and behaviour may feature highly.

Examples 3(a) and 3(b) share their mode and differ from the other examples in this respect: the channel of communication here is written. The two letters will take very different forms, however, because of differences between the two situations in tenor and field. Even if you have not met your French penfriend before, the letter is likely to be relatively informal, because neither of you has a more powerful position than the other (although your abilities in a foreign language may affect the tenor). The bank, on the other hand, has a lot of power, specifically the power to grant or refuse your request for a raise on your overdraft limit. There is likely to be no common ground between the field of these two letters.

TASK 7.9   Identifying register from extracts

How would you describe the field of the following two extracts?

Extract A: 'right, that's right um, he he allows seven years to go by well anyway he gets ready to depart, mkay uh, I'm again on the first page towards the bottom, and we have a description of his wife Miyagi. his wife Miyagi, who was beautiful enough to stop any man's eyes, had always taken good care of Katsushiro. but at this decisive moment she disapproved of his purchase of goods and of his projected journey to Kyoto. she did her best to dissuade him, but in the face of his impetuous nature all her efforts were in vain.' [MICASE transcript ID LEL140SU074]

Extract B: 'and so one question is well, uh you know if we wanted to send a crew of astronauts to a distant star, would they die of old age before they got there? and the answer is not necessarily. if, we get the ship going fast enough. for example, suppose that we get a rocket ship going so fast, that this square root factor is point-one for the gamma, and one over point-one is ten. and let's say, so the speed will be very close to the speed of light then, and let's say there's a star, a hundred light years away. and the ship is moving at close to the speed of light. how long does it take to reach the star? about a hundred years, moving at the speed of light. now. okay.' [MICASE transcript ID LEL485JU097]

What were the most important linguistic clues for you? Do these concern lexis, grammar, discourse?

Can you establish the tenor and mode of these extracts from other linguistic clues? Remember you can check the attributes of the speaker and the text in MICASE.

Here we have begun with a situation and established the factors which are likely to have an effect on the language produced. But the reverse approach is also possible. Halliday (in Halliday and Hasan 1985, p. 38) explains that:

Any piece of text, long or short, spoken or written, will carry with it indications of its context. We only have to hear or read a section of it to know where it comes from. This means that we reconstruct from the text certain aspects of the situation, certain features of the field, the tenor, and the mode. Given the text, we construct the situation from it.

Tasks 7.9 (above) and 7.10 ask you to identify the situation behind extracts from online corpora.

TASK 7.10   Indicators of tenor

The adjective *wee* functions in Scottish English and Scots to mean 'small' and also to convey the level of formality of the speech. How would you characterise the tenor of the following concordance lines: formal or informal?

- Did she have her **wee** alcoholic friend with her?
- You know that sonsie sorta face that **wee** babies have in their pram
- AGNES: (TO BETH) You huv a **wee** seat, hen.
- Juist you hae a **wee** rest or ye gether yeirsell!
- If you want to wait a **wee** second I'll take you to it
- You can help wi some o the **wee** particularities.
- [laugh] Make you look like a **wee** old fart.

Replace *wee* with the more neutral adjective *small* in each example. Is it fair to say that *wee* is the Scots equivalent of the English (and Scottish English) *small*? If you feel it is not, why not? How can you compensate for the effect of *wee* if it is lost in translation?

Now perform an Advanced Search to find a text in SCOTS which is a conversation between family members. What indicators can you find in the transcription of informality?

The final exercise in this chapter aims to bring together this discussion of the field, tenor and mode of a text by looking at how it is possible to draw on the expectations of a register within the context of another type of text.

TASK 7.11   Clues to register

How would you describe the register of a fairy tale in terms of its field, tenor and mode?

Using the TIME corpus of US journalism from 1923 to the present day, available at http://corpus.byu.edu/time/, search for examples of the expression *once upon a time*.

- Can you find examples where the expression is part of a fairy tale?
- Can you find examples where the expression is being used to recall the genre of a fairy tale? What does that contribute to the text?
- When the expression recalls a fairy tale, can you find any further clues in the co-text to reinforce this (e.g. specific lexis, discourse structure).
- In what other ways is the expression used?

Summary

This chapter pulled together strands from previous chapters concerning how online corpora can be used to investigate issues relating to the co-text and, more particularly, the context in which linguistic items (words, grammatical structures, phonemes etc.) occur. We discovered that we are very much at the mercy of the corpus builders in this respect, but that relevant metadata can be mined for significant correlations between language form and sociolinguistic and contextual features and allows us to come to a more nuanced understanding of the linguistic variation which is evident in data. In particular, the notions of *field, tenor* and *mode* were useful in enabling different registers of language to be described with reference to different features in their context of situation.

FURTHER READING

Biber, D., Conrad, S. and Reppen, R. (1998). *Corpus Linguistics: Investigating Language Structure and Use.* Cambridge: Cambridge University Press.

Crystal, D. (1995). *The Cambridge Encyclopedia of the English Language.* Cambridge: Cambridge University Press.

McEnery, T., Xiao, R. and Tono, Y. (2006). *Corpus-Based Language Studies: An Advanced Resource Book.* London and New York: Routledge.

Meyerhoff, M. (2006). *Introducing Sociolinguistics.* London and New York: Routledge.

O'Keeffe, A., McCarthy, M. and Carter, R. (2007). *From Corpus to Classroom.* Cambridge: Cambridge University Press.

Romaine, S. (2000). *Language in Society: An Introduction to Sociolinguistics.* Oxford: Oxford University Press.

Conclusion: Issues in the Use of Corpora in Teaching and Research

8

This book has had two main aims. We have sought to introduce you to the following:

• empirical, that is, evidence-based ways of exploring aspects of the English language systematically
• a range of online resources, especially electronic corpora, that provide both data and search tools to enable your explorations.

We have now looked at how electronic resources can support you in your investigations of different levels of spoken and written language, namely the lexical, phonological, grammatical and discourse levels. We have also touched on ways of linking language use to different contexts. This concluding chapter revisits some general issues in the use of corpora in teaching and research, considers where you might go next and speculates about how online corpora in general seem to be developing.

Using corpora in teaching

The instant availability of searchable, online corpora has much to offer the teacher of English in both first and second language contexts. An excellent introduction to corpora in educational contexts is O'Keeffe, McCarthy and Carter (2007). The interactive and 'authentic' nature of the texts in the corpora makes them a rich teaching resource both for native speakers and speakers of English as a second or other language. For example, the language section of the 2005 Scottish Qualifications Authority Higher English examination included a typical question inviting candidates to discuss the extent to which English has 'borrowed' words, phrases and idioms from other parts of the world. By combining a dictionary and a suite of online corpora, the teacher of English can design a project that actively involves pupils in exploring this topic. Task 8.1 gives an example.

TASK 8.1   Borrowings in English

1. Look up the following words in a good dictionary. What do they mean? Which languages did they come from? What is the date of the first recorded use in English? *pièce de résistance, déjà vu, juggernaut, dervish, kamikaze, karaoke, banshee, samba, voodoo, alcohol, coffee, creek, boomerang.*
2. Go to the TIME corpus, at http://corpus.byu.edu/time/.
3. Click on Chart. Search for each of the words in turn. The results of this search will show you the use of each term, decade by decade in the American magazine *TIME* from 1923 to 2006. To see the context of the words in each decade, click on the relevant bar on the chart.
4. Note down your observations about the words, e.g.

   - are they used consistently throughout the period 1923–2006?
   - if not, why not?
   - how frequently are they used?
   - are they used in particular contexts, e.g. to what kind of things does *pièce de résistance* generally refer?
   - are the terms used to describe other nouns?
   - does a particular set of adjectives or nouns describe them?
   - are any markers of their 'foreignness' still evident in the contexts in which they are used?

5. Write a brief description, giving the sources of these borrowings and discussing how they have been used in *TIME* magazine over eight decades.

The availability of the TIME corpus and the search function that allows the user to see the distribution of items decade by decade together allow the imaginative teacher to devise activities that can engage learners in exploring how aspects of language – in this case 'borrowings' – are used in almost a century's worth of American journalism. The words and phrases here show a range of types of borrowings into English: while *kamikaze* is attested in the TIME corpus before Second World War, its usage unsurprisingly peaks in the 1940s. *Karaoke*, on the other hand, is unknown in the TIME corpus before the 1980s: in the few examples where it does occur, in discussions of imported Japanese culture, its meaning has to be explained:

Now thousands of closet Sinatras and Madonnas are publicly vocalizing, thanks to a nifty electronic device from Japan called the **karaoke**.

In the 2000s, its cultural popularity remains unabated, and the link to Japan is generally diminished:

Lebanon has never won an Olympic medal, but recently a Lebanese woman won the world **karaoke** championship in Finland, singing the 1980s classic Fame.

This activity can be adapted to some degree to explore British texts using the BYU-BNC, though instead of decades, the chart will show types of text. Even so, it is interesting to see if, say, *juggernaut* is more commonly found in speech, journalism, fiction or academic prose.

Teachers of English as a first language can, of course, adapt many of the activities in this book to meet the demands of their courses. In addition, as we have seen above, corpora can provide a wealth of easily searched texts that can be used in language projects investigating a range of themes, such as the impact of borrowings on English over time. At present, corpora are probably more frequently used by teachers of English as a second language than by teachers of English as a first language. The promise that corpora would provide learners of English as a foreign language with a wealth of data about 'authentic' language use in different contexts, though critiqued by Widdowson (1996, 1998), meant that writers and publishers of course books and reference books quickly took advantage of available corpora and began compiling their own. While their concerns might overlap, teachers and learners of English as a foreign language tend to have different interests from teachers and learners of English as a first language.

One obvious, traditional way for teachers and learners to engage with corpora is to use them as a source of information about particular patterns of usage. A typical concern for EFL teachers and learners, for example, is the meaning and use of two-word verbs such as *get into, get over, get through*, particularly when they mean things like *become interested in, stop being upset by* and *endure*.

TASK 8.2   Exploring 'Got + Preposition'

1. Go to the BYU-BNC, at http://corpus.byu.edu/bnc.
2. Click on Chart.
3. In the 'Word(s)' box, type 'got [pr*]' to find results for *got* + any preposition.
4. From the chart, identify in which type of English texts this sequence is most frequently found. Click on that type of text.
5. You will now see a list of examples of *got + preposition* in that text type. Choose one example, e.g. *got into*, and click on it to see the examples in context.
6. Choose a sample of 20 examples in context and group them according to meaning, e.g. *became interested in, became involved with, moved physically into*, etc. Identify the most frequent meanings in your sample.

This kind of activity engages the learner in active 'consciousness-raising' activities that make them pay attention to the meaning of particular patterns of English. This kind of activity has been a staple of language classrooms for decades, and it might be objected that such activities place an emphasis on 'output' or 'product' as determined by other language users. In other words, learners in the above activity are exploring how other people have used sequences like *got into* in their own utterances. While this might well be useful in helping learners internalise the meanings of sequences like *got into*, it does not involve learners in the process of *using* the target language.

It is possible to use corpora as input into language-learning tasks that have more of a focus on process than product. Two particular benefits of the increasing frequency of specialised and multimedia corpora are the availability to teachers and learners of EFL of (i) unfamiliar examples of language use in particular contexts and (ii) recordings of speakers of English in many contexts that are not usually found in textbooks and their accompanying audio-visual resources. The MICASE corpus, for example, is rich in material that can be used to prepare learners of English for Academic Purposes for university study. The SCOTS corpus is particularly rich in adult-child spoken discourse of the type that has generally escaped the attention of EFL materials writers, but which nevertheless can be adapted to provide interesting classroom activities.

One issue of relevance to EFL teachers is the potential role played by corpus data as a model for classroom production. There is a longstanding debate in language education about 'product' oriented teaching versus 'process' oriented teaching (Richards and Rodgers 2001, pp. 24–25). In product-oriented teaching, learners are generally required to imitate native-speaker models, which might well be supplied by corpus data. In process-oriented teaching, learners refine their language knowledge by completing successively more demanding communicative tasks. There has been a considerable swing towards process-oriented teaching over the past few decades, and so there is understandable anxiety amongst some EFL professionals about simply using corpora as a source of language for learners to imitate. This anxiety is intensified by further developments in the EFL profession that have questioned the status given to native-speaker performance as a general model for language acquisition and suggest a new model based on non-native speaker, 'lingua franca' interaction (Jenkins 2007).

Despite these anxieties, native speaker corpora have much to offer EFL teachers who favour a process-oriented approach. Rather than using a corpus purely as a source of language for learners to imitate, corpora can be mined for instances of actual language use that can inform learners' performance. Typically, in process-oriented classes, learners are given a communicative task to perform. Their performance may then be compared with corpus data featuring speakers performing similar tasks. Learners' attention is drawn to the expressive resources used by these speakers – which may be adopted or rejected by learners. In short,

---

TASK 8.3   Anticipating a Dialogue

1. Ask learners to role-play a dialogue in which a 5-year-old child tells an adult how Spiderman became Spiderman.
2. Play an excerpt from the SCOTS corpus [Document 798: Conversation 15- Glasgow father and his 5-year-old son].
3. Ask learners to compare their own performance of the dialogue with that of the father and child. What do they notice about the child's language?
4. Repeat the activity, this time asking learners to role-play a dialogue in which a 5-year-old child tells an adult how Superman became Superman.

corpus data is not used as a model for learners to mimic slavishly but as examples of communicative behaviour against which they can critically compare their own performances.

An example of a process-oriented classroom activity using corpus data is given in Task 8.3. The activity requires EFL learners to 'anticipate' a dialogue between a father and his son, excerpted from one of the recordings in the SCOTS corpus.

The relevant excerpt from the SCOTS corpus is given below. M804 is the father; M805 is the 5-year-old child.

M804: [laugh] Okay. So, ehm, I was wondering if maybe you could tell me about how Spiderman became Spiderman?

M805: Ehm, so this guy wa-, called Peter Parker was in a place and officer um [?]crogrammes[/?] and there was a spider, //radioactive//

M804: //mm//

M805: spider.

M804: Oh!

M805: And it climbed up Peter Parker and it bit him and then he tu- and then he was poisoned by that spider and he, and he was turning into a spider himself!

M804: Oh //He turned in-//

M805: //[?]With a[/?]// human head!

M804: Oh so he had a spider's body and a human head?

M805: Yeah.

M804: Oh! So how did he become Spiderman that's not got the spider's body?

M805: Um, and there was actually a dream and a- and he walked onto the road and a car was coming //for him//

M804: //Oh!//

M805: and he jumped and he was sticking to the wall!

M804: Really?

M805: Erm, and he noticed he had superpowers, so he would call himself Spiderman!

There are various reasons why this exchange would not work as a model to be imitated in a product-oriented classroom. The first reason is that the child is simply wrong in his answer to his father's question: Peter Parker does not turn into a spider, either in the comic book or the films. Secondly, at this stage of development, the child tends to use quite vague language, such as 'Peter Parker was in a place'. The excerpt, therefore, is best seen as a resource for the comparison of the learner's and the native-speaker's performance, not a text that should be used as a strict model to guide the learner's performance.

In the process-oriented classroom, there are some characteristics of this dialogue that could be usefully adopted by learners. First, if you listen to the recording, you will hear that the child is very expressive, particularly in the final utterance: 'he would call himself Spiderman!' Secondly, the adult provides lots of 'backchannelling' and 'scaffolding' to encourage the child to continue.

In other words, he responds with lots of 'Oh's' to the child's utterances and asks him questions that check and summarise the child's contributions and elicit further information. These are useful conversational skills to acquire, and this kind of activity encourages learners to engage in the process of acquiring them; it does not simply encourage them to observe the products of other language users.

The mere existence of an increasing number of online corpora does not in itself indicate how best they can be used in any given course to teach English to native speakers and second or foreign language learners. They can obviously be used to explore English in the ways suggested in the earlier chapters of this book. However, they can also be used by native speakers as the basis for more general language projects and by non-native learners and their teachers as a source of material for both product-oriented and process-oriented classroom tasks.

Developing your own research interests

Some of the readers of this book will be embarking on longer-term language study at university level. As you read more about the discipline, you will realise that linguists have mixed feelings about empirical data such as corpora provide. This is not surprising, since linguists, like most scholars, have different interests and research agendas. Some are fascinated by the sheer variety of forms of language and how these varieties correspond to factors such as geographical region, social class, ethnicity, gender, age, profession and so on. Others are more intrigued by how the human mind formulates the utterances and sentences that speakers and writers produce. Yet others find their curiosity piqued by the pressures that result in language change over time. All these are legitimate research interests; however, a consequence of different research goals is a range of sometimes conflicting stances towards actual data and where it comes from. In a well-known discussion, the American linguist Charles Fillmore (1992, p. 35) proposed a vivid distinction between corpus linguists and 'armchair' linguists, that is, the kind of theoretical linguists whose evidence for their insights comes not from corpora, large or small, but from reflection on their knowledge of the language. Armchair theoreticians tend to favour research into the individual's internal knowledge of language, that is, his or her *competence.* No amount of *performance,* that is, evidence of actual language, such as we find in corpora, can substitute for theoretical insight. The major figure in theoretical linguistics in the modern era has been Noam Chomsky, whose dissatisfaction with the largely descriptive project of earlier twentieth century linguistics led him to develop his early grammars that sought to model the mental processes by which individuals form and transform phrases and sentences. Only with the potential, afforded by computers, to gather, store, search and analyse vast quantities of language has there been a general swing back towards description as a lively avenue of research. And yet, as Fillmore noted (ibid), mutual suspicion can characterise the engagement of one group of linguists with the activities of the other. He imagined the armchair linguist proudly displaying his or her latest theoretical breakthrough to a corpus linguist. The corpus linguist would look at the model of language presented by the theoretician and say, 'Yes, that's interesting, but is it true?' In response, the corpus linguist would sift through an immense amount of data to come up with a pattern hitherto unsubstantiated, about which the armchair linguist would comment, 'Yes, that's true, but is it interesting?'

As later commentators (e.g. Leech 1992, pp. 108–113; Meyer 2002, p. 4) have observed, ideally linguists should combine aspects of both the armchair and the corpus linguist, although Meyer holds out less hope that generative linguists will ever enthusiastically adopt corpora as primary sources of data. Even so, as you progress with your linguistic studies, you will develop your own fascinations and preferences, formulate your own hypotheses and develop your own stances towards evidence. You will develop your own taste for what in language study intrigues you most and determine the best means to answer the questions you set yourself. To achieve this, obviously, you have to be aware of the rewards and limitations both of theoretical and empirical analyses. If you have formulated a theory about, for example, a particular constraint on language behaviour in a particular context, you may wish to test this out using an available corpus, or even, ultimately, build a corpus of your own.

The future of online corpora

The world of corpus linguistics is changing all the time, as technology changes, and researchers and teachers realise new ways of employing technology to address research issues and teach the language. Predicting the future is a dangerous thing to do, particularly where technology is concerned, but given recent developments, the following trends can be observed (cf. O'Keeffe, McCarthy and Carter 2007, pp. 246–248).

Large-scale corpora of national standard Englishes

Despite the time, expense and copyright issues involved, large-scale corpora are still being produced, and this trend looks set to continue. The 100-million word British National Corpus established a benchmark for 'national' corpora, and this was trumped by the 360-million word BYU-Corpus of Contemporary American English, which went online only a few weeks before this book was completed. Arguably, large-scale corpora of national standard varieties attract some of the prestige that motivates, say, dictionaries of a national variety such as the *Oxford English Dictionary, Webster's Dictionary, The Macquarie Dictionary of Australian English*, and so we may see other 'national' standard varieties of English represented online in coming years.

Smaller corpora of specialised English

An area of more rapid growth has been the rise of smaller corpora of specialised domains of English. The Michigan Corpus of Spoken Academic English

(MICASE) serves as a good example of this. By focusing on specific situations, a smaller corpus can identify features of language that might get lost in a larger reference corpus such as the BNC or the BYU-Corpus of Contemporary American English. We can expect to see further specialised corpora, probably representing professional domains, coming online in the future.

Corpora of non-standard varieties of English

Perhaps because they were initially motivated by the desire to provide resources for lexicographers and teachers of English as a foreign language, most corpora have focused on standard English. An exception is the SCOTS corpus, which sought to include a spectrum of varieties, spoken and written, ranging from standard English as it is used in Scotland through to different regional and social varieties of Broad Scots. There is scope for the availability online of corpora of English that focus entirely on particular non-standard varieties, such as Appalachian English, Yorkshire English, African-American Vernacular English and so on.

Corpora of World Englishes

In the twenty-first century, more people speak English as a second or foreign language than speak it as a first language, to the extent that English as a Lingua Franca is now being considered as a variety of English in its own right (cf. Kirkpatrick 2007). Corpora recording interactions between different speakers of English as a second or foreign language provide insights into the strategies and linguistic forms that characterise such interactions. One example is the VOICE corpus, the Vienna-Oxford International Corpus of English, available at www.univie.ac.at/voice/index.php. Corpora of Learner English have already been compiled but these are not yet readily available online. As the debate in educational circles about the viability of English as a Lingua Franca continues to excite attention, this situation may well change.

Parallel corpora

The availability of corpora that allow the interrogation of two or more languages, such as English and French, or English and Polish, is currently limited. This is partly because such corpora present more of a challenge in design, presentation and searching than monolingual corpora. However, as corpora become more sophisticated, storage space becomes cheaper and search tools become more flexible, the technical aspects of putting a parallel corpus online should decrease. The question then is how such a corpus is to be explored. Researchers and teachers who use parallel corpora to investigate linguistic and literary issues across cultures are a lively group, but inevitably they are more specialised than monolingual researchers, and it may be some time before parallel corpora become widely available online.

Diachronic corpora

Most online corpora are made up of more or less contemporary texts. The BNC draws its samples largely from the 1980s and 1990s, while the BYU-Corpus of Contemporary American English samples texts from 1990–2007. We have seen in this chapter how the TIME corpus, which contains eight decades of the magazine, gives some evidence of how language changes over time. This is the aim of diachronic corpora. One such corpus which will appear online in the relatively near future is the successor to the SCOTS corpus, the Corpus of Modern Scottish Writing (1700–1945), currently underway at the University of Glasgow (see www.scottishcorpus.ac.uk).

Multimedia corpora

The earliest corpora were text-only. More recently, MICASE and the SCOTS corpus have given online users the possibility of hearing, and in the latter case seeing, some of the participants speaking. The technical challenges involved in delivering online the sounds and images of speakers in action have been successfully addressed; however, it is still laboriously time-consuming and expensive to produce the accurate transcripts of recordings that are necessary if the recordings are to be searchable.

The search tools used in online corpora such as those outlined above are also continuing to improve. As we have seen in this book, concordances, map searches, synonym searches and some basic statistical operations can already be carried out online with a range of corpora. Not all tools are available for each corpus, but over time we can expect to find the most popular search tools becoming available for the major online corpora. Areas which could be improved include searches for spelling and dialectal variants. The SCOTS corpus, for example, currently requires separate searches for spelling variants such as *football, footba, fitba* and *fitbaw* and for dialect variants such as *above, abune, abuin* and *abinn.* Automatic parsers could be refined and delivered online for untagged corpora. For general users, frequencies and collocations could be presented in more attractive ways than lists and bar charts.

A major constraint in the development of online corpora will continue to be copyright and intellectual property laws. While these rightly protect the authors of written text and 'performers' of speech, they do restrict the kinds of material which can be made freely available online. Changes in such laws in future would clearly affect the availability of material online. The main spur to advances in online corpora, such as those suggested above, will be determined by people such as the readers of this book. The rise of online corpora promises to take corpus linguistics out of the domain of a relatively small group of expert users and into the wider sphere of students, teachers and interested members of the general public. If this takes place, the use of corpora should become securely embedded in mainstream language and teacher education courses. Students, teachers and users generally will then have an increasing say over what resources are developed for them, and what tools are devised to serve their own requirements. We hope that this book helps further that process.

FURTHER READING

Fillmore, C. (1992). '"Corpus linguistics" or "Computer-aided armchair linguistics"' in Svartvik, J. (ed.) *Directions in Corpus Linguistics: Proceedings of Nobel Symposium 82, Stockholm 4–8 August 1991*. Berlin: Mouton de Gruyter, pp. 35–60.

Kirkpatrick, A. (2007). *World Englishes: Implications for International Communication and English Language Teaching*. Cambridge: Cambridge University Press.

Leech, G. (1992). 'Corpora and theories of linguistic performance'. In Svartvik, J. (ed.) *Directions in Corpus Linguistics: Proceedings of Nobel Symposium 82, Stockholm 4–8 August 1991*. Berlin: Mouton de Gruyter, pp. 105–122.

Meyer, C.F. (2002). *English Corpus Linguistics: An Introduction*. Cambridge: Cambridge University Press.

O'Keeffe, A., McCarthy, M. and Carter, R. (2007). *From Corpus to Classroom: Language Use and Language Teaching*. Cambridge: Cambridge University Press.

Widdowson, H. (1996). 'Comment: authenticity and autonomy in ELT'. *English Language Teaching Journal*, 50(1), 67–68.

Widdowson, H. (1998). 'Content, community and authentic language'. *TESOL Quarterly* 32(4), 705–716.

Appendix: Online Corpora

In this section, we list in alphabetical order corpora of English, of which at least a sample of texts are available free of charge online and which, in most cases, may be explored using integrated analysis tools. More detailed information about the main corpora from which the discussion and tasks in the book draw is contained in the introduction. Many other corpora are available which can be downloaded and analysed using free or commercial software packages.

British Academic Spoken English corpus (BASE)

A companion to the British Academic Written English corpus (BAWE), the BASE corpus can be accessed online, www.coventry.ac.uk/researchnet/d/503, through the Sketch Engine interface, which requires subscription but for which a free trial is available. Individual transcripts of corpus texts can be accessed freely online. BASE contains spoken material (160 lectures and 39 seminars) from a range of academic disciplines, totalling over 1.6 million words.

British Academic Written English Corpus (BAWE)

Like BASE, limited analysis of BAWE can be carried out online, at www.coventry.ac.uk/researchnet/d/505. The corpus contains over 3000 pieces of assessed student writing, representing various academic disciplines and levels and a sample of the corpus can be accessed and searched online.

British National Corpus (BNC) / BYU-BNC

The BNC contains 100 million words of British English texts from the late twentieth century. Ten per cent of the corpus is transcribed spoken language; ninety per cent is written language of a wide range of genres. The corpus is part-of-speech tagged. Information about the BNC can be found at: www.natcorp.ox.ac.uk. Simple searches can also be carried out through this site; these indicate the total number of hits for a search word and retrieve a random sample of fifty examples in context. Searches may be restricted by part of speech.

The complete BNC can also be explored through the user-friendly interface created by Professor Mark Davies at Brigham Young University, available at http://corpus.byu.edu/bnc/. This interface offers the facility of identifying collocates, comparing words across registers, and viewing all hits for search terms in the corpus. Full texts are not available but an expanded context of several sentences can be viewed.

BYU Corpus of Contemporary American English

The BYU Corpus of Contemporary American English, at www.americancorpus. org, contains 360 million words of text in American English, covering the period 1990–2007, and further texts will be added every subsequent year. The corpus contains roughly even quantities of five genres: spoken (transcripts of unscripted media talk), fiction, magazine, newspaper and academic. The interface offers the same facilities as the BYU-BNC, including the possibility of narrowing a search by part of speech, comparing search terms across genres and sub-genres, comparing collocates and creating customised lists.

Collins WordbanksOnline English Corpus Concordance Sampler

The corpus behind the Collins WordbanksOnline resource, available at www.collins.co.uk/corpus/CorpusSearch.aspx, is a 56-million-word sample of the Bank of English, or COBUILD corpus, which was created by HarperCollins publishers and Birmingham University. The Concordance Sampler works on part-of-speech tagged text, and the search system can also deliver collocate information.

Compleat Lexical Tutor

The Compleat Lexical Tutor is a set of online data-driven language learning tools: www.lextutor.ca. Among many other features, it offers a concordancer which can be used on a selection of corpora of English including the 1-million-word Brown Corpus and the BNC Sampler (a 1-million-word subset of the BNC).

English Language Interview Corpus as a Second-Language Application (ELISA)

The ELISA corpus, at www.uni-tuebingen.de/elisa/html/elisa_index.html, contains orthographic transcripts of interviews conducted with native speakers of English around the world, talking about their occupations. The corpus is small, with roughly 60,000 words, but also contains video clips, a concordancer and full texts.

Freiburg English Dialect Corpus (FRED)

FRED at www2.anglistik.uni-freiburg.de/institut/lskortmann/FRED/index. htm contains spoken language, recorded in nine major dialect areas of the UK. The complete corpus consists of 2.5 million words of text, equating to 300 hours of speech. The complete corpus cannot currently be searched or browsed online, but a small number of transcripts and audio files can be accessed.

GlossaNet

GlossaNet, at http://glossa.fltr.ucl.ac.be/, run by the University of Louvain in Belgium, facilitates concordance analysis of daily updated corpora of news-paper texts in many languages. Users can specify language and search term requirements, and receive concordances by email. The GlossaNet Instant facility provides concordances online.

Intonational Variation in English (IViE)

The IViE corpus at www.phon.ox.ac.uk/IViE contains recordings of speakers of English urban dialects in England, Wales, Northern Ireland and the Republic of Ireland. Speakers are recorded in a number of speaking styles, from stimuli sentences to free conversation. The corpus recordings can be searched according to various criteria, downloaded and listened to online, and prosodic transcripts can be displayed using external software.

Lexware Culler corpora

The Culler corpus tool at http://bergelmir.iki.his.se/culler/, and Lexware Culler corpus of English prose at www.nla.se/culler/, can be used to access collections of texts on biomedicine, European Union administration and English prose. The corpora are lemmatised, and wildcards, filtering and sorting are all possible.

Michigan Corpus of Academic Spoken English (MICASE)

Available to search and browse at http://quod.lib.umich.edu/m/micase/, MICASE contains close to 2 million words of audio recordings and transcripts of academic speech events which can be searched according to various criteria such as the academic role of the speaker, the type of speech event, academic dis-cipline, and so on. Complete transcripts can be viewed and also downloaded. Searching for a word gives a sortable concordance view, and additional context can be shown.

PolyU Language Bank

The PolyU Language Bank resource at http://langbank.engl.polyu.edu.hk/indexl.html offers access to a bank of corpora (of English and other languages), all of which can be searched and concordances created. The available corpora include the BNC Sampler, and corpora in the domains of business, academia, travel and tourism, medicine and fiction.

Scottish Corpus of Texts & Speech (SCOTS)

SCOTS, available at www.scottishcorpus.ac.uk, contains 4 million words of texts in Scottish English and varieties of Scots, covering a wide range of genres from conversations and interviews to prose fiction, poetry, correspondence and official documents from the Scottish Parliament. Twenty per cent of the corpus is made up of spoken texts, which are presented as orthographic transcripts synchronised with streamed audio/video recordings. Features include a concordancer and map visualisation. Complete texts can be viewed and downloaded, and audio/video recordings can also be downloaded. Extensive demographic and textual metadata is available for each text and can be used to refine a search.

The Speech Accent Archive

The Speech Accent Archive, http://accent.gmu.edu/, is a collection of recordings and phonetic transcriptions of native and non-native speakers of English reading the same paragraph. The web resource allows users to browse and search the archive, to compare accents and explore speakers' demographic and linguistic backgrounds.

TIME Corpus of American English

The TIME Corpus, available at http://corpus.byu.edu/time/, and developed by Mark Davies at Brigham Young University, uses the same interface as the BYU-BNC and BYU Corpus of American English. The corpus contains more than 100 million words of text from the US *TIME* Magazine from 1923 to the present day and enables exploration of how words have changed in meaning and use over time.

Virtual Language Centre Web Concordancer

The Virtual Language Centre Web Concordancer at http://vlc.polyu.edu.hk/concordance/ contains, among other language tools, a concordancer which can be used on a number of small corpora, including the Brown and LOB corpora and several banks of genre-specific texts.

WebCorp

WebCorp allows the user to harness the World Wide Web for use as a language corpus of English and other languages: www.webcorp.org.uk. WebCorp features collocation analysis, the possibility of filtering results according to date and collocates and a word list generator, which creates word lists for individual web pages. While it is very difficult to use the Web to make quantitative statements about language, because the overall quantity of data and proportions of different registers is almost impossible to establish (not least because it is constantly changing), the unparalleled quantity of authentic language data which the Web offers makes it a valuable resource for exploring features of language such as uncommon words and neologisms.

Bibliography

Adolphs, S. (2006). *Introducing Electronic Text Analysis: A Practical Guide for Language and Literary Studies*. London and New York: Routledge.

Anderwald, L. (2001). '*Was/were*-variation in non-standard British English today'. *English World-Wide* 22(1): 1–21.

Baayen, H. (2008). *Analyzing Linguistic Data: A Practical Introduction to Statistics Using R*. Cambridge: Cambridge University Press.

Baker, P. (2006). *Using Corpora in Discourse Analysis*. London, New York: Continuum.

Baker, P., Hardie, A. and McEnery, T. (2006). *A Glossary of Corpus Linguistics*. Edinburgh: Edinburgh University Press.

Barbieri, F. (2005). 'Quotative use in American English: a corpus-based, cross-register comparison'. *Journal of English Linguistics* 33(3): 222–256.

Bazerman, C. (2004). 'Intertextuality: how texts rely on other texts'. In Bazerman, C. and Prior, P. (eds). *What Writing Does and How It Does It: An Introduction to Analyzing Texts and Textual Practices*, Mahwah, NJ: Lawrence Erlbaum Associates, pp. 83–96.

Biber, D. (1988). *Variation Across Speech and Writing*. Cambridge: Cambridge University Press.

Biber, D. (1990). 'Methodological issues regarding corpus-based analyses of linguistic variation'. *Literary and Linguistic Computing* 5(4): 257–269.

Biber, D. (1992). 'Using computer-based text corpora to analyze the referential strategies of spoken and written texts'. In Svartvik, J. (ed.). *Directions in Corpus Linguistics: Proceedings of Nobel Symposium 82*, Stockholm, 4–8 August 1991, Berlin: Mouton, pp. 213–252.

Biber, D. (1993). 'Representativeness in corpus design'. *Literary and Linguistic Computing* 8(4): 243–257. Republished in Sampson, G. and McCarthy, D. (eds). (2004). *Corpus Linguistics: Readings in a Widening Discipline*. London: Continuum, pp. 174–197.

Biber, D., Connor, U. and Upton, T. (2007). *Discourse on the Move: Using Corpus Analysis to Describe Discourse Structure*. Amsterdam: John Benjamins.

Biber, D., Conrad, S. and Reppen, R. (1998). *Corpus Linguistics: Investigating Language Structure and Use*. Cambridge: Cambridge University Press.

Biber, D., Finegan, E., Johansson, S., Conrad, S. and Leech, G. (1999). *The Longman Grammar of Spoken and Written English*. London: Longman.

Biber, D., Leech, G. and Conrad, S. (2002). *The Longman Student Grammar of Spoken and Written English: Workbook*. London: Longman.

Braun, S. (2007). 'Designing and exploiting small multimedia corpora for autonomous learning and teaching'. In Hidalgo, E., Quereda, L. and Santana, J. (eds). *Corpora in the Foreign Language Classroom*. Amsterdam and New York: Rodopi, pp. 31–46.

Brown, G. and Yule, G. (1983). *Discourse Analysis*. Cambridge: Cambridge University Press.

Brown, P. and Levinson, S. (1987). *Politeness: Some Universals in Language*. Cambridge: Cambridge University Press.

Campione, E. and Véronis, J., ([2001], 2004). 'Semi-automatic tagging of intonation in French spoken corpora'. In Sampson, G. and McCarthy, D. (eds). *Corpus Linguistics: Readings in a Widening Discipline*. London: Continuum, pp. 462–470.

Carter, R. and McCarthy, M. (2006). *Cambridge Grammar of English: A Comprehensive Guide to Spoken and Written English Grammar and Usage*. Cambridge: Cambridge University Press.

Chambers, A. (2007). 'Popularising corpus consultation by language learners and teachers'. In Hidalgo, E., Quereda, L. and Santana, J. (eds). *Corpora in the Foreign Language Classroom*. Amsterdam and New York: Rodopi, pp. 3–16.

Charteris-Black, J. (2004). *Corpus Approaches to Critical Metaphor Analysis*. Basingstoke: Palgrave Macmillan.

Chomsky, N. (1965). *Aspects of the Theory of Syntax*. Cambridge, MA: The MIT Press.

Clear, J. (1992). 'Corpus sampling'. In Leitner, G. (ed.) *New Directions in English Language Corpora*. Berlin: Mouton de Gruyter, pp. 21–32.

Cloran, C., Butt, D. and Williams, G. (eds) (1996). *Ways of Saying: Ways of Meaning: Selected Papers of Ruqaiya Hasan*. London: Cassell.

Crystal, D. (1995). *The Cambridge Encyclopedia of the English Language*. Cambridge: Cambridge University Press.

Crystal, D. (1997). *The Cambridge Encyclopedia of Language*. Second edition. Cambridge: Cambridge University Press.

Douglas, F. and Corbett, J. (2006). ' "Huv a wee seat, hen": evaluative terms in Scots'. In Caie, G.D., Hough, C. and Wotherspoon, I. (eds) *The Power of Words: Essays in Lexicography, Lexicology and Semantics*. Amsterdam and New York: Rodopi.

Fillmore, C. (1992). ' "Corpus linguistics" or "Computer-aided armchair linguistics" '. In Svartvik, J. (ed.) *Directions in Corpus Linguistics: Proceedings of Nobel Symposium 82, Stockholm 4–8 August 1991*. Berlin: Mouton de Gruyter, pp. 35–60.

Firth, J.R. (1957a). 'A synopsis of linguistic theory, 1930–1955'. *Studies in Linguistic Analysis*. Special Volume of the Philological Society. Oxford: Blackwell, pp. 1–32.

Firth, J.R. (1957b). *Papers in Linguistics: 1934–1951*. London: Oxford University Press.

Fowler, H.W. (1926). *Dictionary of Modern English Usage*. Oxford: Oxford University Press.

Fries, C.C. (1952). *The Structure of English*. New York: Harcourt Brace.

Gadamer, H.-G. (2003). *Truth and Method*. Second edition. New York: Continuum.

Gimson, A.C. (1980). *An Introduction to the Pronunciation of English*. Edward Arnold: London.

Grabe, E. and Post, B. ([2002], 2004). 'Intonational variation in the British Isles'. In Sampson, G. and McCarthy, D. (eds). *Corpus Linguistics: Readings in a Widening Discipline*. London: Continuum, pp. 474–482.

Halliday, M.A.K. (1966). 'Lexis as a linguistic level'. In Bazell, C.E., Catford, J.C., Halliday, M.A.K. and Robins, R.H. (eds). *In Memory of J.R. Firth*. London: Longman.

Halliday, M.A.K. (1978). *Language as Social Semiotic*. London: Edward Arnold.

Halliday, M.A.K. (1994). *An Introduction to Functional Grammar*. Second edition. London: Arnold.

Halliday, M.A.K. and Hasan, R. (1976). *Cohesion in English*. London: Longman.

Halliday, M.A.K. and Hasan, R. (1985). *Language, Context and Text: Aspects of Language in a Social-Semiotic Perspective*. Victoria: Deakin University Press.

Hamawand, Z. (2007). *Suffixal Rivalry in Adjective Formation: A Cognitive-Corpus Analysis*. London: Equinox.

Hasan, R. (1987). 'The grammarian's dream: lexis as most delicate grammar'. In M.A.K. Halliday and R. Fawcett (eds). *New Developments in Systemic Linguistics.* Vol. 1: *Theory and Description.* London: Frances Pinter, pp. 184–212.

Hewlett, N., Matthews, B. and Scobbie, J. (1999). 'Vowel duration in Scottish English speaking children'. In Proceedings of the XIVth International Congress of Phonetic Sciences. Vol. 3, pp. 2157–2160.

Hockey, S. (2000). *Electronic Texts in the Humanities.* Oxford: Oxford University Press.

Hoey, M. (1983). *On the Surface of Discourse.* London: Allen and Unwin.

Hoey, M. (1991). *Patterns of Lexis in Text.* Oxford: Oxford University Press.

Hoey, M. (2000). 'About sixty: the collocations, colligations and semantic prosodies of a number'. In Heffer, C. and Sauntson, H. (eds). *Words in Context: A Tribute to John Sinclair on His Retirement.* Birmingham: University of Birmingham, pp. 95–109.

Hoey, M. (2005). *Lexical Priming.* Abingdon: Routledge.

Hunston, S. (2002). *Corpora in Applied Linguistics.* Cambridge: Cambridge University Press.

Hunston, S. and Francis, G. (2000). *Pattern Grammar: A Corpus-Driven Approach to the Lexical Grammar of English.* Amsterdam: John Benjamins.

Jenkins, J. (2007). *English as a Lingua Franca: Attitude and Identity.* Oxford: Oxford University Press.

Jordan, M. (1984). *Rhetoric of Everyday English Texts.* London: Allen and Unwin.

Kennedy, G. (1998). *An Introduction to Corpus Linguistics.* London: Longman.

Kirkpatrick, A. (2007). *World Englishes: Implications for International Communication and English Language Teaching.* Cambridge: Cambridge University Press.

Leech, G. (1992). 'Corpora and theories of linguistic performance'. In Svartvik, J. (ed.). *Directions in Corpus Linguistics: Proceedings of Nobel Symposium 82, Stockholm 4–8 August 1991.* Berlin: Mouton de Gruyter, pp. 105–122.

Leech, G., McEnery, T. and Wynne, M. (1997). 'Further levels of annotation'. In Garside, R., Leech, G. and McEnery, A. (eds). *Corpus Annotation.* London: Longman, pp. 85–101.

Levey, S. (2003). 'He's like "Do it now!" and I'm like "No!": some innovative quotative usage among young people in London'. *English Today* 19(1): 24–32.

Levinson, S. (1983). *Pragmatics.* Cambridge: Cambridge University Press.

Louw, B. (2000). 'Contextual prosodic theory: bringing semantic prosodies to life'. In Heffer, C. and Sauntson, H. (eds). *Words in Context: A Tribute to John Sinclair on His Retirement.* Birmingham: University of Birmingham, pp. 48–67.

Macafee, C. (1994). *Traditional Dialect in the Modern World: A Glasgow Case Study.* Frankfurt am Main: Peter Lang.

MacMahon, M. (2002). *Basic Phonetics & Phonetics of Poetry.* Thirteenth edition. Glasgow: Department of English Language, University of Glasgow.

Malinowski, B. (1923). 'The problem of meaning in primitive languages'. Supplement to Ogden, C.K. and Richards, I.A., *The Meaning of Meaning.* London: Kegan Paul.

McEnery, T. and Wilson, A. (2001). *Corpus Linguistics: An Introduction.* Edinburgh: Edinburgh University Press.

McEnery, T., Xiao, R. and Tono, Y. (2006). *Corpus-Based Language Studies: An Advanced Resource Book.* London and New York: Routledge.

Meyer, C.F. (2002). *English Corpus Linguistics: An Introduction.* Cambridge: Cambridge University Press.

Meyerhoff, M. (2006). *Introducing Sociolinguistics.* London and New York: Routledge.

Moon, R. (1998). *Fixed Expressions and Idioms in English.* Oxford: Clarendon Press.

Nunan, D. (1993). *Introducing Discourse Analysis*. London: Penguin.

Oakes, M.P. (1998). *Statistics for Corpus Linguistics*. Edinburgh: Edinburgh University Press.

O'Keeffe, A., McCarthy, M. and Carter, R. (2007). *From Corpus to Classroom: Language Use and Language Teaching*. Cambridge: Cambridge University Press.

Oxford English Dictionary, available online at www.oed.com.

Partington, A. (1998). *Patterns and Meanings*. Amsterdam and Philadelphia: John Benjamins.

Popper, K. (1959). *The Logic of Scientific Discovery*. London: Hutchinson.

Quirk, R., Greenbaum, S., Leech, G. and Svartvik, J. (1985). *A Comprehensive Grammar of the English Language*. London: Longman.

Renouf, A. and Sinclair, J. (1991). 'Collocational frameworks in English'. In Aijmer, K. and Altenberg, B. (eds). *English Corpus Linguistics*. London: Longman, pp. 128–144.

Richards, J.C. and Rogers, T.S. (2001). *Approaches and Methods in Language Teaching*. Second edition. Cambridge: Cambridge University Press.

Roach, P. (2000). *English Phonetics and Phonology: A Practical Course*. Third edition. Cambridge: Cambridge University Press.

Romaine, S. (2000). *Language in Society: An Introduction to Sociolinguistics*. Second edition. Oxford: Oxford University Press.

Schiffrin, D. (1994). *Approaches to Discourse*. Oxford: Blackwell.

Schiffrin, D., Tannen, D. and Hamilton, H. (eds). (2001). *The Handbook of Discourse Analysis*. Oxford: Blackwell.

Scott, M. (1997). 'PC analysis of key words – and key key words'. *System* 25(2): 233–245.

Scott, M. (1999). *WordSmith Tools*, version 3.0. Oxford: Oxford University Press. Versions 4 and 5 available from www.lexically.net/wordsmith.

Siepmann, D. (2005). 'Collocation, colligation and encoding dictionaries. Part I: Lexicological aspects'. *International Journal of Lexicography* 18(4): 409–443.

Sinclair, J. (1991). *Corpus, Concordance, Collocation*. Oxford: Oxford University Press.

Sinclair, J. (2003). *Reading Concordances: An Introduction*. London: Longman.

Sinclair, J. (2004). *Trust the Text: Language, Corpus and Discourse*. London: Routledge.

Smith, J., Durham, M. and Fortune, L. (2007). 'Community, caregiver and child in the acquisition of variation in a Scottish dialect'. *Language Variation and Change* 19: 63–99.

Stenström, A.-B. (1994). *An Introduction to Spoken Interaction*. Harlow: Longman.

Stubbs, M. (1983). *Discourse Analysis: The Sociolinguistic Analysis of Natural Language*. Oxford: Blackwell.

Stubbs, M. (1996). *Text and Corpus Analysis*. Oxford: Blackwell

Stubbs, M. (2001). *Words and Phrases: Corpus Studies of Lexical Semantics*. Oxford: Blackwell.

Tadros, A. (1985). *Prediction in Text*. Birmingham: English Language Research, University of Birmingham.

Tagliamonte, S.A. (2006). *Analysing Sociolinguistic Variation*. Cambridge: Cambridge University Press.

ten Have, P. (1999). *Doing Conversation Analysis: A Practical Guide*. London: Sage.

Teubert, W. and Čermáková, A. (2007). *Corpus Linguistics: A Short Introduction*. London: Continuum.

Tognini-Bonelli, E. (2001). *Corpus Linguistics at Work*. Amsterdam: John Benjamins.

Tottie, G. and Hoffmann, S. (2006). 'Tag questions in British and American English'. *Journal of English Linguistics* 34(4): 283–311.

Truss, L. (2003). *Eats, Shoots and Leaves: The Zero Tolerance Approach to Punctuation*. London: Profile Books.

Widdowson, H. (1996). 'Comment: authenticity and autonomy in ELT'. *English Language Teaching Journal* 50(1): 67–68.

Widdowson, H. (1998). 'Content, community and authentic language'. *TESOL Quarterly* 32(4): 705–716.

Widdowson, H. (2000). 'On the limitations of linguistics applied'. *Applied Linguistics* 21(1): 3–25.

Widdowson, H. (2004). *Text, Context, Pretext: Critical Issues in Discourse Analysis*. Oxford: Blackwell.

Winter, E. (1977). 'A clause-relational approach to English texts: a study of some predictive lexical items in written discourse'. *Instructional Science* (special issue) 6(1): 1–92.

Winter, E. (1994). 'Clause relations as information structure: two basic text structures in English'. In Coulthard, M. (ed.). *Advances in Written Text Analysis*. London: Routledge, pp. 46–68.

Wordsworth, D. (2006). 'Grammar is a question of manners'. *The Telegraph*, 22 March 2006. Available online at www.telegraph.co.uk/opinion/main.jhtml?xml=/opinion/2006/03/22/do2203.xml

Glossary

Accent – a speaker's inventory of sounds, which serve to identify him or her geographically or socially.

Adjacency pairs – mutually relevant turns which are usually found together in discourse. For example, an offer is typically followed by an acceptance or refusal of the offer.

Adverbial – in **SPOCA**, a component of the clause realised by adverbial or prepositional phrases, giving extra information about time, location, direction, manner.

Analysis tools – computer software designed to analyse language, which may be either integrated with online corpora, or stand-alone for use on downloaded or self-built corpora.

Annotation (see also **mark-up, tagging**) – the practice or process of adding information to text so that it is possible to search for and retrieve instances of features which lie below the surface of language, such as part of speech information.

ANOVA, Analysis Of Variance – statistical tests which facilitate the calculation of differences *between* data sets compared with differences *within* data sets.

Archive, text archive – a collection of texts. A corpus and an archive can be distinguished by the fact that a corpus aims to represent a language, language variety or genre(s), while an archive is normally constructed with no particular linguistic motivation.

Articulation of sounds – the movement required in the vocal apparatus to form the sounds of language. Consonants are defined by their place of articulation, manner of articulation and voicing.

Aspect – a verb system where the verb form expresses meaning related to duration, completion and non-completion (e.g. simple aspect, continuous aspect, perfect aspect).

Assimilation – changes which occur in a sound so that it becomes more similar to the other sounds around it.

Chi-square – a measure of statistical significance which compares observed corpus frequencies with expected frequencies, to determine how likely it is that frequencies are due to chance.

Coherence (compare **cohesion**) – the underlying connectedness of a text, which allows us to recognise it as a text rather than an unconnected collection of sentences.

Cohesion (compare **coherence**) – surface features of language which serve to bind a text.

Colligation – the typical grammatical patterning into which a word or grammatical construction enters.

Collocation – the typical lexical patterning of a word or lexical item, which may depend on the textual genre or register.

Comparable corpus (see also **parallel corpus**) – a type of corpus used to study patterning across languages. An example of a comparable corpus is one which contains 1 million words of texts in each of two different languages, each following the same design.

Competence (compare **performance**) – an individual's unconscious knowledge of the rules of language.

Complement – in **SPOCA**, the component of the clause which describes the subject or has a relationship of identity with the subject.

Concordance – a list of all of the occurrences of a word or phrase in a corpus, presented in their immediate context. Often called a KWIC (Key Word In Context) concordance.

Context, context of situation (compare **co-text**) – the non-linguistic situation in which a text is produced. Features of the context may have an influence on the language produced in that context.

Conversation analysis – the linguistic study of the mechanisms of conversation, including aspects such as turn-taking and overlap.

Coordinate clause – a clause which is linked to another by a coordinating conjunction, such as *and, but, or*.

Copyright – a set of rights that regulate the use of creative and intellectual works, which have a material form, such as novels, poems, images and screenplays. Detailed information on copyright in the UK is available from the UK Intellectual Property Office: www.ipo.gov.uk/copy.htm.

Corpus (plural: corpora) – a collection of texts designed for linguistic analysis, normally held in electronic form. Corpora vary in size, containing anything from tens of thousands to hundreds of millions of words. Corpora are often designed to be representative of a language or genre, that is, they aim to contain a balanced sample of that language or genre.

Corpus linguistics – a set of methods for the analysis of language based on the evidence provided by corpora of texts.

Co-text (compare **context**) – the language which surrounds a unit of language form (word, phrase, passage, etc.). Studying co-text allows us to see the typical environment of units, in terms of patterning with features of phonology, grammar, lexis and discourse.

Data-driven models of grammar – descriptions of grammar which are established empirically, that is, derived from the study of the language behaviour of many people.

Delexicalised verbs – 'empty' verbs, with little inherent meaning, which are used in conjunction with a noun containing the bulk of the meaning. In the example, *making progress, make* is delexicalised, and the meaning is contained in the noun *progress*. The same concept could be expressed with the 'full' verb *progressing*.

Diachronic corpus (compare **synchronic corpus**) – a corpus which samples texts from across a period of time, to enable analysis of how language changes over time.

Dialect – a variety of language defined geographically (or sometimes socially), with characteristic features of pronunciation, lexis and grammar.

Discourse – the organisation of language above the level of the sentence; particular ways of talking and writing in a given social context.

Discourse markers – features of language which serve to organise speech. For example, *I mean* typically signals that the speaker will explain or clarify something already mentioned.

Dispersion plot – an analysis tool, available for example in WordSmith Tools, which shows where in a text instances of search terms occur. For example, instances of a chosen search term may cluster at the beginning of a text, or may be spread quite evenly through it.

Ditransitive verbs (compare **transitive verbs** and **intransitive verbs**) – verbs which take two objects. In the example *hand me a tissue, me* is an indirect object and *a tissue* is a direct object.

Elision – the phenomenon whereby certain sounds disappear completely in fast, connected speech.

Empirical analysis – in linguistics, the use of authentic language, rather than one's **intuition**, as evidence for a description of how language works.

Field of discourse (see also **tenor of discourse**, **mode of discourse**) – the focus of activity, or subject matter, of language. The field of discourse has an influence on features of language such as lexis.

Finiteness – within the verb system, the capacity of a verb phrase to signal tense or not. The verb phrase in *I wend my way home* is finite, indicating that the action is taking place in the present; in *Wending my way home* the verb phrase is non-finite, as tense is not signalled.

Genre – a category of texts defined by common function or social role.

Grammar – the organisation of words and phrases into sentences or utterances in speech.

Head, head word – the main word in a phrase, around which the other words are organised, for example the noun in a noun phrase or the verb in a verb phrase.

Hypothesis – an assumption or supposition based on little evidence which can be investigated, for example, by using the evidence provided by a corpus.

Idiom – a sequence of words where the overall meaning cannot be understood from the meaning of the component words. For example, the idiom *paint the town red* (meaning to go out and celebrate) is understood through knowledge of the whole expression and is not closely related to the meanings of the individual words *paint, town, red*.

Idiom principle (see also **open choice principle**) – a term coined by the linguist John Sinclair: 'The principle of idiom is that a language user has available to him or her a large number of semi-preconstructed phrases that constitute single choices, even though they might appear to be analysable into segments' (Sinclair 1991, p. 110). That is, the fact that language users select more than one word at once in producing language.

Interface – a program or website which allows a user to access an online corpus and perform certain types of linguistic analysis on it.

Intertextuality – the study of the relationship between texts and how texts draw on other texts to create meaning.

Intonation – the meaningful variation of pitch in spoken language. For example, questions in English are typically recognised by a rising intonation.

Intransitive verbs (compare **transitive verbs**, **ditransitive verbs**) – verbs taking neither a complement nor an object. Compare for example *She whistled* (where the verb is being used intransitively) and *She whistled a jaunty tune* (where the verb takes the direct object *a jaunty tune*).

Intuition – a language user's reflections on their own knowledge of language and feelings about what is acceptable and unacceptable in language. Corpus linguistics can be used to test intuitions about language against authentic language use.

Inventory of sounds – the set of sounds that make up a speaker's accent.

IPA, International Phonetic Association – the association which devised the most commonly used system for describing the sounds of language. IPA symbols are conventionally transcribed in slash brackets: e.g. /e/.

Key words – expressions that have a significantly higher or lower frequency of occurrence in a text or corpus than we would expect based on a quantitative analysis of a larger corpus.

Lemma (see also **word-form**) – The 'dictionary form' of a word, an abstract form which encompasses all the possible forms in which the word is found in language. For example, GO is the lemma relating to the word-forms *go, goes, went, gone*.

Lemmatisation – a corpus which has been lemmatised has been annotated so that related word-forms are all treated as instances of a lemma. Thus *be, being, are, is, were* would all be tagged as being examples of BE, and therefore a corpus search for the lemma BE would return all of the related word-forms in the data.

Lexical items – the basic units of meaning in a language. The term can be used to cover both words and items larger than words (such as idioms) which cannot be broken down into smaller semantic units. In *look up a word in the dictionary*, the phrasal verb *look up* is a lexical item because its sense cannot be further analysed.

Lexicogrammar – the level of language which includes both lexis and grammar and accounts for the 'wording' of language. The concept is used particularly in the work of the linguist M.A.K. Halliday (see Halliday 1994).

Lexicography – the practice of dictionary-making, one important application of corpora.

Log-likelihood – a measure of statistical significance which compares observed corpus frequencies with expected frequencies, to determine how likely it is that frequencies are due to chance.

Mark-up (see also **annotation**, **tagging**) – the process of adding information about the text structure to the texts in a corpus. For example, a corpus of drama texts might be marked up to show the lines spoken by individual characters.

Mean, arithmetic mean – a type of average, calculated by dividing the sum of a set of figures by the number of figures (e.g. the mean of the set *1, 3, 7, 8, 11* is *6*, calculated by dividing their sum, *30*, by the number of figures, *5*).

Metadata – contextual information about the texts in a corpus, including, for example, information about the social background of speakers, or the context in which a text was produced. Metadata often accompanies the texts in a corpus, to allow for **sociolinguistic** analysis.

Metaphor – non-literal language use, in which one thing is described in terms normally associated with something else. Metaphor is very pervasive in language: conceptual metaphors (such as GOOD IS UP) may be seen to underlie our whole language system (exemplified by expressions such as *be riding high, go out on a high, in seventh heaven*, all from the BNC).

Modality – a verb system, involving the use of modal auxiliaries to express concepts like possibility and obligation.

Mode of discourse (see also **tenor of discourse**, **field of discourse**) – the medium of communication or role which the language plays in discourse.

Monitor corpus – a corpus to which texts are continually added, so that it continues to reflect current usage, and neologisms can be studied. The Bank of English is a well-known monitor corpus.

Mood – the verb system which expresses the distinction between statements, questions and commands (the indicative, interrogative and imperative moods, respectively).

Multimedia corpus – a corpus which contains examples of language use in more than one medium: e.g. text, audio footage, video footage, images.

Mutual Information, MI – a statistical measure used in corpus linguistics to indicate the strength of collocation of two words. MI works by comparing the frequency of two words occurring together in a corpus, compared with the frequency of each word occurring independently. A high MI score suggests a significant association between words.

Neologism – a new lexical creation. Recent years have seen a lot of neologisms in the field of computing, such as *download, podcast, wireless connection, social networking site.*

Node word – the search word in a concordance; the word whose occurrences are presented in their immediate co-text.

Normalised frequencies – frequencies which have been brought to a common base to allow them to be compared. For example, a raw frequency of 100 instances of a word in corpus A (50,000 words) and a raw frequency of 800 instances of the same word in corpus B (2 million words) may both be normalised to compare the frequencies per 1000 words: 2 instances per 1000 words in corpus A and 0.4 instances per 1000 words in corpus B.

Object – in **SPOCA**, a noun phrase element which does not have a relationship of identity with the subject.

Observer's paradox – in linguistics, the problem that it is impossible to observe a speaker's language use in a situation when he or she is not being observed. That is, the presence of an observer or recorder affects the language production.

Open choice principle (see also **idiom principle**) – a model of interpretation of language according to which the only factor governing the choice of the next word is grammaticality. It assumes that there is no co-selection between lexical items. See Sinclair (1991).

Parallel corpus (see also **comparable corpus**) – A type of corpus used particularly in translation studies. An example of a parallel corpus is one which contains the original text of a novel, alongside translations of the same novel in one or more languages.

Part-of-speech tagging, **POS tagging** – the practice of **annotating** a corpus to indicate the class of words (noun, adjective, adverb, etc.). Automatic POS tagging is common but is not 100 per cent accurate.

Performance (compare **competence**) – the spoken and written language that people actually produce.

Phonemic symbol (see also **phonetic symbol**) – one of a set of symbols designed to show contrastive sounds of language.

Phonetics – the study of the sounds of speech, as they are articulated and perceived.

Phonetic symbol (see also **phonemic symbol, IPA**) – one of a set of symbols designed to describe the sounds of language.

Phonology – the study of the sounds of languages, focusing on the sounds which serve to make meaningful contrasts.

Population (of texts) – the set of all texts which meet defined criteria and which may be sampled to form a corpus.

Pragmatics – the linguistic study of speaker meaning, often contrasted with **semantics**.

Predicator – in **SPOCA**, the verb phrase element in a clause.

Qualitative analysis (compare **quantitative analysis**) – in linguistics, the study of language based on in-depth, interpretative analysis of patterns and tendencies, often focusing on contextual factors behind language.

Quantitative analysis (compare **qualitative analysis**) – in linguistics, the study of language based on numerical data, such as relative frequency counts and distributions. Corpus linguistics often uses a quantitative approach as a first step in analysis.

Received Pronunciation, RP – a regionally neutral, prestigious reference accent of English, sometimes known as the Queen's English.

Reference corpus – a corpus used as a background against which to compare findings from another corpus. Typically, reference corpora are large and contain texts from multiple genres.

Register – a form of language defined by its social features. In Hallidayan linguistics, the register of a stretch of language is defined by its **field**, **tenor** and **mode** (see Halliday 1978).

Relative clause – a type of clause which is dependent on a noun phrase and refers back to the noun (the antecedent of the relative pronoun). Relative clauses may be defining (e.g. *Her interest has been aroused by some new paintings which she has seen in a SoHo gallery*, in which the relative clause identifies a particular set of new paintings) and non-defining (e.g. *all went to form his own peculiar style, which is apparent for the first time in these frescoes*, where the relative clause simply provides additional information about his style) (examples from the BNC).

Representativeness – a corpus which is representative is one whose component texts have been selected carefully from the total **population** of texts which meet defined criteria in order to act as a valid **sample** of a language, language variety or genre.

Rhotic – a dialect or variety of a language in which the *r* sound is pronounced in all phonetic environments (before a consonant, before a vowel, at the end of a word) is rhotic. Some varieties, such as **RP**, are non-rhotic, which means that *r* is normally only pronounced before a vowel.

Sample text corpus (compare **whole text corpus**) – a corpus containing extracts or samples from texts, rather than complete texts. The Brown corpus for example contains 2000-word samples from larger texts.

Sampling – the practice of carefully selecting texts for inclusion in a corpus, in order to give a fair representation of the total **population** of texts which meet the criteria governing the corpus design.

Semantic preference (compare **semantic prosody**) – a form of **collocation** where the relationship is between one unit (e.g. word, phrase) and a semantically related set of words. For example, in the SCOTS corpus, *a bottle of* . . . has a semantic preference for words denoting (particularly alcoholic) drinks, including *whisky, gin, vodka, sherry, champagne*.

Semantic prosody, discourse prosody – a form of **collocation** where there is a relationship between one unit (e.g. word, phrase) and a type of meaning. For example, the verb *cause* has been found repeatedly in corpora to occur typically with negative outcomes (*cause a riot, cause a lot of noise, cause a stooshie*, examples all from the SCOTS corpus). The term 'discourse prosody' is sometimes used in preference to 'semantic prosody' in order to stress the role of such semantic relationships in the construction of discourse.

Semantics – the linguistic study of word and sentence meaning, often contrasted with **pragmatics**.

Sociolinguistics – the branch of linguistics which investigates the relationship between language and society, including aspects such as the influence of speaker variables (sex, age, education) on the language produced, the relationship between standard and non-standard language varieties and language planning.

Span, collocational span – the words surrounding the **node word**. Many corpus linguistics typically consider a span of about 5 words to the left and to the right of the node.

SPOCA analysis – the components of a clause, comprising the **subject, predicator, object, complement** and **adverbial**.

Standard deviation – in statistics, a measure of the dispersion of a distribution.

Statistical significance – a measure of how confident we can be that a particular finding is not simply a matter of chance.

Statistics – quantitative data which can be analysed, for example, in order to compare linguistic findings in two different varieties of language.

Sub-corpus – a component of a larger corpus, which is delimited and analysed as a corpus in itself. For example, to investigate spoken language in English, one could define a sub-corpus of all of the transcriptions of spoken texts in the BNC, comprising 10 million words.

Subject – in **SPOCA**, the element, usually a noun phrase, about which something is predicated in the rest of the clause.

Subordinate clause – a clause which cannot stand alone and is dependent on another main clause. Subordinate clauses may contain subordinating conjunctions, such as *although, if, because*; or may contain non-finite verbs, as in 'there might be a requirement *to disclose the surveillance to the suspect*' (subordinate clause in italics; example from SCOTS corpus).

Synchronic corpus (compare **diachronic corpus**) – a corpus which contains texts all from the same or broadly similar time, which allows a user to investigate the state of the language at that time.

t-test – a measure of statistical significance, like the **chi-square** test, which compares observed corpus frequencies with expected frequencies, to determine how likely it is that frequencies are due to chance.

Tag questions – a question attached to the end of an utterance, typically comprising, in English, an auxiliary verb and a pronoun (e.g. *isn't it? aren't they?*).

Tagging (see also **annotation, mark-up**) – the process of adding information to a text or corpus (either automatically or manually), particularly part of speech or other linguistic information which is not consistently reflected in the form of language.

Tenor of discourse (see also **field of discourse, mode of discourse**) – the relationship between the participants in discourse. For example, the tenor may be formal, as a result of the different status of participants (as in a job interview, where the participants are the potential employer and an applicant). Tenor has an influence on features of language, such as grammar and lexis.

Tense – a verb system which encodes the time at which the action indicated by the verb takes place, e.g. present, past, future. The relationship between tense and time is not straightforward, however; for example, the present tense may indicate past, present and future time.

Text – a coherent unit of discourse, either written or spoken.

Token, word token (see also **type, word type**) – an individual instance of a word. For example, the sentence *The wheels on the bus go round and round* contains nine word tokens (but seven **types** because *the* and *round* are repeated).

Transcription – the rendering of one form of language in another form, in particular the process of turning spoken language into the written form through a system of notation. The end result of the process is known as a transcription or a transcript.

Transitive verbs (compare **intransitive verbs, ditransitive verbs**) – verbs which take a direct object (e.g. *close the door*, where *the door* is the direct object of the verb *close*).

Type, word type (see also **token, word token**) – a word form. For example, the sentence *The wheels on the bus go round and round* contains seven word types (but nine **tokens**, because *the* and *round* are repeated).

Vocabulary 3 – a term developed by Winter (1977, 1994) to cover lexical items such as nouns and verbs which perform signalling functions in discourse.

Voice – a verb system which encodes the relationship between the subject and object of a verb. In English, the active and passive are voices of the verb: *the student downloaded an audio file* (active); *an audio file was downloaded (by the student)* (passive).

Whole text corpus (compare **sample text corpus**) – a corpus which contains complete texts rather than extracts of a determined length. Whole text corpora are necessary for many types of discourse analysis.

Wildcard characters – characters used by corpus search tools to stand for other characters or groups of other characters. For example, * (asterisk) can often be used to stand for any number of characters, including zero (so searching for 'sa*d' will retrieve instances of *sad, said, sand, saved, sacred*, etc.), and a full-stop (.) often stands for any single character ('sa.d' will retrieve only *said* and *sand* of the list above).

Word-form (see also **lemma**) – each possible sequence of characters which represent a lemma. *Sleep, sleeps, slept, sleeping* are all word-forms related to the lemma SLEEP.

Word list – a list of all of the lemmas or word-forms in a corpus, ordered alphabetically or by their frequency of occurrence.

Index